DEMOCRACY AND DICTATORSHIP
IN VENEZUELA
1945-1958

CONNECTICUT COLLEGE MONOGRAPH NO. 10

Democracy and Dictatorship

in Venezuela,

1945-1958

by
Glen L. Kolb

CONNECTICUT COLLEGE
in association with
ARCHON BOOKS

Library of Congress Cataloging in Publication Data

Kolb, Glen L. 1914-
 Democracy and dictatorship in Venezuela, 1945-1958.

 (Connecticut College monograph no. 10)
 Bibliography: p.
 1. Venezuela—Politics and government—1935-   I.
Title. II. Series: Connecticut College for Women, New Lon-
don. Connecticut College monograph no. 10.
F2326.K64   320.9′87′063   73-17111
ISBN 0-208-01416-0

Orders should be placed with
Archon Books
The Shoe String Press, Inc.,
995 Sherman Avenue
Hamden, Connecticut 06514

Printed in the United States of America

Contents

Preface

This book deals, in its thirteen chapters, with an important period of Venezuelan history: 1945-1958. The Introduction is a summary of the decade from the death of Dictator Juan Vicente Gómez, in 1935, to the October Revolution of 1945. It was my original intention to concentrate only on the period of dictatorship dating from the fall of the constitutional government of Rómulo Gallegos in November, 1948, to the overthrow of the Pérez Jiménez tyranny in January, 1958. Then it became apparent that no adequate study existed in English of the three-year period of democratic rule, 1945-1948, dominated by Rómulo Betancourt, and it was evident that the succeeding decade of dictatorship could be properly studied only in terms of Venezuela's first attempt to establish a democratic way of life. I therefore decided to enlarge the scope of the project to include the entire thirteen-year period treated in this work.

In preparation for the present study, I spent several months in Venezuela, traveling to all parts of the country, collecting documentation, and interviewing government officials, labor leaders, university professors, student representatives, politicians, businessmen, and ordinary citizens. I went first to the Instituto de Estudios Hispano-Americanos at the Central University in Caracas. I was immediately impressed by the friendly and generous attitude of the faculty members of that institution. Many of them put aside their own busy schedules to come forward with helpful suggestions on travel, bibliography, persons to be interviewed, offers of useful books, and information pertinent to the project.

I wish to express my heartfelt gratitude to the following people: Dr. Rodolfo Luzardo, a generous and hospitable Venezuelan gentleman who gave me unstintingly of his time, provided much valuable documentation, and placed his excellent private library at my disposal; Dr. Eleazar Córdova-Bello, of Central University, who kindly provided transportation and put me in contact with many useful scources of in-

formation; Drs. Eduardo Arcila-Farías and Ildefonso Leal, of the same
institution, who contributed generously to my bibliography; and Professor Julio Febres-Cordero, of the University's Instituto de Investigaciones de la Prensa, who gave me much friendly help and advice in
matters relating to the Venezuelan press. I am also grateful to Dr. Simón
Alberto Consalvi, of the Central Information Office at Miraflores
Palace, for the time he spent in discussion of my research project and
for the documentation that he supplied.

I wish to express special thanks to Dr. Ramón J. Velásquez, editor of
the Caracas paper *El Nacional,* for much necessary information on
Venezuelan journalism; to Dr. Luis Barrios Cruz, Director of the National Library, for permitting me unrestricted access to research materials;
and to Dr. Horacio López Guedez, of the University of the Andes in
Mérida, and Orestes Di Giacomo, of the Casa Nacional of Acción
Democrática, for long and informative conversations on Venezuelan
history and problems.

Unfortunately it was not possible to utilize the resources of the U.S.
State Department for this project. In answer to my request for information concerning U.S.-Venezuelan relations for the period in question,
departmental functionaries replied that all records pertaining to the
subject were "completely closed."

Although I believe that a study of this kind should stand on its own
merits, without excuses of any sort, I wish to make the following statements about myself. I have devoted my adult life to the general field
of Hispanic studies—language, literature, and history—and it is obvious
that I am pro-Latin American. This does not, I trust, make me anti-U.S.A.
On the contrary, I am convinced that a better understanding of Latin
America is important to the survival of our way of life. Part of this
understanding has to do with the reasons why it has been so difficult
for democracy to take root and flourish in the countries south of the
Rio Grande. Recent Venezuelan history is instructive on this point, and
the present study attempts to clarify it.

I am grateful to Professors Mackie L. Jarrell, Walter F. Brady, Frances H. Jacobs, W. Rafael Ramírez-de-Arellano, and Marion E. Doro,
all of Connecticut College, who kindly read the manuscript and offered
suggestions to improve it. And I wish to express special gratitude to
Professor Robert J. Alexander, of Rutgers University, whose constructive criticism has been most helpful.

I am indebted to Connecticut College and to the American Philosophi-
cal Society (Penrose Fund) for the research grants which made this
study possible.

Quaker Hill, Connecticut   Glen L. Kolb

DEMOCRACY AND DICTATORSHIP
IN VENEZUELA
1945-1958

Introduction

When the 27-year dictatorship of Juan Vicente Gómez ended with the tyrant's death in 1935, it seemed for a moment that Venezuelans were once again a free people. Hundreds of political prisoners, suddenly released from jails, joined the crowds of workers and poor people in looting and burning the dictator's palace at Maracay, and ransacking the homes of his relatives and favorites. Thousands of exiles, some of whom had lived abroad for fifteen or twenty years, returned to their homeland with the hope of taking part once more in Venezuela's national life.

In reality there was reason to expect that, in a spirit of goodwill and co-operation, Venezuela could look forward to an increasingly bright and prosperous future. Despite the grinding poverty of the great majority of citizens—ill-housed, ill-clothed, ill-nourished, and illiterate—the nation had, in its vast petroleum deposits, a source of wealth unequalled by any other Latin American country. At the time of Gómez' death, Venezuela had no national debt, nor any need to borrow from any quarter. Since the discovery of oil in the country in 1918, the dictator had dealt shrewdly with both American and European petroleum interests, with steadily-increasing benefits to his Treasury. By 1935 Standard Oil of New Jersey was producing nearly half of the crude oil from Venezuelan fields, principally in the area of Lake Maracaibo. Royal Dutch-Shell produced about 36%, and Gulf (known in Venezuela as Mene Grande) the remaining 14%.[1]

Human resources, of no less importance, were not lacking. Venezuela had produced many eminent men in the fields of letters and science. Not a few of the returning exiles had studied in universities in Europe and the United States, and had much to offer in the renovation of the political, economic, and social life of their country.

Nevertheless, the new freedom of 1935 was more apparent than real, and the unrestrained exuberance of repatriates was soon to be tempered by contact with hard realities. Gómez was dead, but *gomecismo* was very much alive. The last of the six repressive Constitutions sponsored by the dictator (promulgated July 9, 1931) provided that his successor should be the Minister of War. In this case, it was General Eleazar López Contreras, a native of the southern Andean State of Táchira, like his two immediate predecessors, Juan Vicente Gómez and Cipriano Castro. López Contreras, although more literate and enlightened than the defunct tyrant, soon made clear that he intended to run a fairly "tight ship" while giving Venezuelans as much liberty as he thought the country could stand. Against the will of his *gomecista* Congress, he permitted the formation of labor unions, student organizations, and political groupings.

One of the exiles who came back to Venezuela in 1935 was Rómulo Betancourt, later to be President of his country, whose name will appear frequently in this study. A member of the "Generation of 1928" and participant in innumerable scuffles and demonstrations against the Gómez dictatorship, he had been cast into a dungeon in Puerto Cabello in that year with three other men, each laden with 60-pound leg irons. Two of the men died, one of tuberculosis and another of beatings inflicted by guards. The other survivor was Jóvito Villalba, who in later years would become leader of another political party. After some months of captivity, they were released and sent out of their country. They would not return for eight years.

Both inside and outside Venezuela, 1936 was an eventful year. In the United States Franklin D. Roosevelt, having built a powerful political machine through support of labor unions, aid to farmers and small business, and the WPA programs, swept to a landslide victory over the conservative Alfred M. Landon; it was a lesson not lost upon Rómulo Betancourt, Raúl Leoni, and the other young reformers who sought to establish a liberal regime in Venezuela. Mexican President Lázaro Cárdenas, having done much to fulfill one goal of the Mexican Revolution by distributing millions of acres to landless peasants, was soon to nationalize the petroleum industry. In Europe, by contrast, events were moving in a contrary direction. The tragic Spanish Civil War had erupted, and a traditional alliance of rightwing military factions, the Church, and wealthy individuals had undertaken to overthrow the Republican government. Spain was soon to be a bloody proving ground for great quantities of military hardware and advisers sent from Nazi Germany, Fascist Italy, and the USSR.

In Venezuela, young would-be reformers, including labor leaders, students, intellectuals, and repatriated exiles, formed a loose political grouping called Organización Venezolana (ORVE). Although they represented many different shades of political beliefs, including social-Christians, democrats, and even Communists, they were unanimous in pointing out the need for reform and renovation of their country's way of life. Some of their members delivered impassioned radio addresses denouncing the reactionary Congress for its failure to pass much-needed liberal legislation. Others published increasingly bitter attacks in the newly-unfettered press.

When one member of Congress demanded immediate censorship of radio and press, the reformers called a general strike in protest. They then gathered in the Plaza Bolívar on the evening of February 14, 1936, to hear orators condemn the continuation of *gomecismo.* In the midst of their meeting troops stationed on the balcony of a government building opened fire on the crowd, killing about a dozen people and wounding some two hundred. The enraged populace then marched to the presidential palace and forced President López Contreras to promise that press and radio would remain free, the perpetrators of the massacre would be punished, and the most reactionary members of Congress would be removed from their posts. These promises were fulfilled.[2]

Reform-minded Venezuelans in 1936 were speaking and writing most insistently in favor of the following changes: 1) direct election of the President by the people rather than by Congress; 2) a one-term limit on Presidential incumbency; 3) constitutionally guaranteed freedom of press and of speech, and complete freedom of political participation for all citizens; and 4) the passage of a new petroleum law which would give Venezuela a larger share of the profits, and the oil companies would be required to pay taxes on imports and furnish better living conditions and wages to their employees.

The new López Contreras Constitution, promulgated in July, 1936, was in many respects a sharp disappointment to most Venezuelans. There was to be no electoral reform of the kind demanded by liberals. Instead, three electoral levels were set, culminating in the designation of the President: 1) only literate males above the age of 21—a very small percentage of the population—would be allowed to vote for state assemblies and municipal councils; 2) these assemblies and councils would elect the Congress; 3) the Congress would then elect the President and appoint the members of the Supreme Court. Election of the Chief Executive was thus as much out of the hands of the general citizenry as had been the case during the Gómez dictatorship. The new charter did, however, set a single five-year term for the President, who could not become a candidate for that office again until another term had intervened.

Despite all the eloquent speeches, essays, and articles concerning the necessity of a new petroleum policy for the nation, the Constitution of 1936 also failed to make provision for any law revising the conditions under which the foreign-owned companies operated in Venezuela, the share of profits of those concerns, or the taxes they should pay. There was, however, a firm legalization of labor's right to organize and to negotiate with employers.

Most disturbing for those who had hoped for political freedom were the provisions of Article 32 of the López Contreras Constitution. Set forth as a measure to "define and control subversion", this article authorized the President to imprison or deport any individual who, *in his judgment,* was a Communist, an anarchist, or a terrorist.

In the face of these threatening provisions, and the danger of prison or exile to any citizen who incurred the displeasure of the regime, Venezuelans continued to speak out in favor of change. In the second half of

1936 a rash of strikes swept the petroleum-producing areas of the country, especially in the States of Zulia and Falcón, caused by the refusal of companies to improve working and living conditions. Nearly all oil workers at that time lived in unsanitary shacks and received a bare subsistence wage. The right to unionize and to bargain collectively was not very meaningful because the company representatives were instructed to make no concession whatever. The government finally intervened in February, 1937, granting the petroleum employees minimal increases in daily wages and a few small concessions in improved living conditions.

Also in February, 1937, the liberal political organization ORVE managed to have some of its candidates elected to various state assemblies and municipal councils. The government reacted with fear and rage. The President delivered speeches by radio filled with virulent denunciations of the liberal group, and the Caracas paper *La Esfera,* the regime's mouthpiece at the time, mounted an attack to discredit and condemn those who were agitating for reform.

In July of the same year López Contreras, seeing his political power threatened, issued a list of several dozen individuals—mostly repatriated exiles, union leaders, journalists, and liberal political leaders—whom he declared to be Communists, anarchists, or terrorists, in conformity with provisions of his new Constitution. Ordered dissolved by executive decree were the three main opposing political entities: ORVE, the Partido Republicano Progresista, and the Bloque Nacional Democrático. Rómulo Betancourt, leader of ORVE, and a few other leaders evaded the police round-up by hiding with friends. All other blacklisted persons, 47 in all, were arrested and deported for an indefinite period. Another group, the conservative and Church-oriented Unión Nacional Estudiantil (later to become Copei), headed by Dr. Rafael Caldera, was not dissolved by the executive order.

Members of the liberal and left-wing ORVE, once driven underground in their activities, separated according to their differing ideologies. Those who favored representative democracy followed the 30-year-old Betancourt in forming a new party called Partido Democrático Nacional (PDN). The extreme left-wing elements joined the Marxist leader Gustavo Machado to form the Partido Comunista de Venezuela (PCV). The López Contreras regime then sponsored the formation of a rightest political entity called Agrupaciones Cívicas Bolivarianas (ACB) whose sole function was to support the President's program.

During the three remaining years of López Contreras' term the outlawed parties carried on a clandestine campaign of anti-government propaganda, their leaders scurrying from one hideout to another. The Communists, as usual, worked mainly to gain control of labor unions and to. infiltrate student organizations. The PDN leader, Betancourt, wrote hundreds of articles on the problems of workers, the country's petroleum policy, and the need of electoral reform. These were published unsigned, as editorial notes, in the Caracas daily *Ahora.*[3]

In 1940, as López Contreras approached the end of his term, he indicated that he wished the Congress to elect as his successor General Isaías Medina Angarita, Minister of War. The 43-year-old Medina, a member of the Táchira military clan and long-time confidant of López Contreras, was considered a safe candidate to maintain the political and social *status quo*. The prospect of *continuismo* was obvious: by placing his own man in the Presidency, it was very probable that López would be able to return to that office in 1946.

Faced with this situation, Betancourt changed the name of his party to Acción Democrática and announced that it would present as a candidate for the Presidency the respected novelist Rómulo Gallegos. With great vigor but little hope of success, the AD partisans (soon to be known as *adecos*) undertook a campaign to liberalize and modernize the voting procedure by having the President elected by direct ballot throughout the country rather than by Congress. Their efforts came to nothing: government spokesmen simply ignored the clamor and refused to discuss the issues. On April 28, 1941, the Congress dutifully elected Medina Angarita to the Presidency. He received 130 votes, the AD candidate only 13. Nevertheless, the "symbolic candidacy" of Rómulo Gallegos had awakened Venezuelans to the possibility of meaningful changes in the future.

Shortly after his inauguration President Medina, proving more liberal than most people had anticipated, permitted the return of political exiles. Rómulo Betancourt, arrested by the political police late in 1939 while returning from a stay in Chile, had been exiled again for the remainder of López Contreras' term in office. In February, 1941, under the new amnesty, he came back to Venezuela to campaign for the desired reforms. Accompanied by Raúl Leoni and other *adeco* leaders, he approached the new President to request legalization for Acción Democrática. As Medina remembered this interview in his memoirs, he had found it "painful that men versed in the political struggle, who ought to know how to use their rights, should come to the First Magistrate to consult about the exercise of a right that the Constitution guaranteed to them."[4]

Betancourt's recollection of the event was somewhat different. According to the AD leader, he and his associates were referred to Dr. Luis Gerónimo Pietri, governor of Caracas and legal counsel to petroleum interests. This official subjected the petitioners to an inquisitorial examination, demanding their assurance that they were zealous defenders of the sanctity of private property, and that they harbored no notions of changing the existing social order in any significant way. For this reason, says Betancourt, the announced program of AD "had to be a vague enunciation of general principles, and not a concrete and sincere revolutionary focus of the country's problems and their possible solutions."[5]

After legalization, AD used its party newspaper *El País* to launch a steadily increasing attack on the shortcomings of the Medina administration. Making no effort to seek the support of the oligarchy, the party devoted its attention to the development of political awareness in the Venezuelan population, particularly petroleum workers, industrial laborers, and the peasantry. To this end AD strove during the period of the Medina government—1941-45, the years of World War II—to build a broadly-based support in all parts of the country. Representatives were dispatched to the most remote sections to explain the *adeco* program, the aim being to establish a party unit in every village in the nation.

Peculation, the age-old curse of governments, involving high officials from the President down, was also exposed and denounced by the apostles of Acción Democrática. It was clearly realized, however, by AD members as well as by the incumbent regime, that no basic changes of lasting benefit to the country could be realized so long as the means of self-perpetuation in power remained in the hands of the ruling oligarchy. Therefore AD agitated constantly for electoral reform and sought to make the country realize that direct election of the President and Congress by the Venezuelan population was an absolute necessity.

With the outbreak of World War II in September, 1939, Venezuela's oil had suddenly assumed much greater importance as a strategic commodity. Although Acción Democrática favored the Allied cause from the beginning, the López Contreras regime, like other right-wing Latin American governments, did not at first identify its own interests with those of the democracies. The Venezuelan Communists, faithful to the Moscow party line, had initially assumed an attitude of strict neutrality in the hopes that the Allies and the Axis Powers would destroy each other. But after Hitler attacked the Soviet Union in June, 1940, Machado and his PCV became ardent supporters of the Medina administration, anxious that there should be no interruption in the flow of vital petroleum in the effort to defeat Russia's enemies.

Shortly after the Japanese attack on Pearl Harbor, the war brought a petroleum crisis to the Medina government. On February 14, 1942, German submarines sank seven oil tankers that were on the way from Venezuela to the refineries of Aruba and Curaçao. The resulting tanker shortage soon caused a 25% drop in production of crude oil in the country, creating unemployment in the industry and a decrease in the government's revenues.[6]

The problems brought by these developments stimulated the Medina administration to seek a revision of Venezuela's business relationship with the foreign-owned petroleum companies. In March, 1943, the Congress passed a new law which, at the time of its inception, was considered a kind of legal contract between the government and the petroleum industry. It provided for a greater percentage of profits for the nation, an added capacity for refining Venezuelan oil within the country, and increased taxes on a variety of company activities. The government agreed, in return, to cancel all previous legal claims against the companies and to abide by the terms of this arrangement for a period of forty years.[7]

This legislation was denounced both before and after its passage by Juan Pablo Pérez Alfonso, a petroleum expert who represented Acción Democrática in the Chamber of Deputies, as being much too favorable to the oil companies and because it did not forbid the granting of new concessions for exploration and exploitation. It did, however, represent a great improvement over previous practices and brought an immediate increase in revenues to the government.[8]

President Medina used a large part of these funds to renew and expand the program of public works begun by López Contreras. He did much for education by undertaking the construction of the Central University in Caracas, as well as high schools, nursing centers, military schools, and specialized institutes in various parts of the country. He also made an honest effort to aid industry and agriculture through loans to small business and the building of roads and irrigation systems in the interior.[9] Labor unions organized freely and the press was at liberty to analyse, propagandize, and belabor the government's program in every way.

The liberal measures undertaken by Medina, although condemned by Acción Democrática as inadequate, alienated the very right-wing forces that had brought him to power. López Contreras, unable to control the President's tendency to grant a measure of democratic reforms, began to gather support from the most conservative elements: big landowners, the clergy, the industrialists, and the Armed Forces, with the clear intention of returning to the Presidency for the period 1946-1951. Medina could not legally succeed himself without an intervening term, but he wished to nominate a successor who would carry on his program. Finding himself pressed on the left by the *adecos* and on the right by the *lopecistas,* the President decided to fortify his position on the state and local levels by forming a new political party prior to the 1944 elections of state and municipal councils. This was a necessary step, since those bodies would choose the Congress of 1945 which would, in turn, elect the new President. Medina's new party became known as the Partido Democrático de Venezuela (PDV).

The President began the year 1944 with a mid-January visit to the United States, where he was received by President Roosevelt at the White House, addressed the House of Representatives, and did his best to cement relations with his country's best petroleum customer. In March, First Lady Eleanor Roosevelt returned the visit, and her photograph appeared beside that of Medina in Venezuelan newspapers. While the President built his public image, his PDV made preparations to assure the election, in October, of *medinista* legislators and councilmen in all parts of the country.

In July Medina made a deal with the Communists, who exercised more influence in the labor unions than any other political group; in return for their support, the government would grant them legal existence as a political party. On July 14, under the new name of Unión Popular Venezolana (UPV), the leftists held their first rally, at which speakers solemnly gave public assurance that their group was "not the Communist Party in disguise", but a new party of "national structuration". And on the following day, the Caracas paper, *El Nacional,* thoroughly *medinista* at that time, gave front-page treatment to the formation of the "absolutely democratic" new party, which put forward no candidates of its own, but hastened to endorse those of Medina's PDV.

By early October, the forthcoming electoral contest had attracted great attention, and it was certain that its results would be regarded as an indication of the national preference for or against Medina's middle-of-the-road policies. In a frenzy of pre-election activity, the PDV used public funds to finance the campaigns of its candidates. Government vehicles transported food purchased in agricultural zones to depressed areas where it was sold to the poor at low prices, and government planes carried campaign literature to all parts of the republic.[10]

As for the attitude of the citizenry, there is evidence that although Medina's opposition at the polls would be the candidates sponsored by Acción Democrática, the literate and politically aware segments of the population were concerned that a repudiation of the *medinista* brand of democracy might well result in a resurgence of *lopecismo* and a return to the stifling repressions of earlier days. On October 7, for example, *El Nacional* carried a "Public Letter to the President of the Republic" signed by more than seventy well-known writers and artists, including not only leftists, but such prominent and democratically-inclined scholars as Mariano Picón Salas, Joaquín Gabaldón Márquez, and Eduardo Arcila Farías, who declared their admiration and support for the Medina administration. On October 17, the Teatro Hollywood was the scene of a mammoth rally featuring orators of the "Generation of '28" who evoked the terrors of the Gómez tyranny in an effort to convince the public that the enlightened rule of Medina was a blessing to be cherished.

Although Acción Democrática conducted a vigorous and hard-hitting campaign, with a good slate of qualified candidates, Betancourt's young and poverty-striken party was no match, as yet, for the well-oiled machine of Medina's PDV in alliance with the Communist-run UPV, and the government won an overwhelming victory at the polls on October 23.

Venezuelan events of the spring and summer of 1945 do not belong in this Introduction, for they lead inexorably to the "October Revolution" of that year, a *coup d'état* resulting in the coming to power of Acción Democrática in alliance with a group of young military officers. We devote the remainder of this space to a judgment of the administration of President Isaías Medina Angarita.

If his period in office was not precisely "four years of democracy", marked by clean and constitutional government, as the ousted President claimed in the defense of his rule, neither was it as bad as his detractors would have us believe. Measured against the ruthless tyranny of the Gómez dictatorship or the capricious and heavy-handed authoritarianism of López Contreras, the Medina government can be seen as a period of transition from dictatorship to democracy. As will be noted in the following chapter, an investigative board subsequently proved that President Medina and his associates had indulged in graft on a fairly impressive scale, though their peculative efforts could scarcely be compared to the systematic looting of national wealth as carried out by Trujillo, Batista, Perón, and Pérez Jiménez.

It is to the credit of President Medina that the period of his tenure in office saw progress in many important areas of the national life; whatever the provocations from his opponents, he did not jail or exile them. Neither did he crush labor unions nor muzzle the press. He chose to defend his program within the democratic framework of free speech and a free press, while maintaining most of the conservative forms and practices of government with which he was familiar. Many Venezuelans remember his time in office as the best and happiest period that the country has ever known.

Chapter I

The October Revolution

At the beginning of 1945, as Venezuela approached the end of another presidential term, the politically astute Medina Angarita appeared to have outflanked his opponents on both the right and the left by preparing the electoral base for the membership of the new Congress. It seemed certain that he could impose a successor of his own choosing, and that his only problem was the selection of a man who would be amenable to his wishes and continue his program, but who was also of sufficient prestige to command the respect of Congress and of the people.

If we accept, as do most Venezuelans, the basic sincerity of Medina's intention to modernize and democratize his country's political system, and to do this by retaining some of the safeguards of the old order while attaining the advantages of a new one, it is difficult to fault the President on the logic of his political methods or on his skillful handling of the 1944 electoral campaign.

It was not, however, on the political front but on the military flank that President Medina neglected to insure the success of his program. As a man who had risen through the hierarchy of the Armed Forces to the rank of General, and who had directed the Ministry of War for five years before moving to the Presidency, he could not fail to be aware of the Latin American custom of the *coup d'état* and the fact that every change of government in Venezuelan history had been effected by the military. Yet it is clear that he did not realize the danger to his regime from the very organization that he knew best and upon which the safety of his government depended. The fact is that the young officers who secretly organized the Unión Patriótica Militar (UPM) in 1945 were bitterly disappointed in President Medina. Let us see why this was so.

During the long decades of dictatorship prior to the death of Juan Vicente Gómez in 1935 the Venezuelan military was one of the most primitive organizations of its kind in Latin America. Intended primarily for the control of internal revolt rather than resistance to a foreign invader, the Army was composed largely of illiterate recruits commanded by regional caudillos responsible only to the dictator. In the first decades of the twentieth century, as in earlier periods, many of the barracks commanders in Caracas and Maracay were merely *jefes de montonera* (tough bosses of armed cowboy bands) transplanted from Táchira or Mérida to urban areas closer to the center of power. Many of these "officers", although loyal to the dictator, had little or no knowledge of military science or tactics, and were concerned mainly with maintaining their own authority and positions.[1]

When General Medina Angarita was appointed Minister of War in 1936, this backward situation in the military establishment began to change. In keeping with his desire to modernize Venezuelan life, Medina arranged to send promising young officers to study in military academies in the United States, Peru, and elsewhere in the Hemisphere. By the early 1940s, when Medina occupied the Presidency, many of these young men had returned to Venezuela imbued with the desire to renovate the military schools and to bring their country's defense organization abreast of the times. They were disappointed to find that senior officers did not share their enthusiasm for change and modernization. Some young lieutenants fresh from study in the United States were appalled to find that common soldiers stationed in barracks throughout the country were still forbidden to listen to radio programs or to read books, magazines, newspapers, or any printed material except leaflets on military rules approved by the Defense Ministry. Also irksome to the serious-minded career officers was the fact that promotions and honors were still often awarded by reason of family connections or social influence rather than in recognition of efficiency and merit.[2]

President Medina's effort to improve the preparation of military personnel by sending officers to study abroad while maintaining the defense establishment at home in the traditional state of backwardness can be seen as a dangerous half-way measure, made in good faith but inimical to the interests of his regime.

The principal organizer and foremost conspirator of the Unión Patriótica Militar was the young artillery expert, Major Marcos Pérez Jiménez. Born on April 25, 1914, in the village of Michelena, Táchira State, he was one of four children of a poor farmer in a remote and backward area of the Andes. The father, Juan Severo Pérez, had been a widower for some time when he remarried in 1907, and he was seventy years old when Marcos was born. The mother, a Colombian by birth, had been a village school teacher. Marcos attended primary school in Michelena and high school in the Colombian town of Cúcuta. According to his official biographer, he was a "brilliant and exemplary student" whose conduct at all times was above reproach.[3]

After graduation from high school in 1931, Pérez Jiménez entered the Military School at Maracay where, it is alleged, he was quiet and studious and liked to discuss scientific subjects, but never took part in arguments about politics. After graduation from that institution in 1934, he was assigned to the Ayacucho Artillery Regiment in Maracay. The following year he was commissioned to the same post as a lieutenant. In 1936, he was transferred to the Military School in Caracas, where he served as instructor in artillery methods for three years.

Arriving in Lima, Peru, in March, 1939, as a member of a group of young Venezuelan officers who were to receive special training in new military methods, Pérez Jiménez enrolled in a six-month course in the School of Applied Artillery. He displayed such aptitude and proficiency in tactics with new field weapons that, after a visit home in August, War Minister Medina Angarita sent him back to Peru to enroll in the three-year course in Command and General Staff at the Escuela Superior de Guerra. During that prolonged period he also attended classes at the artillery School in Chorrillos.

Pérez Jiménez' stay in Lima coincided with the administration of Peruvian President Manuel Prado (1939-45), a pro-American political moderate who co-operated with the Allies during the War, but there is no indication that the Venezuelan ever made the acquaintance of the Peruvian President. In it known, however, that he became the friend, disciple, and admirer of General Manuel Odría, Chief of the General Staff of the Peruvian Armed Forces, who was to overthrow the elected President and impose his own illegal rule as dictator of Peru.

In January, 1944, during President Medina's visit to Washington, Pérez Jiménez returned to Caracas, was promoted to the rank of Major and appointed Chief, First Section, of the Estado Mayor General. What-ever the validity of the complaint about the backwardness of the Vene-zuelan defense establishment, the principal organizer of the anti-Medina *coup d'état* could not claim a personal grievance of mistreatment or neglect.

Another prominent member of the UPM conspiracy was the young Army engineer, Major Carlos Delgado Chalbaud, 36, who joined the group somewhat later than others, after the principal objectives and intentions had already been established. He is introduced at this point, not by reason of any decisive part played in the October Revolution, but because of the increasingly vital influence that he wielded in Venezuelan affairs for the five years following that event, until his assassination in November, 1950. Born in Caracas in 1909 of wealthy and aristocratic parents, the course of his life was largely conditioned by the tragic career of his father, Román Delgado Chalbaud, who had twice tried and failed to overthrow the dictatorship of Juan Vicente Gómez.[4]

Exiled from Venezuela at the age of ten because of his father's fall from favor, Carlos Delgado had accompanied his mother to France and spent his most formative years in that country, somewhat embittered by his father's imprisonment. He acquired a good education in the best French schools and a concept of democratic institutions in the Western European sense. He entered the French Academy of Saint Cyr to special-ize in military engineering, in 1933 married a Rumanian student named

Lucie Berliand, and graduated shortly before the death of Gómez in 1935. He then returned to Venezuela and was commissioned a Captain by President López Contreras. Of all the young officers who constituted the membership of the conspiratorial UPM in 1945, the most cultured and the least military-minded was Carlos Delgado Chalbaud. Perhaps for this reason, as well as his tendency to remain aloof, he never enjoyed great popularity in military circles.

Lieutenant-Colonel Julio César Vargas, another member of the UPM steering committee, had received advanced military training in the United States. After the fall of the Medina regime he would be promoted to the rank of Major and appointed Chief Inspector of the Armed Forces. His brother, Captain Mario Vargas, also educated in the United States and one of the principal planners of the October Revolution, later to occupy the post of Minister of the Interior, was probably the best liked and most influential of all the young officers of the Armed Forces. The two remaining members of the six-man Comité Directivo were: Horacio López Conde, Captain of Aviation at the time of the *coup*; and Lieutenant Francisco Gutiérrez. Various other officers were closely associated with this group in organizing the action against the Medina regime. We shall refer to them in the following account.

We have noted that the October Revolution was the result of an alliance between the UPM and the leaders of the political party Acción Democrática. Certainly Pérez Jiménez and his associates did not share the AD motives of undertaking a general rectification of the social, political, and economic backwardness of Venezuela. The young officers simply identified their own advancement, prosperity, and well-being with the greater glory of their country. They envisioned national dignity and prestige primarily in terms of military strength, organization, and efficiency; and they perceived the possibility of attaining their objectives through the formation of a conspiratorial organization in combination with some political entity.

Neither the leaders of Acción Democrática nor those of the UPM could know, in the summer of 1945, what candidate Medina would present to the nation as the next President of Venezuela. Since both groups were equally dissatisfied with the incumbent regime, though for very different reasons, neither of them had any cause for optimism. It was in this mood of uncertainty and apprehension that the UPM conspirators, having decided to overthrow the Medina government, first approached the leaders of Acción Democrática. The initial contact between the two groups took place in early June, 1945, at the home of Dr. Edmundo Fernández, a mutual friend of Rómulo Betancourt and UPM member Horacio López Conde.[5] Both Dr. Fernández and the AD leader himself report the latter's astonishment and hesitation at the thought of any contact between his party and members of the Armed Forces. Betancourt was opposed in principle to the *coup d'état* as a means of changing the form of government, and suspected that any intervention by the military must conceal dictatorial intentions. He agreed, however, to meet the UPM delegation, he and Raúl Leoni being the only AD representatives present. The officers were those listed above as comprising the UPM steering committee with the exception of Carlos Delgado Chalbaud, who did not join the conspiracy until autumn.

Major Marcos Pérez Jiménez, as senior officer and organizer of the group, served as spokesman to set forth the UPM objectives to the AD leaders. According to the other officers present, he explained the ideals of his organization "in clear and categorical form", reducing them to the five following points (verbatim translation):

1. The supreme goal of the movement is to implant in Venezuela a general order of things in which honesty, justice and qualification shall be the rule.
2. The movement has as its immediate objective to bring about the commitment of morally sound and intellectually capable officials of the Armed Forces, so that we may act effectively in favor of the goal already set forth.
3. The movement is not intended to carry the Armed Forces to the exercise of power; it purposes to bring to high office honorable and capable men who will have genuine popular support.
4. It is stated categorically that the private interests of members of the movement are of marginal consideration; we shall always work exclusively in behalf of the interests of the Nation and the interests of the Armed Forces.
5. This movement is intended to head up a movement of national concentration against the present state of things. Consequently, we are contacting civil organizations who fully share the ideas set forth and are disposed to give full aid and support to the action of the Armed Forces.[6]

As for the immediate reactions of the AD leaders to the words of Pérez Jiménez, there is a marked difference of opinion in the reports. Dr. Fernández recalled that after Betancourt and Leoni talked with the military men, "they understood the sincerity of their promises and their disinterest concerning power. There was no doubt . . . , These young men had no thought of military dictatorship. Later meetings, arranged on that occasion, convinced them of the purity of their intentions."[7] Gonzalo Barrios, another life-long friend of Betancourt, later to be Governor of the Federal District under the Revolutionary Junta, remembered that "Betancourt and Leoni came back very well impressed by the military representatives."[8]

Nearly all who heard Pérez Jiménez speak on that occasion or later have remarked that he was inclined to be extremely brief, succinct, and sparing of words. Rómulo Betancourt, however, writing in exile more than ten years later, at a time when Pérez Jiménez had bludgeoned his way to dictatorial power in Venezuela, recalled that the future tyrant had looked to him, at first glance, like "a provincial bookkeeper", and "seemed a timid and talkative person, fertile in words rather than ideas, lost in the dark jungle of obscurities." Betancourt found that the conspirator's "long and wordy speech contained only two concrete ideas: the young Army officers repudiated both López and Medina; and they were ready to stage a *coup d'état.*"[9]

All accounts agree that the AD leaders made no commitment at this first meeting, nor during many subsequent meetings held in various places and including different members of the two organizations. Nevertheless, the fact that the two groups did not break off contact, but met for discussions over a period of many weeks, is a clear indication that despite the serious reservations on the part of Betancourt and Leoni, the possible advisability of collaboration with the UPM was recognized from the beginning.

Acción Democrática, devoted to political reform, was not primarily concerned with the modernization of the Armed Forces, while the UPM thought almost exclusively in terms of military reorganization. Since the objectives of the two groups had so little in common, it would appear astonishing, at first glance, that either would consider joint action with the other. The explanation, however, is simple. The AD leaders were aware that the military conspiracy had developed with great speed during the period of their exploratory talks, acquiring many hundreds of sworn adherents in the Armed Forces, and they were convinced that the UPM would attempt the *coup* with or without AD co-operation. As for the officers' choice of Acción Democrática as a partner in revolution, several of them mentioned in later interviews that they had needed some political group to take charge of the government, and there was no other party in Venezuela except the Communist UPV, which they abhorred, and the PDV of Medina, whom they wished to overthrow.

In the midst of the developing conspiracy, and while Betancourt continued to seek some political solution as an alternative to the violent overthrow of the regime, there was mounting speculation concerning Medina's choice of a successor. Early in 1945 had come the news that the President had offered the nomination to Dr. Diógenes Escalante, the Venezuelan ambassador in Washington, a cultured and experienced diplomat of pronounced liberal tendencies. The ambassador, however, notified Medina in April that, for reasons of health, he could not accept the nomination. Nothing further was heard of the candidacy of this diplomat for several months, during which time a bitter under-cover feud took place between Medina and ex-President López Contreras.

Early in July President Medina, although fully informed of the precarious state of Ambassador Escalante's health, again appealed to him to reconsider his decision and to accept the Presidential nomination. To explain the political crisis and to plead the urgency of his request, the President sent his brother, Julio Medina Angarita, to visit Dr. Escalante in Washington. At the same time Rómulo Betancourt and Raúl Leoni flew to Washington and explained to the ambassador that only his acceptance as a unity candidate could prevent the violent overthrow of the Medina regime. Faced with this obvious crisis, Dr. Escalante accepted. He returned to Caracas, received the plaudits of the crowds, and almost immediately became seriously ill. He was forced to relinquish the nomination, thus returning the political situation to its former state of crisis.[10]

Medina then cast about for a substitute candidate, and soon offered the nomination to Angel Biaggini, the Minister of Agriculture, a lackluster politician who had no national standing whatever. Some members of the President's own Cabinet were appalled at the choice, particularly Interior Minister Arturo Uslar Pietri, who predicted that Biaggini would be too weak to maintain himself in power. Medina's political adversaries pounced at once upon this action as a brazen attempt at *continuismo,* the imposition of a puppet President who would do his bidding.

Faced with what they regarded as a return to the methods of Juan Vicente Gómez, the leaders of Acción Democrática prevailed upon their party president, Rómulo Gallegos, to try to persuade Medina to a different course of action. The AD proposal was that the President should consult with other political parties in order to select some eminent but nonpolitical figure who could serve for only one year, during which time a constitutional reform would be carried out providing for direct election of the President by the people. Medina rejected this idea out of hand. The name of Angel Biaggini was formally submitted to Congress on September 11 and his pre-candidacy announced. On October 1, by a vote of 252 to 7, he was approved by that body as the sole Presidential candidate of the Venezuelan Democratic Party.[11]

There now remained, for the Venezuelan people, only the prospect of routine election of Biaggini by the same Congress that had confirmed his candidacy or, even worse, a bitter showdown in Congress between *medinistas* and *lopecistas,* resulting in a return to power of ex-President López Contreras. The latter possibility was by no means remote. The political mentality of many congressmen was still reactionary and typically *gomecista,* and Medina had aroused their suspicions and distrust by his tactical alliance with the Communists, his mild agrarian reform program, and the political liberties permitted by his regime.

Some months earlier, several reactionary groups, all favoring the return to power of López Contreras, had combined to form an organization called the Venezuelan Democratic Republican Party. Not legalized by the government, this faction had carried on through the press, by propaganda leaflets, and in public speeches, a vitriolic campaign against the Medina regime and the candidacy of Biaggini. By mid October, these factors had greatly increased the probability of a last-minute struggle for power between the supporters of Medina and the partisans of López.

In this situation Acción Democrática, having been rebuffed in every effort to achieve democratic reforms through legal methods, was left with no alternative but to co-operate with the UPM in the overthrow of Medina in order to form a more representative government. It was inevitable that the AD decision to come to power through the undemocratic act of the *coup d'état* should bring forth accusations of insincerity and demagoguery from both the reactionary right and the Communist left. In the interests of historical accuracy, it must be pointed out that the AD leaders did not seek the alliance with the UPM, nor did they "incite" or "stimulate" the officers of that organization to rebel against the government, as has been alleged by some writers.[12] It was conspirator Marcos Pérez Jiménez and his fellow UPM members who sought the initial contact with AD in June, 1945, and, as we have seen, they had already determined at that time to carry out an armed revolt against the government with, or without, the collaboration of civilian political leaders.

Meanwhile, several significant political developments took place in rapid succession. On October 9 President Medina, encouraged by the electoral victory obtained in 1944 by the tactical manoeuver of legalizing the Communist-front UPV, now took another step in the same direction by openly granting legal existence to the Communist Party in return for its support of the candidacy of Biaggini. On the evening of the 13th, in the Teatro Boyacá, the partisans of López Contreras staged a tumultuous convention to proclaim the candidacy of the former President. On October 16 more than 8,000 wildly-cheering leftists gathered in the Nuevo Circo to hear speeches by a panel of Red orators, including Juan Bautista Fuenmayor, Secretary-General of the PCV, who praised the accomplishments of Medina and endorsed the Angel Biaggini candidacy. On the following night the Nuevo Circo filled again, this time by impatient and frustrated *adecos* who heard Rómulo Gallegos announce that Acción Democrática would put forward no candidate for the Presidency, "so as not to contribute to the farce" of Biaggini's election by the *medinista* Congress. They also heard Betancourt explain why AD had endorsed Dr. Escalante, but could not support Biaggini.[13]

Even as the AD rally was taking place on the evening of October 17, several UPM conspirators were holding a tense meeting at the home of Captain Mario Vargas. According to the original plan conceived by Peréz Jiminéz, the *coup* was to take place in the latter part of December. But for several days the plotters had been aware that Medina and members of the Army High Command were suspicious of their activities and intentions. The UPM leaders had therefore agreed that when the first member of their group was arrested, they would strike without delay. When they learned, on October 17, that many officers had been summoned to the Military School for questioning, they realized that only prompt action could save their plans.

On the following morning, when two of the principal conspirators, Major Delgado Chalbaud and Captain Vargas, on regular duty at the Military School, received news that Peréz Jiménez had been arrested and was under interrogation by Defense Minister Delfín Becerra, they immediately took command of the institution for the insurrection, arresting the officer who had been sent to conduct them for questioning. Other UPM members were then dispatched to the barracks of San Carlos, Ambrosio Plaza, Miraflores, and the Defense Ministry itself to seize control according to pre-arranged plans. At Miraflores and the Ministry the insurgents took command with surprising ease, but Medina and members of the Army General Staff barricaded themselves in the Ambrosio Plaza Barracks, where Pérez Jiménez, Julio César Vargas, and other conspirators were confined in jail cells for most of the day.

In less than twenty-four hours the Medina regime collapsed and the insurgents assumed full control of the government. Ex-President López Contreras, who had appeared to constitute a serious threat of civil strife after the announcement of the Biaggini candidacy, was arrested by UPM officers at the gates of Miraflores Palace early on the morning of October 18. He remained in a jail cell until the success of the Revolution was no longer in doubt, when he was sent into exile with many of his followers.

Some three years after the event, Medina himself, writing his memoirs in the exile of his New York apartment, attempted to explain his downfall mainly in terms of his own magnanimity and good faith, the perfidy and restless ambition of the young officers of the UPM and the hypocrisy and lust for power of certain AD politicians. Not all of the ex-President's explanations and assertions are convincing, but he was probably right in declaring that he made no real effort to put down the rebellion because he wished "to spare my country the evils of a prolonged commotion, insecurity, civil war and loss of international prestige."[14]

Chapter II

The Advent
of Acción Democrática

On the evening of October 19, 1945, a group of the principal victors of the October Revolution gathered in the presidential office of Miraflores Palace to form a Revolutionary Junta of Government and to formulate a communiqué to the nation. By unanimous agreement of those present, the seven-man Junta would be composed of four members of Acción Democrática (Rómulo Betancourt, as Junta President, Dr. Raúl Leoni, Dr. Luis B. Prieto, Dr. Gonzalo Barrios); two representatives of the Armed Forces, Major Carlos Delgado Chalbaud and Captain Mario Vargas; and one non-partisan civilian, Dr. Edmundo Fernández. Major Marcos Pérez Jiménez, though undoubtedly the foremost organizer and co-ordinator of the *coup d'état,* was not mentioned as a possible member of the Junta, nor was he present at the Miraflores meeting. The absence of the future dictator from these organizational deliberations has been tentatively explained by Rómulo Betancourt as caused by resentment on the part of Pérez Jiménez, who felt that the AD leader had deliberately slighted him in favor of Delgado Chalbaud.[1]

In its message to the nation the Junta, after listing its own membership, expressed its intention to hold general elections at an early date, featuring direct and universal suffrage and the secret ballot, in order to give the country a democratic government and a new constitution. The Junta also declared that all those who had profited from the graft and corruption of previous regimes would be brought to trial, judged severely, and stripped of their illicit wealth. Former Presidents López Contreras and Medina Angarita were specifically included among such *reos de peculado.* Immediate steps would be taken to lower the cost of living and to improve economic and social conditions, especially for the middle class, laborers, and farmers. Public order would be maintained and the suspension of constitutional guarantees would remain in effect for a time. The Junta's foreign policy was to include the maintainance of "perma-

nent relations with all the democratic nations, especially the countries
of Latin America, the United States, Laborite England, and the Soviet
Union."[2]

In the early period of AD government, during which Rómulo Betancourt ruled by decree from Miraflores Palace, the prevailing Venezuelan
mood was one of enthusiasm and excited anticipation of things to come.
As successive liberal rulings emanated from the Junta Revolucionaria,
various civic and professional groups declared their support for the new
government. A Cabinet was appointed, and recognition of the regime
came quickly from seven American nations, including the United States.
On October 21, only three days after the *coup,* the Junta announced
that elections for a constituent assembly would be held in April, 1946,
and that all political parties would be free to organize and participate,
including even the *medinista* PDV and the Communist Party. At the
same time, Rómulo Betancourt made known that no member of the
governing Junta would be a candidate for the Presidency, and that
Acción Democrática would put forward the candidacy of the famous
novelist, Rómulo Gallegos, who had been the "symbolic candidate"
against Medina in 1941. As further evidence of political non-exclusivism,
the Junta appointed as Attorney General the former student leader
Dr. Rafael Caldera. Such opposition groups as the PDV and the Communist PCV responded at once with manifestos and organizational
meetings, while Jóvito Villalba's Unión Republicana Democrática (URD)
and Copei (Comité Organizador Pro Elecciones Independiente) were in
the process of re-grouping.

By the first week of November the Betancourt government, having
been recognized by nearly all countries, made several important an-
nouncements: the rupture of diplomatic relations with Franco Spain
and the Trujillo dictatorship in the Dominican Republic; the reduction,
by executive decree, of the cost of staple foods; a drastic cut in the
salaries of government officials, including members of the Junta and
the Cabinet; and the publication of a definitive list of about 150 Venezuelans who would be tried by a special court (Jurado de Responsabili-
dad Civil y Administrativa) for corruption in government, or for having
profited from illegal use of public funds. This list, which was published in
nearly all Carcas newspapers on November 11, 1945, included the two
ex-Presidents, Medina and López Contreras, and their immediate families and the *medinista* Cabinet members, most of whom were still in
prison, dozens of descendants and other relatives of Juan Vicente
Gómez, and many other wealthy citizens lumped together as *gomecistas.*
Their prosecution was placed in the hands of newly-appointed Attorney
General Caldera, and their trial was to proceed according to the terms
of a retroactive law embodied in the Junta Decree No. 64, published by
the Venezuelan press on November 28. On the following day, however,
the two ex-presidents and fourteen members of the Medina government

The Communists were split into two rival factions. The more orthodox of these groups, the Partido Comunista Venezolano (PCV), led by Gustavo Machado, was known as the Red Communists. The other faction, headed by Rodolfo Quintero and known as Black Communists, comprised that part of the Marxist movement legalized by Medina the previous year under the name of Unión Popular Venezolana (UPV). This group was known during the campaign of 1946 and later as the Partido Comunista Proletario.[9]

In mid March the Junta decreed the restoration of constitutional guarantees. Having determined in the Electoral Statute that suffrage was to be granted to illiterates, it was necessary to provide a method for those who could not read to vote for the parties of their choice. This problem was solved by assigning a different color to each party. Acción Democrática was given white and its candidates were known as Blancos. The members of Copei were Verdes (Greens); the candidates of URD, also called *urredecos* or *urredistas,* became Pardos (Browns); the orthodox Communists of the PCV were Rojos (Reds); and the Negros (Blacks) were the Communists of the UPV.[10]

With the new freedoms brought to the Venezuelan political arena by the Revolutionary Government, the opposition began to attack what they considered the arrogant exclusivism and insufferable tactics of Acción Democrática. Despite the exaggerations of some of the charges, many of the grievances were well founded. Careful and objective analysts of the situation have been explicit in stating that the conduct of Junta President Betancourt and his associates on the top level of government was meticulously correct in dealing with the business community, labor unions, and other political parties. The previously-cited Dr. Rodolfo Luzardo, a well-known Venezuelan financial expert who has been Chief of the Bureau of Economic Research, Director of the Venezuelan Institute of Social Security, and Secretary to the President, recalls that the Junta made every effort to acquire the services of experts in the various fields of governmental activity, and that "no pressure from the highest levels of government was ever put upon them." However, he adds:

> In the secondary posts, the party pressure of Acción Democrática was indeed becoming more and more intense and conspicuous. In the important departments of government the "Party Faction", under the direction of one or two leaders employed in those departments, created situations which did not square with a democratic order, and which on the contrary, did the government a great disfavor. There was, then, a fundamental difference in the way in which the situation developed on the levels of immediate contact with President Betancourt, and on the lower levels of administrative organization.
>
> The aforesaid is no secret, because all Venezuelans outside the said affiliation saw it and suffered it in their daily lives. The press condemned it with furious emphasis. What is not generally known. but which we shall repeat, is that no such state of affairs was ever

fomented from Miraflores. The Junta President himself never tired of urging his co-partisans to desist from such an attitude; but directors of intermediate level who, in important numbers, occupied posts of leadership in official departments, remained in a state of stubbornness that might be termed anarchical: they conducted themselves with annoying arrogance in the offices they held.[11]

There was truth also in the bitter charges from the Communist sectors that the AD regime sought to reap political advantage from its support of unionism and of labor's demands for higher wages. Through deals with the Medina regime, Rodolfo Quintero's Black Communists had maintained a dominant influence in the labor movement. But the benefits accruing to the workers under this arrangement were minimal: wages remained low while the prices of necessities were high; hours were long, and working conditions unsatisfactory. There is ample evidence in the writings of Betancourt that the AD leadership was aware of the phenomenal success of Franklin D. Roosevelt in building an effective political machine as champion and defender of unionism in the 1930s. Dr. Raúl Leoni, Minister of Labor in the Betancourt Cabinet, undertook to achieve similar results in Venezuela. And it must be admitted that Leoni's efforts, despite the chagrin of Stalin's disciples, were at least as justified as those of FDR in the United States: in the mid-1940s, the average Venezuelan working man was still miserably poor, downtrodden and exploited.

The Copei Party found more immediate cause for complaint in alleged "ruffian tactics" used against its campaigners. In his telegram of resignation from the post of Attorney General, sent to Betancourt from San Cristóbal, capital of Táchira, Dr. Caldera accused AD of sending hecklers and stone-throwing hoodlums to break up his rallies in that state. The *copeyanos* complained of similar incidents in Puerto Cabello and and elsewhere. As the campaigning progressed, the political atmosphere became increasingly tense. The government party, while combatting the efforts of the opposition to impugn its motives and discredit its program, joined other liberal and left-wing groups in denunciations of the Copei Party for its reactionary attitudes. On June 10, thousands of citizens representing labor unions, student federations and youth groups gathered in the Plaza Urdaneta, in the section of downtown Caracas known as El Silencio, in support of liberalism. Its principal slogans were "Down with Copei" and "Down with reaction." The *copeyanos* replied with a giant rally of their own, held on June 19 in the Nuevo Circo. This meeting, attended by numerous left-wing hecklers, ended in the death of two students and the wounding of several others when shots were fired to silence shouts of "Abajo el Copei".[12]

As if these dissensions were not enough, former President López Contreras had installed himself in neighboring Colombia and was busily plotting to overthrow the AD Junta, or at least to create sufficient turmoil to obstruct democratic elections. These subversive schemes came to light in July, on the eve of a projected trip by Junta President Betancourt to cement Venezuelan relations with the government of Cuban President Ramón Grau San Martín and that of Mexican President Manuel Avila Camacho. The government made numerous arrests and tightened security by dismissing known subversives from their posts, but announced that elections would be held as scheduled, and Betancourt made his trip as planned.[13]

Elections for the constituent assembly took place throughout the nation on October 27, 1946. It was an historic and significant event in many respects: no more than 5% of Venezuelans had voted on any previous occasion, but on this date 36% of the population, constituting 92% of registered voters, cast their ballots. And the people deserved high marks for their conduct as they put aside the partisan passions of the campaign and, in the manner of more experienced democracies, went quietly to the polls without a single incident of violence or bloodshed.

Although the landslide victory of Acción Democrática brought forth predictable cries of fraud from the losers, no responsible investigator has expressed any doubt that the elections were admirably free and honest. A total of 1,395,200 ballots were cast, and of these more than one million were for candidates of Acción Democrática. The *copeyanos,* in second place, received only 180,000 votes, and all other parties were far behind. The resulting distribution of seats in the Constituent Assembly was: 137 for Acción Democrática, 19 for Copei, and two each for the URD and the Communist Party. The authenticity of these results was attested in a sworn affidavit signed by Carlos Delgado Chalbaud, Marcos Pérez Jiménez, and Luis Felipe Llovera Páez, under whose supervision the election had taken place. The document states, in part: "The National Constituent Assembly is representative of the popular will, freely elected on October 27, 1946, in elections which were under our vigilance, and we can therefore attest that they were carried out with the greatest purity."[14]

The Constituent Assembly, under the presidency of AD leader Andrés Eloy Blanco, faced the tasks of writing a new and democratic Constitution for Venezuela, legalizing the *de facto* government of the Revolutionary Junta, reviewing decrees and decisions made during the preceding months, including sentences passed on peculators of previous regimes, and fixing the time and conditions for the election of a Constitutional President, National Congress, Legislative Assemblies, and Municipal Councils.

The Assembly's work was unnecessarily prolonged by the obstructionist tactics of rabidly hostile minority-party representatives who insisted that loudspeakers be installed outside the assembly hall so that the public could follow the debate. Many Assembly members engaged in virulent and tasteless diatribes, couched in vulgar and insulting language, that produced an atmosphere totally inappropriate to the importance of their legislative functions. On leaving the Capitol building various legislators were interpellated, insulted, and even manhandled by irate party followers in the streets.[15]

Despite these obstacles, the Assembly produced a new and generally admirable Constitution which was formally adopted on July 5, 1947. In sharp distinction from the Venezuelan Constitution of 1811, which was modeled after that of the United States, and therefore federalist and marked by the decentralization of powers, the Venezuelan document of 1947 was unitarian and centralist. In its provisions for social legislation (labor laws, child welfare, health and medical coverage, land reform, separation of Church and State, *habeas corpus,* basic freedoms, legal redress, etc.) it compares favorably with the most modern of Latin American charters. Like the Mexican Constitution of 1917, it provided for residual ownership by the State of subsoil wealth. One very controversial part of the new Constitution was Article 77, the so-called "Ley Alfaro Ucero", which empowered the President to arrest and detain for a period of ten days any citizen suspected of involvement in seditious plans or activities against the Constitutional Government. Such suspect might be held for longer periods only with the approval of Congress and, in certain cases, by the Supreme Court. Considering the carefully controlled conditions of this authorization, and the many safeguards provided here and elsewhere in the Constitution, as well as the numerous subversive activities of which the Junta was aware, Article 77 does not appear to the North American reader to constitute any great threat to the freedom of honest citizens.[16] In most respects the Constitution appeared to satisfy the minority parties. Even the URD's chronically dissident Jóvito Villalba declared, on the day of its promulgation, that the document was "one of the most advanced, one of the best, on the American continent."[17]

National elections for President and Congress, and for Legislatures of the Territories and Federal District were set by the Constituent Assembly for December 14, 1947. The AD presidential candidate would be Rómulo Gallegos, a man of little political experience, but of enormous prestige as a novelist, former teacher, and ex-Minister of Education. Rafael Caldera was put forward as the candidate of Copei, a centrist party still far behind Acción Democrática in national influence, but growing in political strength as a result of defections from the ranks of other minority groups. The Communist Party, its power and influence much diminished by failure to compete successfully with the AD program and strategy, nominated Gustavo Machado as presidential aspirant. The Unión Republicana Democrática offered candidates for the Senate, the National Assembly, and Municipal Councils, but made no attempt to capture the Presidency.

Despite subversive plots, attempted *cuartelazos,* and dissensions within the Armed Forces, voters again went quietly to the polls on December 14 to elect a President and a national government by democratic processes, thus winning the respect of other democratic nations and lending credibility to the claims that Venezuela was ready for representative government.

Again Acción Democrática won a resounding victory, although the proportions of the landslide were less overwhelming than in 1946. Gallegos won the Presidency with a wide margin of 871,752 votes, as compared to Caldera's 262,204. Communist Machado trailed with a mere 36,514. In the National Assembly, AD won seats for 83 deputies, Copei 19, URD 4, the Communists 3, and the Liberal Party 1. In the Senate, AD received 38 seats, and Copei 6, while URD and the Communists had one each. The number of citizens participating in the election of 1947 was about 200,000 fewer than in 1946, and AD's share of the votes fell in this interval from 78.8% to 70.83%, while Copei's rose from 13.2% to 20.48%.

Betancourt is probably correct in attributing the fall in the number of voters to "political fatigue" on the part of the electorate, caused by the frequency of elections, and in considering Copei's gain as a healthy trend toward the development of a two-party system. It was only in the states of Mérida and Táchira that AD again ran a poor second to Copei. In Táchira the *copeyanos* received 54,000 votes compared to AD's 27,000. This result showed two things: first, that the southern Andean region comprising these two states still found its loyalty to the conservative and clerical traditions more attractive than the idea of social progress through democratic reforms; and second, the election was indeed honest, and wherever the opposition had sufficient votes, it could win.[19]

The transition from junta control to constitutional government by a duly elected executive was smooth. The Cabinet appointments of President-elect Gallegos were in no sense a shake-up of the government, but a considered shifting of responsibilities at the top levels of power that reflected the wishes of Betancourt and other AD leaders.

Four of the ministers continued in the Cabinet posts they had held under the Revolutionary Government: Carlos Delgado Chalbaud, Minister of National Defense; Juan Pablo Pérez Alfonso, Minister of Development; Edmundo Fernández, Minister of Health and Social Welfare; and Raúl Leoni, Minister of Labor. Three new Cabinet members came directly from the governorships of states: Eligio Anzola Anzola, from Lara, became Minister of the Interior; Ricardo Montilla, of Guárico, a conservation expert, was assigned to the Agriculture Ministry; and Leonardo Ruiz Pineda came from the governorship of Táchira to become Minister of Communications. Andrés Eloy Blanco, former president of the Constituent Assembly, was appointed Minister of Foreign Affairs. Valmore Rodríguez left the Interior Ministry to preside over the Senate. Betancourt, although formally out of the government, continued to exert a strong influence in national policy. In April, 1948, he headed the Venezuelan delegation to the Ninth Inter-American Conference in Bogota.[20]

In the spring of 1948 the Gallegos government, which was to endure less than a year, appeared to be off to a good start. The story of its downfall, and the beginning of a new and oppressive regime dominated by the military, will be considered in a later chapter. We turn now to the problems, accomplishments, and shortcomings of the three-year rule of Acción Democrática, 1945-1948.

Chapter III

The Rule
of Acción Democrática,
1945-48

One of the most pressing problems facing the Junta following the October Revolution was the development of a national petroleum policy that would redound to the greatest benefit of the nation. For many years prior to that time, Acción Democrática had propounded the doctrine that the vast petroleum wealth belonged to the Venezuelan people, that it was not the property of any government leader, and did not exist for the enrichment of the foreign-owned companies. The AD leaders preached further that the oil wealth was expendable and must one day come to an end. It was imperative to use all of the government's authority and influence in firm bargaining with the companies to obtain the largest possible share of profits for Venezuela. It was equally necessary to invest the enormous oil revenues in the development of a diversified national economy (agriculture and industry) against the day when the mineral wealth would be depleted. As previously noted, the Petroleum Reform Law of 1943 had brought an increase in Venezuela's share of the profits, but from the AD point of view, the whole petroleum situation still left much to be desired.

Within two months of coming to power, the Junta made its first move in the direction of a new oil policy. By special decree, an income tax was imposed on 1945 incomes of more than Bs. 800,000. This decree, applicable only once, was aimed squarely at the oil companies, for although some 20,000 persons were subject to income tax, only 75 were affected in this case, and the companies paid 98.5% of this surtax which amounted to more than Bs. 93,000,000 of added revenues to the Treasury.

The principal architect of AD's policy on petroleum was Development Minister Juan Pablo Pérez Alfonso, whose thesis, adopted by Acción Democrática, was that Venezuela must always receive at least half the petroleum profits in any given year, that it might make more than the companies, but never less. In 1947 the companies earned more than their

50% of the total profits, and the government required them to compensate for the imbalance by investing the difference in Venezuelan enterprises. The nation's income for that year, including regular and special taxes, machinery, salaries and services paid to Venezuelans, and reserve funds amounted to more than two billion bolivars. This greatly increased income resulted partly from the sharp rise in both the demand and the price of petroleum in the post-war period, and partly from the special income tax of 26% imposed on incomes of more than 28 million bolivars.[1]

According to Betancourt, the AD government never considered nationalizing its oil. The Venezuelan negotiators pushed the companies to the extreme limits in order to obtain the best possible terms. But they knew when to stop; they had studied the nationalization experiences of Mexico and Bolivia, and they knew that such action was not to their advantage if it could be avoided.

Another new concept on petroleum brought by the AD leadership was that the government must adopt the policy of permanent refusal to grant any new concessions of oil lands to private parties for exploration and exploitation. Naturally the companies were firmly opposed to such a policy, and threatened a gradual reduction of investments and activities in Venezuela in order to transfer their operations to the Middle East. The government demonstrated, however, that the companies already controlled vast areas of proven oil reserves, granted by previous regimes, of which they were currently exploiting only a very small part.

In 1947, in a determined effort to extract for Venezuela the maximum benefits from her mineral wealth, the government decided to claim part of its royalties in kind, and to barter it on world markets for needed foodstuffs. Here again the companies objected strenuously; they had no desire to see Venezuela enter the petroleum business on a competitive basis. The government prevailed, trading crude oil to Argentina for frozen meat, and to Brazil and other Latin American countries for their products.[2]

In March, 1948, Venezuela extended its direct involvement in the oil business by appointing a commission to establish a state refinery to process the nation's share of oil royalties. This program, as well as the policy of refusing to grant new concessions to companies, was attacked in Congress by Copei's Rafel Caldera, URD's Jóvito Villalba, and the PCV's Gustavo Machado as being contrary to the national interest by keeping the country ignorant of the extent of its reserves and precluding Venezuelan capital investment in the petroleum industry. The legislation proposed to this effect was nevertheless approved in Congress by a large majority.[3]

Closely related to the foregoing considerations was the government's doctrine of conservation of petroleum as an exhaustible natural resource. This involved the co-ordination of extraction rates in particular zones by competing companies, and the saving of natural gas by pumping it back into the earth instead of burning it off. By 1948 there were various pilot-plants in operation, set up by the Venezuelan Development Corporation, to utilize the gas in the reduction of iron ore, and plans were being made by the regime to pipe gas from oil fields to cities for industrial and domestic use.[4]

In June, 1947, Nelson Rockefeller, of the Creole Petroleum Corporation, proposed to the Venezuelan government the formation of a joint company to be financed by several oil companies in partnership with the government for the purpose of stimulating aspects of the economy not related to the petroleum industry. After many months of negotiations, this project came into being with the establishment of the Venezuela Basic Economy Corporation (VBEC). Funded by a combined appropriation of $15,200,000 contributed by Creole, Royal Dutch-Shell and the Mene Grande Oil Company, and an equal amount by the Venezuelan Development Corporation, this enterprise enabled the companies to reinvest a part of their profits in Venezuelan agriculture and industry. Shares with guaranteed interest were to be made available for purchase by Venezuelans after a period of ten years. In this undertaking also the government faced determined resistance from the opposition political parties, whose leaders claimed to fear that the project was a scheme through which the oil companies would gain a monopolistic control of the Venezuelan economy. The government prevailed and the corporation flourished.[5]

Organized labor grew and strengthened as never before under the AD regime. Raúl Leoni, Minister of Labor, used the executive power, backed by provisions of the 1947 Constitution, to help labor in every way. At the time of the October Revolution there were only 252 legalized unions in the country, and these were relatively weak and ineffective. After one year of AD rule, this number had risen to 773, and by the end of 1948, when the Gallegos government was overthrown, there were 1,014 such unions, some 450 of which were agricultural organizations.[6] The petroleum companies were required to bargain collectively with the Federation of Workers in the oil industry. On April 30, 1946, the first work contract ever negotiated in Venezuela's petroleum industry was signed.[7]

The high per capita income from the oil industry had created the false but widely accepted notion that Venezuela was a healthy and prosperous country. In reality, the great majority of Venezuelans were poverty stricken, illiterate, and undernourished. The semi-colonial economy was dependent almost exclusively upon a single source of income, petroleum, which was also her only hope of achieving a diversified economy within a reasonable period. In 1945 the nation's capacity for the production of corn, wheat, rice, meat, and milk was still far below the rate of consumption. It was necessary to divert petroleum revenues from other projects to pay for the importation of food which Venezuelans consumed but did not produce. To correct this deficiency the Junta established, in 1946, the Corporación Venezolana de Fomento (CVF), with a working capital of Bs. 400 million, and named as its director Dr. Alejandro Oropeza Castillo.[8] From the time of its inception the CVF, in co-operation with the State Bank and the Banco Agrícola y Pecuario (Agriculture and

Livestock Bank) strove to increase food production by making loans to small farmers for the purchase of machinery, fertilizer, seeds, fencing, and improved breeding stock.[9]

The difficulties of bringing Venezuelan agriculture abreast of the times were many and complex, and the single task of supplying the population with sufficient amounts of meat and milk of acceptable quality was formidable. The native cattle, known as *ganado criollo,* were and are the unthrifty and degenerate descendants of animals brought to the New World centuries ago by the Spaniards. Like the Texas Longhorns common to the American Southwest in the 19th century, they are thin and leggy, with large heads and ungainly bodies. They bear little resemblance to such beef breeds as the Angus, Hereford, or Shorthorn, or such dairy cattle as the Jersey, Guernsey, or Holstein. Their principal virtue is that they have survived the rigors of tropical climate, centuries of inbreeding and neglect, and the onslaught of countless parasites, and can serve as the basis of scientifically-bred herds of beef and dairy cattle by crossing them with imported bulls. For climatic reasons the Zebu, rather than any of the northern breeds, was chosen to improve the native beef cattle. The improvement of a country's livestock is a fairly long-term undertaking, and the CVF planners envisioned a ten-year period as necessary to achieve meaningful results. Meanwhile, the continued importation of meat was unavoidable, and the government contracted with Argentina for some 30,000 tons of frozen beef annually in exchange for Venezuelan crude oil.[10]

Similar efforts were made to improve the milk supply. Since quality as well as quantity was involved, it was necessary to go beyond the importation of Brown Swiss and Holstein dairy bulls, and establish pasteurization plants and a distribution system. In 1947 the CVF established in Maracay, with a working capital of Bs. 5 million, the first unit of a planned network of milk-producing stations, using modern methods of processing. Following the example of Chile, the Venezuelan government purchased the properties of several large dairy companies and brought about what amounted to the nationalization of the milk industry.[11]

Basic to both the meat and the milk programs was a controlled water supply for pasturage and livestock. In many of the cattle-raising regions the Venezuelan summer, lasting half the year, is a time of intense heat and prolonged drought; water supplies dwindle and grass disappears. The "winter", occupying the remaining months, is a period of torrential rains, overflowing streams, and flooded pasture lands. This seasonal imbalance has been aggravated by the thoughtless destruction, throughout many generations, of forests and other land cover on Venezuelan hills, resulting in soil erosion and climatic changes that accelerated the evaporation of water from natural lakes.[12]

The Ministry of Public Works and the CVF sought to solve these problems by creating numerous artificial lakes which would collect water during the rainy season and serve as reservoirs to be used for irrigation during the dry periods. Although hampered in its inception by the lack of trained agronomists and engineers, and the unavailability of machinery during the immediate post-war years, an ambitious program of dam building was undertaken in 1946 in the states of Aragua, Carabobo, Trujillo, and Anzoátegui, at an initial cost of Bs. 30 million, to provide irrigation for some 20,000 hectares (nearly 50,000 acres) of farm land, representing a ten-fold increase over the irrigation projects of the Medina regime.[13]

Of special interest in the rural renovation efforts was the pilot project known as El Cenizo, in the state of Trujillo. Located in the foothills of the Andes, in proximity to oil fields and cities, and with abundant sources of water, this area included some 100,000 hectares of fertile land susceptible of irrigation. Adopting on a smaller scale the methods used successfully by the TVA in the United States, the Junta sought to build, at El Cenizo, a model agricultural community, scientifically planned and managed. The completion of this project was planned for December, 1948, one month after the overthrow of the Gallegos government. Much remained to be done in fulfillment of the original plan, and this was not carried out by the military junta. Further comment on El Cenizo will be found at the end of this chapter in a general evaluation of the three-year rule of Acción Democrática.[14]

One of the most difficult aspects of the agrarian question was the finding of an equitable solution to the problem of land ownership. In Venezuela, as in most of Latin America, the predominant pattern of land tenure was the *latifundio,* an estate of many thousands of acres held by a single owner or family. The injustice of this colonial system of ownership, in which nearly all of the valuable farm land was concentrated in the hands of a few wealthy *hacendados,* was recognized by Simón Bolívar himself, who in 1816 issued a Ley de Repartos (Distribution Law) providing for the allotment of land to patriot soldiers and to all those who worked the soil. This admirable intention, like many other Bolívar plans, was frustrated by the very people entrusted with carrying it out. Land certificates, rather than actual allotments of real estate, were issued to soldiers and landless peasants. Inevitably, the intended recipients were defrauded of their properties by unscrupulous speculators and military leaders.

Throughout the remainder of the nineteenth century and until the October Revolution of 1945, the ownership of the great estates changed but little, according to the whims of such dictators as Juan Vicente Gómez, who seized for himself vast areas of the most desirable lands. The Venezuelan dirt farmer, or *conuquero,* like the medieval European serf who toiled on a plot owned by the lord of the manor, scratched out a bare living on a patch of corn land on the fringe of a great estate, on which he was permitted to live in exchange for labor.[15]

The AD leaders had long preached the doctrine that the redistribution of Venezuelan land was an absolute necessity, not only in the interest of social justice, but in order to make the country's agriculture efficient and prosperous. Two months after coming to power, Betancourt said to the nation: "So that the land may produce, it is necessary that it be in the hands of those who make it produce. When I sustain this thesis—expounding it in the name of the Revolutionary Government, which has a definite concept of agrarian policy—we do not assume a position of the extreme radical left."[16]

Indeed, despite the fears of landowners and others who could not or would not forget the early Marxist associations of the AD leaders, the methods advocated by Acción Democrática bore little resemblance to the confiscations carried out by Communist regimes. The task of spelling out a land-reform policy was left to the Constituent Assembly, which was instructed to include specific provisions for a new Agrarian Law in the Constitution of 1947. Meanwhile, as a stop-gap measure to alleviate severe tensions among increasingly land-hungry *campesinos,* the government invested several millions of bolivars in the purchase of rural properties, which were immediately parceled and distributed to the neediest farmers.[17]

Article 69 of the new Constitution ordered Congress to enact a "special law" which should provide for the distribution of cultivable lands and "the necessary means of making them produce." This legislation was the Ley Agraria, passed by the Congress of 1948, and signed by President Gallegos on October 18 of that year. The land distribution program was to be financed by an initial appropriation of Bs. 100 million provided by the State, in addition to the value of properties given by the Administración de Bienes Restituidos (Administration of Restored Wealth), *i.e.,* lands and goods confiscated from the heirs of Juan Vicente Gómez. It would also be supported by an annual appropriation of 2% to 4% of the national budget. The same law provided that the reform would be carried out by a central organ, created by Article 4, called the National Agrarian Institute.[18]

According to Betancourt and other defenders of AD aims and methods, these imaginative steps brought an immediate response from the Venezuelan farmers, who awakened from their age-old lethargy of hopelessness to build fences, care for their livestock, fertilize and irrigate their fields, plan the rotation of crops, and look forward to a prosperous future. The same sources assert that such helpful programs by the government could retard, or even halt, the steady abandonment by farm laborers of their ancestral homes in order to move to the cities. Betancourt condemns as "superficial sociologists" those who attribute such migratory tendencies to "congenital nomadism" on the part of rural Venezuelans. The AD leader's view, as of 1956, was that the *conuqueros* and farm workers left their homes and fields only because of hopeless economic and social conditions, and would really prefer to remain there if the situation were improved.[19]

In retrospect, it is clear that despite some positive results of the AD program of rural renovation, the belief that these reforms would retard or reverse the rural-to-urban migratory trend was overly optimistic. Reliable statistics for the period prior to 1950 are difficult to obtain, but recent demographic studies indicate that the flow of rural Venezuelans toward the cities continued at a fairly constant rate throughout the dictatorship of the 1950s and has persisted unchecked despite the restoration of democratic rule and a much expanded program of agrarian reform and aid to farmers.[20] A clear indication of this fact can be seen in the ever-growing slum areas, or shanty-towns, that surround such major cities as Caracas, Maracaibo, Barquisimeto, and Valencia. These ghetto areas continue to expand rapidly through natural increase of the population, as well as by accretion from the rural areas of the interior. These facts are not a denigration of government aid to farmers, but they do indicate that agrarian reforms are unlikely to stem the movement toward urban centers or to cure the social ills resulting from it.

It is not now possible to judge how successful the Gallegos government would have been in carrying out its agrarian program had it not been ousted from power in 1948. Studies are available, however, which set forth the accomplishments and shortcomings of the Betancourt regime when Acción Democrática returned to power ten years later.[21]

A serious impediment to the realization of the various AD improvement schemes in the period 1945-48 was the primitive condition of most Venezuelan highways. Since the 19th-century regime of Guzmán Blanco, very little had been done to extend or improve them. The López Contreras and Medina administrations built some roads, but their efforts involved only piecemeal projects that were unrelated to any concerted plan for a specific purpose. In 1946 the Junta attempted to approach the highway problem as an integral part of the over-all transportation needs of the country, including railroads, airlines, and river transport. A government commission prepared a plan that included construction of 16,000 kilometers of roads, 50 airfields, and various coastal and river ports. As in the case of dam building, irrigation works, and other projects requiring engineering skills, detailed technical knowledge, and special equipment, the regime again encountered a scarcity of personnel and machinery.

Nevertheless, some progress was made: 360 kilometers of highways were completed in 1947 and 400 in 1948. Studies were made and construction begun on several other necessary routes, including the super highway linking Caracas to the Caribbean port of La Guaira, crossing a region whose rough topography imposed many months of blasting, cutting and filling before actual construction could begin.[22]

Meanwhile, perhaps because it was imperative to bring aid on many levels to the backward and poverty-stricken areas of the country, the streets and public squares of Caracas were much neglected by the AD government during this period. Political opponents joined in bitter denunciations of the *adecos* for the eroded streets, pot-holes, and mud puddles to be seen in the capital and in other cities and towns. Commentators of later periods have neither forgotten nor forgiven these conditions.[23]

An accomplishment that brought profit as well as prestige to Venezuela during this period was the creation of a merchant fleet. The very high freight charges exacted by American shipping companies during World War II on foods and other necessities were regarded by Latin American countries as exorbitant and unfair, and made them aware of the need for merchant vessels of their own. Early in 1946 the Junta began negotiations with Colombia and Ecuador for the formation of a joint enterprise to be known as the Flota Mercante Gran-Colombiana, in memory of the original Bolivarian nation comprising those three countries. Beginning with eight small ships representing a capital of only 20 million dollars, the company's stock was owned 45% each by Colombia and Venezuela, and 10% by Ecuador.

In 1947, its first year of operations, the merchant fleet carried less than 200,000 tons, but by 1951 it had expanded to a capacity of more than a million tons, realizing a saving of 25% in freight costs. This enterprise, acting independently of the powerful "Caribbean Conference" cartel, dominated by North American shipping interests, did not find itself unopposed. According to Betancourt, the State Department sought to intervene by reminding Colombia that an old treaty required that country to accord preferential treatment to American carriers, but the Colombian press quickly pointed out that the same treaty guaranteed American recognition of Colombian sovereignty over the Isthmus of Panama.[24] As will be noted in a later chapter, the Flota Mercante Gran-Colombiana did not long survive the fall of the Gallegos government.

In 1946 the Junta began to invest some of the nation's petroleum revenues in the development of native industry. The country was rich in natural resources of many kinds, and industrial power was at hand in the form of petroleum, natural gas, and hydroelectric potential. Manpower was also ample, particularly in the larger cities whose populations had swollen as a result of the rural-to-urban movement of the post-war years. The obstacles to industrialization, however, were numerous and discouraging. The mangement class was without experience or know-how in modern methods. Factory equipment and machinery of all kinds were lacking and, in the period immediately after the war, practically unavailable. And the manpower, although abundant, consisted almost entirely of unskilled and illiterate citizens whose background was typically rural and backward.[25]

The Venezuelan Development Corporation was given the responsibility of supporting the growth and improvement of selected native industries by means of loans, subsidies, duty-free imports, and tax credits. Among those receiving governmental protection were firms involved in producing or processing foods, including edible fats such as corn oil and sesame oil. Loans were made to the owners of fishing fleets operating along the Caribbean coast for the purchase of motorized craft and modern gear. Canneries in Cumaná and Puerto Cabello were subsidized to process the catch.

One reason for the low yields in many Venezuelan crops was the lack of fertilizers. The best soil areas had been worked intensively for centuries and were exhausted, but imported commercial fertilizers were prohibitively expensive and not always suited to local soil requirements. This problem was studied, and by 1948 the CVF had included in its budget appropriations for a fertilizer pilot plant at Puerto Cabello, using native phosphates and other local materials.[26]

Efforts to stimulate and improve the manufacture of textiles and shoes were relatively unrewarding. Both were extremely backward, using antiquated methods for lack of technical knowledge and modern machinery. These industries needed not only subsidies and loans, but complete revision of production methods. In the mid 1940s a large percentage of Venezuelans were still barefoot or wearing only *alpargatas,* or rope sandals. Better quality textiles and leather goods were still imported from Peru, Chile and elsewhere.[27]

One of the most successful of the attempts to stimulate industry was in the manufacture of cement, a material much needed for the construction of rural highways, hospitals, schools, and bridges. It would later be utilized by the Military Junta, and especially the Pérez Jiménez regime, for the great building spree of the 1950s in and near Caracas.[28]

In 1945 electricity was used on only a very limited scale in Venezuela. Millions of people in small towns and rural areas still depended on kerosene lamps, lanterns, and candles. Although there were several sources of electrical power, including natural gas, petroleum, and water power, all in abundance, the companies had followed the general business practice of producing below demand and selling at a high price. Rates charged were not controlled by the government. Betancourt first reduced the prices by presidential decree, then undertook a program to increase the supply of electrical power. Through the CVF many millions of bolivars were spent in the installation of generating plants in many parts of the country. Faced with a shortage of competent technicians for an electrification program of large scale, Development Minister Pérez Alfonso arranged with the Engineering Department of the Central University to inaugurate a course for the training of specialists in this field.[29]

Another natural resource with which Venezuela is richly endowed is iron. A deposit of 100 million tons of 60% pure ore was discovered near the Orinoco in 1932 by Iron Mines of Venezuela, a subsidiary of Bethlehem Steel Corporation, and during the Medina regime there was much debate concerning the best means of exploiting this mineral. The Orinoco was not deep enough to admit ocean-going freighters without costly dredging, and the company proposed to export the ore on barges to a deep-water port in the Caribbean, for trans-shipment on freighters to smelters in the United States. Acción Democrática, then in opposition, urged that the ore be reduced within the country to form a base for the development of a Venezuelan steel industry, and in 1945 a beginning was made in this direction. In 1947 the U.S. Steel Corporation discovered the enormous reserves of Cerro Bolívar, now estimated to contain one billion tons of high-grade ore. Negotiations were under way in the autumn of 1948 between the Gallegos government and a subsidiary of United States Steel for construction of a railroad from the

Orinoco to Puerto La Cruz and the development of foundries and steel mills in that city. This undertaking was brought to a sudden end by the overthrow of the legal government on November 18 of that year.[30]

In 1945, according to Education Minister Luis B. Prieto, only one-third of the 800,000 children of school age were receiving any education at all, and this under unsatisfactory conditions. Classrooms with seats existed for only 55,000 pupils, others having to stand or sit on the floors of makeshift schools. More than a million Venezuelans, comprising 65% of the population between the ages of 14 and 59, were totally illiterate.[31] The government undertook a program of school building and aid to education on all levels. In the three years that this regime existed, primary school attendance increased from 133,000 to 500,000. Similar support was extended to secondary schools, both public and private.

The efforts of Acción Democrática in the field of education did not always meet with public approval. At times the zeal to modernize and liberalize Venezuelan life on all levels led the Junta into extreme and unwise decisions. On May 30, 1946, the government issued the controversial Decree 321, which imposed new and severe regulations on private primary, secondary, and normal schools, affecting the status of teachers. Government support to public education had already attracted many students away from private institutions, and the provisions of the new Decree were widely regarded as an attempt by the regime to weaken the Church-directed private schools. As a result of much public opposition, including protest marches and newspaper editorials, the restrictive measure was rescinded, but it had created much suspicion and ill-will.[32]

Vocational education, long neglected, was aided by the establishment of technical and industrial schools, and gains were made in the fight against illiteracy. The teaching profession, traditionally in low repute, was made more attractive by pay rises, improved working conditions, and the encouraging of teacher participation in political activities and social reforms. Central University, in Caracas, planned and started by the Medina regime, was finished by the AD government at a cost of some Bs. 100 million, and aid was extended to higher education elsewhere in the country.[33]

In the field of public health, the regimes of Betancourt and Gallegos found both challenge and opportunity. The fight against malaria and other endemic diseases and the building of adequate hospitals and rural health centers, neglected by the dictatorial rulers of the past, had received some support from the government of Medina Angarita. In 1945 the Revolutionary Government embarked on an all-out campaign to improve and protect public health. The anti-malarial program was placed in the hands of Dr. Arnaldo Gabaldón, a Venezuelan expert of international reputation and chief of the Division of Malariology at Central University. This undertaking succeeded so well that by 1948, when the Gallegos government was overthrown, malaria was practically non-existent in many parts of the country. Also carried out as part of the disease prevention program was the construction of aqueducts, sewerage systems, and adequate drainage in cities and towns throughout the country.

Recognizing the close relationship between proper diet and the ability to learn, the government in 1945 created the Instituto de Alimentación Popular to study the dietary problems of public school children. In co-operation with the Ministries of Education and of Health and Social Assistance, this organization established student dining halls where, by 1948, some 38,000 children supplemented their daily food supply with balanced meals provided by the government.[34]

Many of the most seriously debilitating diseases afflicting the Venezue-lan population, such as ankilostomiasis and Chagas' disease, were closely related to the unsanitary character of the dwellings of a large percentage of the people. For this reason, the government began a national housing program as a part of the effort to improve the country's health and living standards. The 1941 census had revealed that in 17 of the nation's 20 states and its two territories, the prevailing dwelling was the one-room thatch-roofed hut with dirt floor known as a *rancho*. The Banco Obrero, charged with carrying out the financial aspect of public housing, received an appropriation of Bs. 60 million for 1946, and increased amounts for 1947 and 1948. In the first two years of AD rule, some 5,000 dwellings were built in various parts of the republic, a good beginning, but clearly not enough to satisfy the nation's housing needs.[35]

Among the many long-standing national problems facing the new regime in 1945 were the general cultural and technical backwardness of the Venezuelan people and the paucity of the nation's population in comparison to its geographical size. Developed by the Junta, and later specifically adopted by the Gallegos government, was an "open-door policy" of carefully selected immigrants. In this, the AD position was to some extent a conscious imitation of the policy advocated a century earlier in Argentina by Juan Bautiste Alberdi, whose dictum "Gobernar es poblar" (to govern is to populate) was enthusiastically put into prac-tice by President Sarmiento. The Alberdi plan was a calculated effort, destined to be successful, to make Argentina a white country by popu-lating the vast hinterland with European immigrants, thus outnumbering and eventually absorbing or displacing the "inferior" *mestizo-criollo*; this was done in the sincere belief in the superiority of the white race.

In partially similar circumstances a century later, the government of Venezuela, while rejecting the notion of the innate superiority of the white or the European, nevertheless sought large numbers of immigrants from this same source for the reasons already stated. In the first year of AD rule, the country accepted some 5,000 newcomers, principally from Italy, Spain, and Portugal. They were screened in those countries by Venezue-lan missions charged with the exclusion of criminal elements, psycho-tics, political extremists, and other undesirables. In the remaining two years of the Betancourt-Gallegos period, an additional 32,000 immi-grants arrived from the same areas of western Europe.[36]

In attempting to set forth at this point an objective evaluation of the three-year rule of Acción Democrática, we postpone examination of the charges leveled against the constitutional government by those responsible for its overthrow, *i.e.,* members of the military Junta of Delgado Chalbaud. These accusations were clearly attempts at after-the-fact "justification" of the *coup d'état* of November 24, 1948. We shall consider them in a later chapter. In the opposite direction, but for similar reasons, we must exclude the excessive and self-serving claims of government efficiency and social renovation adduced by Rómulo Betancourt and other *adeco* apologists with respect to that period.

The fact is that the AD regimes of 1945-48 left a mixed record of many beginnings, hopeful gains, partial successes, and some failures. In 1945 and 1946, euphoric with power, and brimming with enthusiasm and political ambition, the *adeco* planners rushed into a multitude of undertakings affecting the national economy in a manner reminiscent of the rulings and interventions of FDR's New Deal "Brain Trust" in 1933. With an eye to the election of delegates to the Constituent Assembly, scheduled for October, 1946, Betancourt and other AD orators toured the country for many months prior to that event, reminding Venezuelans of measures already taken in their behalf by the Revolutionary Junta and promising many more benefits in the future.[37]

As noted earlier in this study, many of the first decrees emanting from the Junta after the October Revolution of 1945 ordered drastic reductions in the prices of such necessities as corn, rice, meat, milk and kerosene. These urgently needed measures, bringing welcome relief to millions of poverty-stricken citizens, undoubtedly did much to win popular support for the new regime. Other actions initiated by the government, particularly those involving the importation of scarce foodstuffs, were less successful. One instance of remarkable bureaucratic bungling and mismanagement occurred when the Junta summoned a group of 20 or 30 Venezuelan wholesalers to inform them that the government wished to import 20,000 tons of Cuban sugar at once and another 20,000 tons a month later. The dealers were asked to submit bids to the Junta for this transaction. Thereupon, more than 20 of the importers applied simultaneously to companies in Havana, each one requesting prices on a purchase of 40,000 tons of sugar! This sudden and unprecedented Venezuelan demand for nearly 1,000,000 tons of Cuban sugar naturally caused a dramatic rise in the price of the product, with the result that the Junta was forced to postpone all action in the matter until the market returned to a normal level. Although imports ordered by the regime were later placed in the hands of a government purchasing commission in order to avoid such problems, confusion and discontent continued, especially in the case of thousands of tons of beef imported from Argentina in exchange for Venezuelan crude oil.[38]

Other mistakes were committed by the AD regimes of Betancourt and Gallegos, whether caused by errors in policy or lack of proper control of governmental functions. The alienation of many Venezuelan Catholics resulting from the anti-clerical provisions of Decree 321, affecting parochial school teachers, was entirely unnecessary. The humiliation of of many prominent citizens, caused by publication of their names in the hastily-prepared list of persons to be indicted for suspected corruption in office during past periods, was the cause of much resentment and bitterness toward the regime. Some individuals, accused by the *adecos* of embezzlements and other crimes, but later vindicated of guilt after great anguish and expense, lost all desire to co-operate with even the most legitimate and admirable aspects of the AD program. The policy of near-monopoly control of all governmental posts and agencies exercised by Acción Democrática during the period, and the favoritism shown to *adeco* businessmen and industrialists in the granting of contracts, was also divisive in effect and contrary to the best interests of the government and of the country.

Some of the more spectacular and ambitious undertakings of the AD regimes to bring about rural renovation and progress have been condemned by qualified experts as ill-planned and unrealistic, serving only as vote-getting propaganda for the party in power. An example of this type of project was El Cenizo, mentioned earlier in this chapter, much touted by Acción Democrática as a complete and balanced agricultural community, but allegedly ill-conceived, poorly managed, and destined to failure.[39]

At the time of the *coup d'état* of November, 1948, many economic dislocations remained in Venezuela. Social justice had not been achieved, and the objectives of the October Revolution of 1945 had not been fulfilled. But there was progress. After the election of Rómulo Gallegos in 1947 as Constitutional President with an overwhelming mandate to govern, the legal and moral position of the government appeared unassailable. Despite the unrelenting attacks by the opposition parties, and the bitter invective and harassment of a large section of the press, the party in power maintained a unified command and a concerted program, and the government enjoyed the wide support of organized labor and the masses of the Venezuelan people.

The danger to the continuation of representative government in the nation did not lie in the relatively weak opposition parties, but in the Defense Ministry itself.

Chapter IV

The Military *Coup* of November, 1948

It was inevitable and even predictable that the tactical alliance, or marriage of convenience, formed in 1945 between the liberal and progressive Acción Democrática and the conservative and authoritarian Unión Patriótica Militar should one day come to a violent and disruptive parting of the ways. The reader will recall that although Marcos Pérez Jiménez was the chief planner and co-ordinator of the October Revolution for the young officers of the UPM, he did not become a member of the new governing Junta headed by Rómulo Betancourt. Lieut.-Col. Carlos Delgado Chalbaud, appointed Minister of Defense, was a Junta member, while Pérez Jiménez became Chief of the General Staff of the Armed Forces. The latter's second in command was his old friend and confidant, Lieut.-Col. Luis Felipe Llovera Páez. This arrangement prevailed until the *coup d'état* of November 24, 1948. Even before the election of President Gallegos, there were constant rumors among AD leaders that the arch-conspirator, Pérez Jiménez, was developing a new plot to overthrow the government. His discontent with the regime's democratic program was well known, and it is entirely possible that he was, indeed, occupied with such a plan. On the other hand, the first rumors of this plot may well have been planted by Delgado Chalbaud himself, for tactical reasons.

It is known that the Defense Minister, key figure in this intrigue, professed absolute and unconditional loyalty to the President, and that a simple and effective solution had been formulated to thwart the alleged plot. This plan, also widely discussed and well known to Pérez Jiménez himself, was to send the Chief of Staff on a "military study tour" through various Latin American countries. While on the trip, Perez Jiménez would receive appointment as Ambassador to Brazil, and would then remain in that country instead of returning to Caracas. Another officer would replace him as Chief of Staff, and the conspiracy would be dissolved. Reports of this scheme have appeared in the writings of so many Venezuelan commentators that it is not possible to consider it as having no basis in fact. Rómulo Betancourt relates some details of the Pérez Jiménez tour through Latin America, but makes no mention of the plan to remove him from his military post.[1] This omission may indicate that the AD leader was, as other writers have asserted, the author of the displacement manoeuver, and that he failed to mention it because it was unsuccessful.[2]

The most interesting aspect of this somewhat bizarre affair, in the light of later events, is that Defense Minister Delgado postponed the Pérez Jiménez trip, on one pretext or another, for many months; and when the Chief of Staff finally departed, early in the spring of 1948, he appeared to do so with no misgivings. There is also the fact that he did not complete his journey according to plan. While visiting Perón in Buenos Aires, he is alleged to have received an "urgent cablegram", after which he began his return to Venezuela at once, stopping only in Lima to confer briefly with his old friend and former teacher of military tactics, Peruvian Dictator Manuel Odría. For reasons important to his own plans, Delgado Chalbaud had made it possible for the Chief of staff to return safely to his post in Caracas.[3]

Perhaps because of the "cultural prestige" of the Saint Cyr-educated Defense Minister, to which nearly all commentators have alluded, it was generally accepted at the time of the November *coup*, especially by United States newsmen, that Delgado's conduct throughout the whole period was guided by motives of patriotism, loyalty to fellow officers, and the desire to avoid a disastrous split in the Armed Forces. From the vantage point of more than twenty years, and in consideration of prior and subsequent events, this interpretation appears somewhat naive. He could not possibly have been unaware of the subversive connivings of Pérez Jiménez and, as top man in the entire defense establishment, he had full authority to take whatever measures were necessary to crush the plot in an effective manner. Instead, the Minister of Defense seems to have played a kind of cat-and-mouse game for his own purposes, maintaining the complete confidence of President Gallegos while permitting the conspiracy to develop unhindered.

Chief of Staff Pérez Jiménez returned to his country imbued with the fascist spirit prevailing in Argentina, Paraguay, and Peru, and began a vigorous campaign among the officers under his command to undermine and discredit the Gallegos administration and Acción Democrática. He took special pains to instill in the Armed Forces the military creed enunciated in 1943 by Col. Juan Domingo Perón: "Civilians will never understand the grandeur of our ideal, and they must therefore be removed from government and given the only mission suitable to them: Work and Obedience."[4]

Unaware of the serious situation developing in the Armed Forces, the attention of the government and of the nation was, during the summer and fall of 1948, attracted much more by the less dangerous but more vociferous activities of the political opposition. The Caracas newspaper *El Gráfico,* mouthpiece of Dr. Rafael Caldera's Christian Democratic Copei, and the even more reactionary *La Esfera* were filled with constant anti-government diatribes written in provocative and inflammatory language. Valmore Rodríguez, founder of the AD newspaper *El País,* and President of the Senate during the Gallegos administration, vigorously defended the government's program, repeatedly scolding and denouncing opposition legislators for statements bordering on treason. On June 25, URD Senator Antonio Pulido Villafañe was formally called to account for having published in the newspaper *Segundo Frente* an article inciting the Armed Forces to rebellion. Senator Pulido was censured and suspended from the Senate by vote of his colleagues.[5] The government's majority in both houses of Congress was overwhelming, and although the censure issue was unusual, its outcome was never in doubt; thus it posed no direct threat to the stability of the regime. The fact that a senator could be guilty of incitement to rebellion does indicate, however, that democratic ways had not yet taken firm root among Venezuela's political parties.

So complete was the confidence of President Gallegos in the loyalty of his Defense Minister and in the strength and popularity of his administration, that in the same month of June, 1948, and while the above-mentioned censure motion was under consideration in the Senate, the Chief Executive accepted an invitation from President Truman for an eleven-day good-will visit to the United States. On this occasion the American President sent his famous private plane, the "Independence", to South America to bring Gallegos to Washington, where he was greeted by a 21-gun salute. Thereafter, the itinerary included the unveiling of a statue of Simón Bolívar in Bolivar, Missouri; a formal address before the assembled delegates of the Organization of American States in Washington; a trip southward to inspect the Norris Dam and other TVA installations; a gala celebration in New Orleans; a trip to Texas; and another to New York City where he received an honorary doctor-of-laws degree from Columbia University President Dwight D. Eisenhower.

To the surprise of many Venezuelans, Gallegos had appointed none other than Defense Minister Delgado Chalbaud to serve as Provisional President during his absence; and to complete the prophetic nature of this arrangement, Pérez Jiménez became Acting Minister of Defense; posts that both men were soon to occupy on a more permanent basis. It is true that other men had been considered to serve in the Provisional Presidency during this period, including Interior Minister Eligio Anzola Anzola and Minister of Health Dr. Edmundo Fernández.[6] Delgado Chalbaud, a last-minute choice, may well have won his own appointment and that of Pérez Jiménez by the passionately patriotic speech that he delivered on Army Day, June 24, just prior to the Gallegos trip. Rómulo Betancourt, writing in exile some years later, was to recall how "Delgado Chalbaud, putting on attitudes of loyalty toward the constitu-

tional government, denounced those civilian inciters of military dis-
obedience with words of deceptive dignity."[7]

In the second week of July, President Gallegos returned to his office
in Miraflores Palace, Delgado and Pérez Jiménez went back to their
respective posts in the Defense Ministry, and internal developments in
Venezuela appeared to have resumed their former course. But the situation had changed, and things would never be quite the same again. The
two top military men in the nation had experienced a temporary increase of power, and they had found it greatly to their liking.

The mood of political discord and gradually rising tension that developed in the country between the return of Gallegos and the *coup
d'état* of November is clearly discernible in the editorial tones of practically all Caracas papers except *El País,* which belonged to Acción Democrática and necessarily reflected the views of the government. Such
frankly conservative or reactionary journals as *La Esfera, El Heraldo,*
and Copei's *El Gráfico* were joined by the centrist and non-partisan
El Universal and *El Nacional* in taking the government to task for
everything that it did or failed to do. Despite the relentless barrage of
criticism, the four-month period in question was a time of legislative
accomplishment. As noted in the preceding chapter, the administration
succeeded in pushing through Congress such important bills as the
Education Law, the Agrarian Law, and the Law of Illicit Enrichment.
These were signed by President Gallegos on October 19, 1948, to become effective at once.[8]

Meanwhile, Chief of Staff Pérez Jiménez had worked zealously in
the barracks and at the Officers Club to prepare the collective attitude
necessary for the seizure of power that he planned. Many young officers,
already conditioned by background and training to the military tradition, had been immediately receptive to the subversive propaganda
offered by their Chief. They were ready to believe that the President
really planned to destroy the Armed Forces, and that the nation could
only be "saved" by a return to military rule. Others, however, proved
less amenable; they had found democracy more admirable than dictatorship, and had no desire to return to caudillo ways. Those who
resisted the campaign of subversion began to receive through the mail
small packages containing women's panties and other articles of femi-
nine apparel, an unsubtle suggestion that they were lacking the necessary
machismo for an uprising against the government.[9] Perhaps Pérez
Jiménez' methods were more effective than he realized, and he may
have achieved his objective of psychological preparation in the Armed
Forces somewhat earlier than anticipated. Or it may be that having
reached the brink of irrevocable action against the legal government,
the conspirator began to have second thoughts about the consequences
of a possible failure. Certainly all was in readiness for the planned *coup*
by the final week of October, including sworn adherents to the conspiracy among commanding officers at barracks in other parts of the
republic.

Yet Peréz Jiménez hesitated. He began to appear frequently at social gatherings in Caracas, cautiously sounding out various guests as to the popularity and strength of the Gallegos regime. Often accompanied by such close associates as Lieut.-Col. Llovera Páez, Major Carlos Pulido Barreto, Major Alberto Paoli Chalbaud, and Major Mario Sosa Puccini, the Chief of Staff expressed few opinions himself, but appeared pleased to hear denunciations of the government. Some of these social scenes are described in detail in the previously-cited book *Escrito de memoria,* by Pérez' faithful friend and ardent admirer, Vallenilla Lanz, a shrewd Caracas speculator who dabbled in real estate, the import trade, journalism, and banking. Assiduous in the cultivation of advantageous friendships among big businessmen, right-wing politicians, and powerful military figures, he was later to become Minister of the Interior in the Pérez Jiménez dictatorship. Vallenilla, who had only recently made the acquaintance of the Chief of Staff, recalls that the latter made a point of insisting that the officers under his command had wanted to overthrow the government for a long time, and that it was only he, Pérez Jiménez, who restrained them, out of respect for legality, although he emphasized that he was not an *adeco* and had no liking for Gallegos or Betancourt.[10]

It will be recalled that at the time of the October Revolution of 1945, Pérez, whose extraordinary conspiratorial talents were responsible for the success of that movement, did not present himself at Miraflores Palace to claim a place on the Revolutionary Junta, as did Delgado Chalbaud and Mario Vargas, who had joined the plot at a later date. His failure to step forward and to claim the authority and prestige that his organizational abilities seemed to have earned for him has been explained by some critics as caused by a naturally gloomy and negative personality, a tendency toward sulkiness and self pity. Others, such as Betancourt and Valmore Rodríguez, have asserted that Pérez was a moral coward, a victim of severe inferiority complex, who was totally incapable of asserting his personality at a decisive moment in the presence of such men as Delgado Chalbaud. Whatever the precise psychological reason may be, it is certain that despite his cunning and meticulous preparations, he tended to be indecisive at critical moments and to postpone direct action in favor of further and more thorough planning. As will be noted, he also displayed this characteristic on later occasions.

In all of this, Delgado Chalbaud had maintained a position of perfect equilibrium. It cannot be ascertained that there was ever any conspiratorial contact between him and any of the plotters, and it is probable that he carefully avoided such communication in order to remain officially "unaware" that a subversive movement existed. Yet it is clear that he had sources of detailed and accurate information, and was thus protected in case of any possible development. If the conspiracy succeeded, he, as Defense Minister, could assume command of whatever situation resulted. If it failed, through betrayal or the accidental leak of vital information, resulting in the sudden arrest of conspirators by order of the President—a common development in subversive movements of the past—, Delgado Chalbaud would be able to show an impeccable record of loyalty to the government.

Sometime during the latter half of October, Pérez Jiménez became convinced that his plans had reached the desired state of perfection, and set the date of November 7 for the overthrow of the Gallegos government. During the first week of November, however, the Chief of Staff and his co-conspirators became aware that certain changes had been made with respect to the stationing of troops under the command of officers who did not belong to the conspiracy, including Lieut.-Col. J. M. Gámez Arellano, chief of the important Maracay Garrison, a loyal supporter of Gallegos. The leaders of the plot suddenly perceived the significance of the new distribution of forces: the President would be removed from power by the *coup d'état,* but Pérez Jiménez, Llovera Páez, and their most important supporters would also be crushed by the military action. Delgado Chalbaud would then remain as the undisputed master of the situation. The execution of the plan was therefore postponed by Pérez Jiménez to November 27 so that necessary adjustments could be made.[11]

After a few days of uncertainty, events moved swiftly toward a showdown. Persistent rumors of an impending military *coup* circulated through the Venezuelan capital and other cities; Delgado's position appeared uncertain and mysterious to nearly everyone. President Gallegos, although still trusting the Defense Minister, was extremely suspicious and watchful. On November 15 Pérez Jiménez, urged to action by impatient comrades and the fear of imminent arrest, presented himself with Llovera Páez and other leading rebels at the President's office in Miraflores. There they presented Gallegos with a list of demands, including the immediate separation of the government from Acción Democrática and the naming of a completely new and radically different Cabinet. The latter was to include a preponderance of military men, as well as representatives of opposition political parties. According to all accounts, President Gallegos indignantly rejected these demands out of hand, pointing out that his government was legal and constitutional, and that they were insubordinate in attempting to impose their wishes upon the Chief Executive. After administering a severe scolding on the evils of military meddling in government and the necessity of respect for law and civil authority, he ordered the officers to return at once to their barracks and to occupy themselves with their own duties. The conspirators left, but first they warned the President that he must comply with their demands or face the overthrow of his government.

In the frantic days that followed, Gallegos and other government leaders were by no means in agreement as to the best means of preventing the threatened *coup.* The President, inexperienced in the intrigues and manoeuvres of power politics, but courageous and morally upright as always, was determined to protect the legality of government structure at all costs, and declared that he would hold the line against the demands of the military. Rómulo Betancourt, political realist, former exile, and agile veteran of power struggles of the past, counseled a more astute course of action. The President, he said, should make partial and temporary concessions to the lieutenant-colonels, in order to gain time for the mobilization of other sources of political power. After that, he could remove the conspirators from their posts and mete out well-deserved punishments. Acción Democrática counted on the loyalty of organized labor, and could threaten the conspirators with paralysis of the entire economy by calling a strike in the petroleum fields. Also, said Betancourt, the President should send at once to the United States for Lieut.-Col. Mario Vargas, Inspector General of the Armed Forces, who was considered entirely loyal to the government as well as popular and influential among officers and soldiers.

It was hoped that Vargas could restrain the Pérez Jiménez group while the government found other means of protecting its position. Gallegos agreed, at least, to this suggestion, and Vargas, although confined to bed in a tuberculosis sanatorium at Saranac Lake, New York, undertook to return to his country at once. As for making any concession to Pérez Jiménez, the President avowed that he would have none of it, nor would he demean his office by seeking tactical support from labor unions. Instead, on November 20, Gallegos issued Presidential Decree No. 119: Suspension of Constitutional Guarantees Relating to Freedom of Speech and Assembly, hoping thereby to maintain law and order, and to preserve the integrity of his regime by the imposition of executive authority.[12]

By this move, however, the President unwittingly deprived himself of the only source of protection and help available to him: the Venezuelan people. The public was not informed of the dire circumstances in which their government found itself; the press was forbidden by decree to explain it. For the same reasons, labor unions were unable to meet or discuss the situation. It is true that Interior Minister Eligio Anzola stated to reporters that the President would soon issue a communiqué explaining the reasons for the suspension of guarantees. Unfortunately Gallegos was never to have the opportunity of making that explanation.

Also on November 20 Mario Vargas arrived by plane from New York, conferred with the President, then with Delgado Chalbaud and other members of the high command. He found the military insurrection so far advanced that it was impossible to arrest it, and counseled only that whatever change in governmental organization was necessary should be carried out by agreement and without violence. On the following day President Gallegos, in a final effort to avert the military takeover, summoned to his office a group of loyal officers, one of whom was Lieut.-Col. Gámez Arellano, commander of the Maracay Garrison. Others present were Delgado Chalbaud, Rómulo Betancourt, and Senate President Valmore Rodríguez. On this occasion Gámez Arelllano became enraged at the ambiguous and equivocal posture of Delgado Chalbaud who, he said, could easily have stopped the conspiracy by removing the plotters from their posts and throwing them into prison. Gámez openly accused the Defense Minister of deliberately permitting the subversion to develop unhindered, and declared that he was therefore to blame for the existing situation. The Maracay commander thereupon turned to the President and demanded permission to place Delgado Chalbaud under arrest then and there. Gallegos, unable or unwilling to believe in the bad faith and treasonable intentions of his Cabinet minister, refused; thus he lost the last slender hope of maintaining himself in office, and of saving Venezuela's first democratic regime.[13]

Events of November 22 and 23 were the hopeless last-ditch efforts of government leaders to prevent total capitulation to the conspirators. At that point it probably did not matter that they moved in opposite directions and at cross purposes. Defense Minister Delgado Chalbaud, acting quietly and unswervingly toward the fulfillment of his own plan, now had the persuasive Mario Vargas to help him convince the President that some concession to the wishes of the military high command was necessary: he must at least consent to the formation of a new Cabinet in which the military would have the preponderance of power.

In the meantime, the leaders of Acción Democrática were moving to bring pressure to bear at other points. Valmore Rodríguez, mindful of the courage and loyalty so recently displayed by Lieut.-Col. Gámez Arellano, made a frantic trip to the military bastion of Maracay in the faint hope of persuading the commander of that garrison to gather all loyal forces under his banner, and to undertake a civil war, if necessary, in order to save the legal government. Gámez, remembering the failure of Gallegos to support him in his confrontation with Delgado Chalbaud, naturally refused.

Betancourt, turning characteristically to the working-class Venezuelans, from whom he had always received inspiration and support, convinced the leaders of labor unions that they held the only remaining power that might frustrate the plans of the military. With their consent, Acción Democrática announced a strike of petroleum workers on November 23. The gesture came too late, and was too hastily prepared, to have the slightest beneficial effect.

Although the government's power and prestige had been effectively eroded by the events described above, November 24 is remembered as the date of the military *coup d'état*. On that morning, as soon as news of the petroleum strike reached the Defense Ministry, Delgado Chalbaud ordered the arrest of the President. Gallegos was confined to his home for two days, then transferred to the Escuela Militar. All government leaders who could be found, including Valmore Rodríguez (who was returned handcuffed from Maracay), were similarly arrested and locked in the jail cells of Miraflores Barracks. From that point, the take-over of power throughout the nation was swift and smooth. The prisons rapidly filled with *adecos,* labor leaders, and all persons who could be considered in any way opposed to the military. Rómulo Betancourt, however, escaped the round-up by hiding in the homes of various friends until December 1, when he was granted asylum in the Colombian embassy.

It was clear that the country would be ruled by a military junta, and the only question that remained was who the top man would be. This doubt was settled on the same afternoon of the *coup* in a brief confrontation between the Defense Minister and the Chief of Staff. Pérez Jiménez was explaining to other officers that there would be a three-man junta, comprised of himself, Delgado Chalbaud, and Llovera Páez, when the Defense Minister asserted quietly and confidently that he, as senior officer of the group, would be President of the Junta. Pérez Jiménez did not argue, and the matter was settled for the next two years. The extent to which there was a "showdown" between the two men for leadership of the Junta must remain in some doubt because of discrepancies in the reports of different witnesses to the event.[14] It is evident, however, that the personality of Pérez Jiménez was less dominant and forceful than that of Delgado Chalbaud. His own keen awareness of this fact was a source of deep anguish and resentment. Artillery expert, master of military tactics, and accomplished conspirator, he would eventually achieve by cunning deception and ruthless force what he could never hope to accomplish through persuasion or the imposition of a strong and charming personality.

It was at this point that Laureano Vallenilla Lanz began to influence the course of events in the government of Venezuela. As noted above, he had only recently made the acquaintance of Pérez Jiménez, but the future dictator appears to have recognized in the shrewd speculator a kindred spirit who could be immensely helpful to him in the realization of his ambitions. Shortly before the *coup* of November 24, the Chief of Staff sent one of his associates, Lieut.-Col. José León Rangel, to ask Vallenilla to draw up a list of candidates for Cabinet posts in the new military government. Vallenilla accepted this assignment, and it is clear that through his preferences for such sensitive and important ministries as Education, Treasury, Foreign Relations, Public Works, and so on, he was in a position to exercise profound influence on future policies and practices of the Military Junta. His nominations were followed almost without exception, and although he refused appointment as Director General of the Secretariat of the Junta, in order to devote his time to private business ventures, he was to continue as unofficial adviser to the group, and especially to the new Defense Minister Pérez Jiménez.

It is significant, and characteristic of Delgado Chalbaud, that he took little part in determining the composition of the new Cabinet, and assignments to other important posts. He had devoted his attention and energies almost exclusively to securing for himself the primacy of command and prestige in the Military Junta. Once that was assured, he seemed content to follow the lead of Pérez Jiménez in the myriad details of organizing the new government. It was, in fact, the new Defense Minister rather than the Junta President, who delivered an official communiqué to the nation by radio on the afternoon of November 24, informing the country of the change of government and stating that the Constitution of 1947 was suspended and would be replaced by the López Contreras Constitution of 1936, as amended by Medina Angarita in 1945. And it was the new behind-the-scenes adviser of the Junta, Vallenilla Lanz, who drew up the "Constitutive Act" of the *de facto* military government, signed in Miraflores Palace at midnight of the same day by Junta members and principal associates, as well as Naval Captain Wolfgang Larrazábal, Air Force Lieut. Félix Román Moreno, Captain Oscar Tamayo Suárez of the Fuerzas Armadas de Cooperación, and the Presidency Secretary Miguel Moreno. This document was published on the front pages of the nation's newspapers the following day.

Reaction to the *coup d'état* on the part of opposition parties was one of instant and extreme jubilation. Rafael Caldera, leader of Copei, and URD's Jóvito Villalba, heedless of the fact that the overthrow of the democratic and constitutional government would be as destructive to their own political freedom as to that of Acción Democrática, hastened to the Defense Ministry to offer their congratulations and support to the Junta.[15] The suspension of constitutional rights, as decreed by Gallegos on November 20, was greatly expanded on November 26, and would continue in effect for some time.

The nation's newspapers, both daily and weekly, partisan and nonpartisan, most of which had indulged in constant vituperative attacks on the Gallegos administration, scarcely had time to express their boundless joy over the fall of the constitutional government when they found themselves tightly muzzled by a censorship code clamped upon them by the Military Junta. The AD mouthpiece *El País* was, of course, permanently closed; and Copei's *El Gráfico,* which at first attempted to express some partisan viewpoints, was quickly brought into line by short periods of suspension from publication. Radio stations were placed under equally severe censorship, and vigilantly watched for any infraction of the rules. Acción Democrática was outlawed, and other political parties were warned that no meetings, parades, or disturbances would be tolerated in any part of the country. Trade union locals throughout the nation were raided by police, their records and funds confiscated, and their leaders thrown into prison.

All of these repressive measures represented nothing more or less than a return to military rule. They were carried out as quietly and efficiently as possible; citizens who resisted were treated roughly, but there was as yet no deliberate terrorism or brutality inflicted on the general public as a matter of policy. The treatment accorded AD government leaders, however, with the exception of President Gallegos, was harsh and vindictive. Valmore Rodríguez, because of his attempt to resist the *coup d'état,* was so severely mistreated in a cell of the Cárcel Modelo in Caracas that he soon suffered two serious coronary attacks. Despite the entreaties of family and friends that he be transferred to a hospital, all proper care was refused for a long period. Pérez Jiménez, in answer to the pleas of a physician who had visited the stricken man, is reported to have replied: "That can be cured by cold baths at dawn."[16]

On December 5, some two weeks after the overthrow of his government, deposed President Rómulo Gallegos was permitted to leave his country for political exile abroad. Accompanied by his wife and daughter, he boarded a plane provided by the Military Junta to take up temporary residence in Havana, Cuba, where he was accorded political asylum by the liberal government of Ramón Grau San Martín. On the following day Gallegos held a press conference to make clear to the world that he had never resigned the Presidency of Venezuela, as alleged by the Junta. He also made a vigorous plea that other nations refrain from granting diplomatic recognition to the new military regime in Caracas. At the same time, the embittered and suspicious Gallegos declared that the government of the United States appeared to have been implicated in the Venezuelan *coup d'état*. The basis of this accusation was the fact that he had noted the presence of U.S. Air Attaché Col. Edward F. Adams at Miraflores Palace and also at the Defense Ministry on the day of his government's downfall. It is good to be able to state that the Venezuelan President was mistaken in the conclusion that he had reached: Col. Adams had gone in search of news about an American plane that had disappeared some days previously in the Gran Sabana region.[17]

The U.S. State Department announced that it had reached no decision concerning recognition of the *de facto* regime in Caracas, and warned that Americans living abroad must refrain from interference in foreign political affairs. The Creole Petroleum Company and Gulf Oil Corporation immediately issued statements denying any participation in Venezuelan political events.[18]

If there is general agreement among the chroniclers of Venezuelan affairs as to the sequence of events that culminated in the downfall of the Gallegos government, the same cannot be said of the reasons for the failure of Venezuela's first attempt to establish a democratic way of life for her people. Various investigators have tried in recent years to marshall the facts and to identify the forces involved in the *coup d'état* of November, 1948. These efforts most commonly point out two principal currents of subversive influence that were operative within Venezuela at the time. The first of these was reactionary political sentiment in collaboration with Peronist military elements supported by the Anglo-Dutch group of investors in the petroleum industry. The other consisted of "those same national groups, oriented and supported by North American imperialism."[19] The present work proposes to look beyond such immediate considerations in order to study some of the underlying aspects of Venezuelan social and political realities.

It is clear that much confusion and misinformation have resulted from the natural tendency of Venezuelan writers to interpret the events of their recent history according to their own political preferences, financial interests, and social attitudes. Commentators of the right, such as Ramón David León and Laureano Vallenilla Lanz, and such Communist writers as Juan Bautista Fuenmayor, have assumed a vengeful attitude by professing to see a kind of "ironic justice" in the downfall of the AD government of President Gallegos simply because Acción Democrática had itself come to power through a *coup d'état* in 1945.[20] This position is simplistic and unjustified, for it overlooks the fact that the Gallegos administration, unlike the Revolutionary Junta of 1945, was a legal and constitutional government which had come to power by the direct vote of an overwhelming majority of the Venezuelan electorate.

Equally unacceptable is the assertion, frequently made even by writers of undoubted integrity and good intentions, that one of the reasons for the fall of the Gallegos government was the refusal of the President and the other AD leaders to share power with the opposition parties: Copei, URD, and the Communists. To anyone accustomed to the political practices of the United States, it is indeed an astonishing proposition that a political party can be entitled to any power which it was unable to win at the polls. As noted in the preceding chapter, all of these minority parties had won seats in the Senate and the National Assembly, and they were in no sense unable to make their positions known to the public on any issue. The opposition press was entirely free and functioned vigorously. Unfortunately, most of that press, including *La Religión,* official organ of the Catholic Church, concentrated much less on the solution of national problems than on bitter invectives and veiled threats against the government, incitement to sedition, and dire predictions of coming disaster.

One might reasonably imagine that the leaders of the minority parties, having experienced the complete denial of political liberties during the dictatorships of the past, would look upon the legality and the democratic freedoms of the Gallegos government as a treasure to be cherished and protected by all possible means. This was not the case. And it would be naive to suppose that the reactionary forces of 1948 could have been contained if the government had frustrated its own popular mandate by sharing power with Copei's Rafael Caldera and URD's Jóvito Villalba, who had been unable to win at the polls. We may conclude, then, that a strong contributing cause of the *coup* of November, 1948, was precisely the inability of opposition party leaders to recognize that their own interests would be best served by accepting the results of the free and honest election of 1947 and adopting an attitude of "loyal opposition" rather than attempting to bring about the violent overthrow of the elected government.

Among the more extreme rationalizations of the 1948 *cuartelada* put forward by some Venezuelan "analysts" is the absurd assertion that some of the articles of the Constitution of 1947 were "formulated under the inspiration of the Soviet Embassy that is operating in Caracas."[21] This allegation, so reminiscent of the "mud-throwing" tactics of the John Birch Society and Senator Joseph McCarthy in the United States, was clearly intended to justify the military *coup* by bringing discredit upon the Gallegos administration; it does not merit serious comment.

Equally unfounded were the charges of embezzlement or peculation made by associates and supporters of the Military Junta against AD leaders, particularly Rómulo Betancourt, who was alleged to have "big deposits in the banks of Canada".[22] Other Venezuelans, saddened and depressed by such calumnies, have taken the trouble to investigate the matter, and have discovered that Betancourt and other *adecos* lived very frugally in political exile.[23] Certainly the military leaders of the November *coup* made no mention, at the time, of any alleged financial irregularities on the part of AD government officials. Indeed, aside from the specific but unrealistic charge of "monopoly of political power," and such vague and general terms as "social unrest" and "economic chaos", Junta members Delgado Chalbaud, Pérez Jiménez, and Llovera Páez made only two definite accusations by which they sought to justify their revolt against the Gallegos government. Both charges were clumsy and inept falsifications, and could scarcely have convinced any intelligent observer.

In a press conference held by Junta President Delgado Chalbaud on December 10, less than three weeks after the *coup,* and reported in *El Nacional* on the following day, the military leader declared that it was "evident to all Venezuelans" that the AD government had "taken unfair advantage of its power" in order to bring about the victory of President Gallegos in 1947. Delgado appeared unmindful of the fact that he and his Junta colleagues had supervised those same elections and had signed a sworn affidavit that they were fair and honest in every way. At that same press conference, Delgado asserted that another reason for the military action against the government was that Acción Democrática had organized a "civil militia", or political police, to counteract or supplant the power of the regular Armed Forces, thus imposing its will by force and maintaining itself in power by means of a general strike supported by the alleged militia. No such militia existed, and the legal government was totally defenseless when it was betrayed by the Ministry of Defense and the Armed Forces on November 24, 1948.[24]

Within the meaning intended, it was undoubtedly true, as claimed by both the U.S. State Department and the Venezuelan MilitaryJunta, that no official of the American government was in any way involved in the *coup d'état.* Probably the American-owned oil companies were equally within the bounds of truth when they issued official statements denying any complicity in that event. But, if such declarations are to be accepted as factual, it must be understood that they meant only that no such official took any active part in the conspiracy prepared by Pérez Jiménez and his associates to overthrow the Venezuelan government. It must be clear, however , that when an advanced industrialized country of such enormous power and influence as the United States has billions of dollars invested in the exploitation of natural resources in a small and underdeveloped country like Venezuela, neither the investing country nor its financiers can remain indifferent to the political climate and social stability of the country in which such resources are located. Nor can the investors feign such total indifference in the name of non-interference in the politics of a foreign country. The attitudes of multi-million-dollar petroleum companies toward a government which grants or withholds desired concessions, imposes taxes, and otherwise determines the extent of profits are common knowledge among military figures and businessmen, as well as the government officials of the country which owns the oil fields. Such attitudes often find their reflection in the cordiality, or the lack of it, that characterizes the diplomatic relations between the two countries.

Other things being equal, investment capital is attracted to areas of political and economic stability; it is repelled by conditions which threaten the loss of investment through confiscation or expropriation. When money is invested in the United States or Canada, where such stability is taken for granted, then this problem does not arise, and the desirability of investment is based on other considerations. In Latin America, however, to which American investors have been attracted by the prospect of enormous profits made possible by the economic backwardness of those countries, and the consequent low standard of living and low wages, millions of dollars of invested capital have been lost through the triumph of liberal or leftist revolutions and the ensuing take-over of foreign investments. Mexico and Bolivia are examples of such expropriation, but the revolutionary governments of those countries paid at least partial compensation to investors for their losses. Fidel Castro's Cuba is a case of outright confiscation, with total loss to investors. Threats of similar developments have occurred in Guatemala, Peru, Chile, and elsewhere.

There are two principal methods of bringing about and maintaining conditions that are safe for foreign investments in Latin America. The first of these, which may be called "short-term safety", is the traditional system, inherited from the colonial period, of maintaining a poverty-striken and illiterate population under the firm control of a military strongman and his coterie of officials, with the support of big landowners and wealthy miners, and the tacit approval of the Church. This method, exemplified by the rule of Porfirio Díaz in Mexico, Juan Vicente Gómez in Venezuela, Fulgencio Batista and his predecessors in Cuba, and the Somozas in Nicaragua, to name but a few, yields the greatest possible returns on investments because the dictator need not divert any appreciable part of the income to the welfare of his country. He can afford to be generous to foreign investors—most often U.S. companies engaged in the extraction of oil, iron, copper, etc.—, for the wealth that he concedes to them is not his own. They, in return, provide him with a princely personal income, besides lavish funds for the uniforms, weapons, and salaries of his small but well-kept army, often trained by U.S. instructors. He is thus able to maintain, sometimes for decades, the condition of stability so necessary for the attraction of foreign capital.

Investors are naturally delighted with this mutually profitable arrangement. The fact that the native population is neglected, exploited, and kept in extreme poverty and ignorance may be considered unfortunate, but necessary to the continuation of profits; most often it is not considered at all.

It should be noted that this system of maintaining safe investment conditions in a Latin American country has acquired its "short-term" character only in recent times, having encountered its first effective challenge in the Mexican Revolution of 1910. More recently, however, the specter of international Communism, previously used as a "bugaboo" to justify every kind of anti-democratic repression, has become an increasingly real threat to the future of democracy in Latin America. Since history has shown that Communist doctrine takes root and thrives only in the midst of hopeless poverty and dire social injustice, it is obvious that the traditional method of preserving political stability in the underdeveloped countries is not only short-term, but short sighted, and it behooves the government of the United States to re-think and reform the attitudes and policies that determine this country's diplomatic and business relations with Latin American regimes.

The second, or "long-term", method of achieving the political and social stability necessary for investment is the same means by which all other social progress may be realized: the building of a free and democratic society in the western sense. This is admittedly a slow and arduous process; democratic institutions cannot be established as quickly as a dictatorship. Venezuela, prior to 1945, had no democratic tradition; but, during the following three-year period, the regimes of Betancourt and Gallegos established the beginnings of a true democratic social revolution, and there should be no doubt that the constitutional government that was overthrown in November, 1948, merited the support of other freedom-loving countries, including the United States.

As noted in the preceding chapter, Venezuela had engaged in some very hard bargaining with the foreign-owned oil companies. Nationalization of the industry was never threatened, nor even suggested, but the government was determined to exact as great a share as possible of the oil revenues. The companies, accustomed to the *entreguismo,* or "handing-over" policy practiced by past regimes, reacted negatively to the increased taxes and larger shares of profits that Venezuela demanded, threatening to "phase out" their operations in that country in order to move to the Middle East. They did not do so, of course, for their profits were still enormous, and they would hardly have abandoned the rich Venezuelan fields to their eager competitors.

It is a matter of record that strained relations existed between the foreign-owned petroleum companies and the Venezuelan government during the entire period of AD rule, beginning in 1945, when the companies were required to negotiate with the Petroleum Workers Union on questions of wages and working conditions, through the next three years of higher taxes and enforced investment of some of the company profits in Venezuelan industries.[25] No doubt it was normal for United States investors to feel some hostility toward a government that was more demanding and less generous than the military regimes of the past.

If the preferences of the petroleum companies were reflected in the policies of the American State Department, it cannot be said that Washington's attitude toward the Gallegos government was anything but scrupulously correct. But when the survival of a democratic and progressive regime in a small nation like Venezuela is at stake, diplomatic "correctness" on the past of a country as overwhelmingly influential as the United States is simply not enough. Unequivocal expressions of warm approbation, sympathy, and understanding are needed; such attitudes cannot be construed as "interference" in the affairs of another nation, yet they can be effective as a deterrent to conspirators. No such enunciation of moral support was forthcoming from the Truman administration during the tense weeks preceding the *coup d'état,* although State Department representatives in Venezuela must have been aware of the impending action by the military. Indeed, it did not escape the notice of Latin Americans that Washington chose the period of greatest tension in Venezuela to announce its recognition of the *de facto* regime of General Manuel Odría, who had overthrown the legal government of Peru in that country's latest *cuartelada.* As noted by Rómulo Betancourt, "the conspirators of Caracas saw in that attitude of the government of the United States a kind of green light for the usurpation of power" in Venezuela.[26]

Even the most democratic and anti-Communist of Latin Americans find it very difficult to understand why the United States, which practices democracy at home, does not hesitate to intervene when a regime, however reactionary and corrupt, is threatened by Communist take-over, yet looks in another direction when a truly democratic government is in peril from a right-wing *coup d'état.* In a later chapter of this work, we shall note how this lack of Latin American "understanding" found violent expression on the occasion of Vice-President Nixon's visit to Caracas in May, 1958, after the fall of the Pérez Jiménez regime.

The conclusion drawn here from the foregoing discussion is that one of the factors contributing to the fall of the Gallegos government in 1948 was the failure of the Truman administration to declare its cordial approval and support of that regime, and opposition to the threatened *coup.*

Whatever the defects of Washington's Latin American policy, however, the principal causes of the democratic government's inability to maintain itself in power are to be found in Venezuela itself. The attitudes of the State Department and the oil companies would have been insufficient to bring about the November *cuartelazo* if powerful elements within that country had not been willing to see the end of popular government and a return to authoritarian control. A share of the blame must be borne by Acción Democrática itself, for its failure to publicize and popularize its many reform programs. These were constantly lampooned in the opposition press in much the same way that the farm program of the early New Deal was ridiculed by many United States newspapers. It is true that the AD paper, *El País,* and its counterparts in other cities, defended and explained the government's programs, but these efforts were insufficient to counteract the steady barrage of the opposition. There were AD agents functioning in all parts of the country, but no petitions were circulated among industrial unions or farm organizations to declare massive support for the government.

It was not that the Venezuelan people had turned anti-*adeco*; the landslide victory of Rómulo Gallegos at the polls only a few months before had shown that Acción Democrática was still the "Party of the People". But, faced with the danger of a military *coup,* the party leadership showed a singular lack of imagination and energy in mobilizing support among the masses. As previously noted, flagrantly subversive speeches had been delivered by anti-government politicians and published in the opposition press as early as June, 1948; and these warnings continued until the government was overthrown. Yet *adeco* leaders Valmore Rodríguez, Andrés Eloy Blanco, and others, who had orated so effectively during the campaign of the previous year, held no mass meetings and gave no radio addresses to inform the Venezuelan people of the rising tide of reaction. It appeared, indeed, as one Venezuelan observer has suggested, that everyone except the directors of Acción Democrática itself could hear the "tic-tac" of the *adeco* clock as it ran out of time.[27]

In assessing the causes of the November *cuartelazo,* it is clear that not even Rómulo Betancourt, in all of his voluminous writings, has found it expedient to point out all of the factors involved in that event. As a perceptive and resourceful politician who hoped to make a successful come-back, the AD leader wrote no analysis of his own shortcomings or those of his party; nor did he assign any word of blame to the obvious tactical blunders of President Gallegos. Instead, Betancourt draws attention to the arrogant vindictiveness and political shortsightedness of the opposition parties, the lack of diplomatic support from the United States government, and above all, the malevolence and treachery of the military conspirators.

For the same reasons of political expediency Betancourt carefully refrains from taking to task either the Catholic Church or the Venezuelan people themselves. It is a fact that the clergy, in expressing its political views through pulpit and newspaper during this critical period, appeared to look mainly to its own interests, and did not lend moral support to the principle of change through democratic means only.[28]

In fairness to the Catholic Church, and in partial justification of its failure to lend enthusiastic support to the administrations of Betancourt and Gallegos, we have already noted that at least two pieces of legislation proposed and passed under AD leadership were distinctly discriminatory against parochial schools. Furthermore, the Catholic Church has never made any pretense of being a democratic institution; from the Pope down to the humblest parish priest, it is, and always has been, frankly hierarchical and authoritarian. In nations that have a long history of democratic practices and institutions, the Catholic clergy has tended to liberalize its views in many matters, and this may some day be the case in Venezuela. But during the period in question, that country had no democratic norms for Church-State relations, and it was hardly reasonable to expect the Venezuelan clerics to perceive the vital importance of lending their support to the Gallegos government, not because it was *adeco,* but because *it was legal and constitutional.*

Someone has said that every nation always has the best government that it deserves. If this is true, it would appear that the Venezuelan people, having failed to protect their constitutional government in 1948, deserved to lose it. Like most general judgments, this one requires some qualifications. Many students of Venezuelan affairs have commented that, at the time of the November *coup* and during the period immediately following, most citizens appeared to accept the change with indifference and little understanding of its meaning or importance. Probably this was indeed the case, but it is well to remember that social reforms in any country are initiated and carried out by intelligent leaders, and not by the general population.

In Venezuela, as in the United States, public apathy and ignorance about vital issues have never been difficult to find. Rómulo Betancourt, like Franklin Roosevelt, won the votes of the impoverished masses, not by preaching the long-term advantages of governmental legality, but by clear promises of immediate improvement in their living standards. The Venezuelan leader, like FDR, built a political machine that depended heavily on protection to labor unions, subsidies and loans to farmers, and assistance to the unemployed. In both cases, the reform programs encountered the opposition of the privileged classes, big business, and conservative politicians. In both cases, the people responded with their votes, not for theoretical reasons, but in return for visible and tangible benefits received. The similarities in the two national experiences are not instructive, however, unless some important differences are also noted.

The United States in which Roosevelt's New Deal took form enjoyed a long and unbroken tradition of stable democratic government. Despite the ravages of the Depression, the average American was literate and reasonably well-behaved. Whatever problems the President encountered, he did not have to undertake the writing of a new Constitution for his country, and he never faced the danger of the overthrow of his government by insurgency in the American Army. In Venezuela, Betancourt and other advocates of representative government found it necessary to preach incessantly against the social injustices and backwardness made possible and perpetuated by the long-established tradition of personalist rule by a military leader. The average Venezuelan was youthful, poverty-stricken, illiterate, and much more interested in improving his condition in life than in the theoretical superiority of democracy over totalitarianism. The leaders of Acción Democrática had to undertake the long and arduous task of educating the masses in the practical advantages of democratic practices and institutions. The educational process was entirely new and contrary to national tradition, and it should not surprise us that Venezuela's first democratic party, despite heroic efforts, did not achieve complete success in the short period of three years.

A spontaneous and heart-felt uprising of the Venezuelan people in support of President Gallegos,—in the way that Czechoslovaks, for example, made known their enthusiastic backing of Premier Alexander Dubcek in 1968—was not to be expected. The reaction of Venezuela in November, 1948, had much more in common with that of Czechoslovakia in that same year, when faced with the death of Jan Masaryk and of Czech democracy: some were delighted and others horrified, but the majority of citizens accepted the return to military rule in confused silence and apathy. Throughout the long years of exile, Rómulo Betancourt never lost faith in the democratic future of his country. He insisted in books, articles, and letters to newspapers that Acción Democrática was not dead, but would one day return to power to carry out its unfinished program. Events were to prove him right. But in 1948 Venezuela had not yet learned her lesson, and she was to pay for that shortcoming with a decade of increasingly brutal and oppressive military rule.

Chapter V

The Military Junta
of Delgado Chalbaud
1948-1950

Having ousted the legitimate government and installed themselves in power throughout the country with a speed and facility that astonished the conspirators themselves, the Junta found that its most pressing need was to secure the recognition of the new *de facto* government by the nations that had maintained diplomatic relations with the Gallegos regime, particularly the United States and other Western Hemisphere nations. Junta President Delgado Chalbaud displayed in this matter a bit of personal delicacy that was typical of his character: he preferred to remain in his old office in the Defense Ministry until a sufficient number of diplomatic recognitions would "justify" his moving to the presidential office in Miraflores Palace. This proved to be a period of two months.

Within forty-eight hours after taking office, Delgado announced formally that the Military Junta would be a transition regime only, that neither he nor any of his associates had the slightest intention of establishing a dictatorship, and that elections would soon be held to choose a new civilian democratic government. In announcing such "early" democratic elections, while at the same time imposing curfews and censorship, and making nation-wide arrests of political figures and labor leaders, the Junta appeared not at all embarrassed that it was, in fact, acting as a dictatorship, and that the legal government it had just overthrown was entirely free, democratic, and representative of the majority of Venezuelans. Delgado also declared that his *de facto* regime supported the United Nations; that it would comply with all international obligations; and that it did not ask for the diplomatic recognition of the Dominican Republic nor of Spain. (Acción Democrática had refused diplomatic relations with the dictatorships of Trujillo and Franco.)

The Military Junta then sent representatives to various democratic governments to plead for early recognition. The new Venezuelan Ambassador-designate José Rafael Pocaterra arrived in Washington on

December 6 for this purpose. Carlos Baptista, a cousin of Vallenilla Lanz, undertook a similar mission to Bogota, working closely with the notorious "fixer", Juan Francisco Franco Quijano, whose unsavory activities will receive some attention in the next chapter of this work. Delgado's group guessed correctly that no urging would be necessary in Buenos Aires, Lima, and Asunción: the dictatorial regimes of Perón, Odría, and Morínigo were only too happy to grant recongition to a government of their own kind in Caracas. In Washington, the State Department announced that it had reached no decision in the matter of recognition, and would consult with other members of the Organization of American States before doing so.[1]

Meanwhile the Junta, following the recommendations of Laureano Vallenilla Lanz, had appointed on November 25 a new Cabinet comprised of four military men, who controlled the ministries involving the security of the regime, and eight civilians. Junta members Pérez Jiménez, in the Ministry of Defense, and Llovera Páez, in the Ministry of the Interior, were the most important of these. Colonel Jorge Marcano became Minister of Communications, and General Juan de Dios Celis Paredes was appointed Governor of the Federal District. The civilian members, all conservatives or reactionaries, were well known for their opposition to the policies and programs of Acción Democrática. Luis Emilio Gómez Ruiz was the new Minister of Foreign Relations, Pedro Ignacio Aguerrevere was appointed Minister of Development, and Gerardo Sansón was put in charge of the Ministry of Public Works. The new Minister of the Treasury was Aurelio Arreaza, and Professor Augusto Mijares, of Central University Law School, became Minister of Education. Doctor Antonio Martín Araujo was appointed to the Ministry of Health and Social Welfare, and Amendoro Rangel Lamus became Minister of Agriculture.[2]

The leaders of Acción Democrática, most of whom occupied cells in the Cárcel Modelo in Caracas in company with members of the Gallegos Cabinet, reacted with greater energy and determination in their new adversity than during their last weeks of political power. Although the party founded by Betancourt was officially dissolved by Junta decree early in December, the AD leaders, whether in jail or in hiding, found ways to communicate and to repudiate the decree. On December 8 it issued a Manifesto of Resistance which read, in part:

> Our Party declares, before the nation, that from this very date it begins its political labor of a clandestine character, designed to organize the fighting vanguard of the people to recover the public liberties and the regime of political sovereignty today suppressed. The Party enters upon a period of sacrifice and of organized resistance, an undertaking for which our movement counts on inexhaustible sources of fervor, mystique, capacity, and integrity. We know that the battle will be bloody and brutal, because our adversaries will use the savage method of violence in order to

silence the people, smother opinion, stabilize itself and survive as a police state . . . With full responsibility for the meaning of this undertaking, with a clear understanding of its immense duty, with sure faith in final triumph, Acción Democrática begins today its determined struggle of underground resistance, until it obtains for Venezuela a regime of liberty, political dignity, administrative honesty and public decency.[3]

As previously noted, Rómulo Betancout had taken refuge in the Colombian embassy on December 1, and he was to remain there for some seven weeks, for although the Chilean government had offered political asylum for him as well as for Rómulo Gallegos, the Venezuelan Junta refused to grant him safe-conduct out of the country. According to one source within the military regime itself, there was a plot at this time to assassinate Betancourt. A small group of right-wing extremists had conceived the idea of gaining entrance to the Colombian embassy in order to kill the AD leader, thus solving the problem of whether to grant him safe-conduct to foreign exile. Junta President Delgado Chalbaud, however, vetoed the plan immediately, finding it most inadvisable to resort to murder at a time when his de facto regime was seeking the recognition of other governments.[4] The same source reveals that a similar plot was prepared for January 23. The Junta had finally granted permission for Betancourt to leave Venezuela by plane for Jamaica, and he was to be driven to the airport at Maiquetía in the Colombian embassy limousine. This time the assassins planned to force the Colombian vehicle to a halt on the highway between Caracas and the airport, and to shoot the AD leader on the spot. But again the Junta discovered the plot in time to prevent the crime. Vallenilla Lanz, the new friend and unofficial adviser of Pérez Jiménez, was charged with dissuading the criminals from carrying out the assassination.[5]

During this same period the Military Junta was informed that the efforts of its representatives in other capitals had brought positive results; recognition would be granted almost simultaneously by Brazil, the United States, Colombia, and Panama. Previous to its decision, the State Department had requested "assurances" that the Venezuelan regime would hold free and democratic elections "soon", and Ambassador Pocaterra, the Junta's man in Washington, hastened to promise that this would indeed be the case. One of the first acts of the new Truman administration was the granting of full diplomatic recognition to the Venezuelan Military Junta on January 21, 1949.

The reasons behind the willingness of the United States government to recognize the new and illegal Venezuelan regime are interesting, but not altogether convincing. As previously noted, the State Department had indicated early in December, 1948, that it would consult with other OAS members before taking action in this case. According to one investigator, the Department, on December 21, "made known to a number of American republics its concern because of recent instances in which

popularly elected governments had been overthrown by military forces."
The Department reportedly solicited suggestions as to appropriate
collective action, but replies to this inquiry are described as "unenthusi-
astic and devoid of constructive suggestions."[6]

The State Department's *Bulletin* does not indicate which countries
were included in the "number of American republics" to which inquiries
on this point were made. One might reasonably suppose that dictatorial
regimes, such as those of Paraguay and Peru, would not be consulted,
since they had themselves come to power by way of military *coups
d'état,* their sympathies were well known, and they had, in any case,
already recognized the new Venezuelan regime. If the Department consulted such democratic and representative governments as those of
Chile and Uruguay, then it is astonishing that the United States preceded
those countries in recognizing the new military regime in Caracas. One
may also wonder at the apparent credulity of the State Department in
accepting promises of democratic electoral practices from a Junta composed of military adventurers who had just overthrown a legal and
democratic government, and were in the process of establishing a dictatorship.

There is a further inconsistency in this matter, and it does nothing to
detract from the impression that the game called diplomacy is a kind of
international charade in which the players must try to attain their objectives without disclosing either their motivations or their methods.
On January 21, 1949, Mr. W. J. Donnelly, American Ambassador to
Venezuela, appeared at the Ministry of Foreign Relations in Caracas
to present his credentials to Chancellor Gómez Ruiz and to announce
recognition of the Junta by the State Department. After the formalities,
and while he was leaving the Ministry, Mr. Donnelly was questioned by
members of the press.

A report of the incident contains the following sentence: "To a question that was put to him as to whether the decision to resume diplomatic
relations with our government on the part of the United States represented the culmination of consultations carried out among the American States, the excellent Mr. Donnelly stated that it was an isolated
decision and was that of the government of his country alone."[7] Although
it is hardly conceivable that the ambassador was unaware of the statements put out by the State Department, all indications are that Mr.
Donnelly's representation of the matter was accurate. Certainly it was
intended for Venezuelan consumption rather than for comparison with
official dispatches from Washington.

While soliciting diplomatic recognition abroad, the Military Junta
had issued pronouncements intended to set at rest the doubts and wor-
ries of the petroleum companies and other foreign investors. Minister
of Development Aguerrevere declared that there would be no change,
for the present, in Venezuela's oil policy or in the granting of concessions. All projects begun by the Gallegos administration, such as the
development of iron mines and diamond mines, and the utilization of

gas would be continued. He also gave assurance that industrial and agricultural projects started by the Venezuelan Development Corporation during the AD regime would be brought to completion, and that enterprises founded by the government in partnership with Nelson Rockefeller would continue as in the past. Aguerrevere announced, however, that the Military Junta, after studying the petroleum situation, would formulate a new and specific oil policy of its own. The foreign-owned oil companies had little to fear from the new military regime. As we shall see, for reasons set forth in the preceding chapter concerning desirably stable conditions for the investment of foreign capital, the government was fully aware of the source of its income, and would prove to be an excellent and agreeable partner in the exploitation of the nation's mineral wealth.

Venezuelan petroleum workers, seeing the Junta's brutal campaign to destroy their unions, were not inclined to co-operate. On January 17, 1949, they responded with a strike in the Maracaibo fields, then producing 80% of the country's oil. But the workers were living in company-owned houses, and the government undertook to break the strike with the most savage and ruthless methods at hand. First the workers' homes were deprived of water and electricity; when this measure did not bring immediate results, police and "goon squads" invaded the houses and carried out all the food in sight. Then road-blocks were set up to keep the workers and their families from leaving. The strike was broken in three days.[8]

During the following weeks, the government intensified its drive to gain absolute control of Venezuelan workers by arresting and jailing union leaders in all parts of the country. On February 25, 1949, the Junta published a decree dissolving the Confederación de Trabajadores de Venezuela (CTV), an organization composed of the leaders of many workers' federations, including the Federación Campesina. This decree did not dissolve the local unions themselves, but effectively deprived them of centralized direction and leadership. Thereafter, meetings could take place only upon authorization of "labor inspectors" from the Ministry of Labor, who would be present at meetings, and whose approval was needed for any union decision. One result of this extreme anti-labor attitude assumed by the government was that many employers tore up the contracts they had signed with unions prior to the November *coup d'état,* dismissed their employees or drastically lowered wages.[9] Other strikes occurred in various parts of the country, particularly in the oil fields, but they were of short duration. The unarmed workers could not cope with the "disciplinary measures" taken by the Junta.

At the time of the November *coup,* each of the political parties had its own following among the country's labor unions. Acción Democrática was outlawed immediately, and unions oriented toward that party were those who suffered the most at the hands of the new anti-labor regime. The other parties, Copei, Unión Republicana Democrática, and the two

Communist fractions (Gustavo Machado's PCV and Rodolfo Quintero's PRP), though repressed and tightly controlled, continued to function legally. In the spring of 1949, the Copei and URD were incurring the increasing enmity of the regime; and the PCV (to be outlawed in May, 1950, and its leaders exiled) never showed any willingness to co-operate with the Junta. Quintero and his Black Communists, however, agreed to support the military government in return for a large share of the control of the labor movement.[10]

In May, 1949, a movement to investigate labor conditions in Venezuela had its inception at a meeting in Montevideo, Uruguay, of the International Labor Organization (ILO), a specialized agency of the United Nations with headquarters in Geneva, and a world membership of more than seventy nations. The Geneva office of the ILO had already heard denunciations of the mistreatment of labor in Venezuela from AD exile Augusto Malavé Villalba, former Secretary General of the CTV. At the Montevideo meeting, these charges were given a thorough airing and then publicized in the world press. To the surprise of many, Venezuelan Labor Minister Rubén Corredor sent an invitation to ILO Director General David Morse to send a representative to Venezuela in order to obtain "complete and impartial information about our social problems, general conditions of work in the different lines of production, the extent of benefits and protection provided to workers by legislation and by the National government, and the development and functioning of union organizations." Mr. Morse accepted, and sent to Venezuela a commission headed by Assistant Director General Jef Rens.

This group arrived in Caracas in June, 1949, and spent the next seven weeks in a thorough investigation of the labor situation in all parts of the country. It was clear from the outset that the Junta was somewhat taken aback, having expected the ILO to send a single individual who could be conducted on a guided tour. The Rens Commission proved strong minded and independent, made its own contacts and discovered the true state of affairs.

Although denied permission to enter Venezuelan prisons to interview union leaders, Commission members gathered detailed information in conversations with workers and their families and neighbors in oil fields, factories, and rural areas throughout the country. The ILO investigators found that the government had completely abandoned the objectives of the Agrarian Reform Law signed by President Gallegos less than a year before. The 446 farmer associations which comprised the Federación Campesina had been forced to desintegrate, and rural workers were once again treated as medieval serfs by the great landowners.

The Rens group also found, as admitted by the Venezuelan Ministry of Labor itself, that of the 1,053 unions that had existed in the country before the November *coup,* only 387 remained, and 666 had disappeared. In numerous interviews with working-class families, the Commission repeatedly heard testimony that the military government had undertaken a campaign to demoralize the national labor force by arbitrarily arresting the wives of workers and holding them incommunicado for indefinite periods. A similar tactic employed by police was to transport independent or unco-operative workers out of the cities and drop them off on the highway, forbidding them to return to their homes under penalty of arrest and punishment. After returning to Caracas from its nationwide tour, the ILO Commission received evidence that many workers who had testified to the investigators in other areas were later arrested and mistreated by police from the Seguridad Nacional.[11]

The report of the Rens Commission, published in 1950 and bearing the title *Freedom of Association and Conditions of Work in Venezuela,* was a devastating indictment of the Venezuelan Military Junta. Predictably, it brought a bitter rejoinder from that regime, which accused the investigators of "exceeding their mandate" and "mixing in social and political matters which were not their business." As we shall note, this report was also to have greater repercussions at a later period.[12]

Almost from the moment of its illegal seizure of power, the Junta of Delgado Chalbaud encountered the implacable hostility of students and teachers in all parts of the republic, but most particularly at the Central University in Caracas. During the first weeks of the new regime, the parades and protest demonstrations of these groups were broken up by police using tear gas and truncheons, with as little publicity as possible. By January, 1949, the government had succeeded in establishing puppet organizations among students, with the hope of displacing the representative and democratically elected federations. When, on January 11, students organized an impressive demonstration near the Central University to protest the repressions of the Junta, police charged with tear gas and dispersed the demonstrators, as usual, and the controlled press reported the event as a "disturbance caused by minority student groups, stimulated by elements from outside the institution." Published with this report, however, was a statement repudiating the demonstration, signed by various students purporting to be leaders of authentic organizations and claiming to represent the majority.[13]

The professional organization of Venezuelan teachers, Federación Venezolana de Maestros (FVM), formed in 1936 after the death of Juan Vicente Gómez and at least tolerated by the regimes of López Contreras and Medina Angarita, expanded and prospered during the period of AD rule under the protection of Minister of Education Dr. Luis B. Prieto. After the November *cuartelada,* Venezuelan educators found their most determined enemy in the person of their erstwhile colleague, Education Minister Augusto Mijares. Many FVM members were imprisoned, exiled, or forced out of the profession in order to forestall any collective action on their part. When he finally granted an interview to Federation leaders on January 3, 1949, Mijares summarily rejected their petition for observance of the Education Law of 1948, which set forth the purposes of education and recognized the organizational rights of teachers.

Persecutions by the Junta continued, including arrests, expulsions, demotions, and arbitrary transfers of position. Federation leaders then sought an interview with the Military Junta itself; failing in this effort, they sent the regime a memorandum, dated November 28, 1949, explaining their problems and expressing their desire to hold the Fourteenth National Teachers Convention. The government's reply was the decision of Minister Mijares to set up a small puppet organization, Grupo de Maestros Independientes (GMI), to compete with the FVM. At the National Convention, which was finally held in Trujillo in August, 1950, both groups were present and were addressed by Mijares, who used the occasion to praise the government-sponsored GMI and to insult and condemn the FVM. In the voting that followed on various resolutions, the vast majority of members supported the positions of the original Federation, with the result that the Mijares group was soundly defeated. The Minister of Education was to have swift revenge: the National Security Police took possession of the Casa del Maestro, a building given to the FVM by the AD government in 1946, arrested and jailed a great many of the loyal members of the organization, and exiled or transferred others.[14]

Rómulo Betancourt arrived in the United States in February, 1949, and immediately undertook to bring to the attention of the civilized nations of the world the despotic nature of the regime that had seized power in Venezuela. On March 28, he submitted to the General Assembly of the United Nations a letter of protest accusing the Military Junta of violating the UN Charter by abridging human rights, destroying freedom of the press, and instituting a "Hitlerian system" of tyranny in the country. Betancourt asked the Assembly to censure the Junta and to demand fair and prompt trials for the "2,000 political hostages" held in the nation's jails. He also revealed that President Truman had sent a letter to Rómulo Gallegos deploring the use of force in political change and promising to give "all possible help in strengthening democracy in the Hemisphere."

The Betancourt charge brought an instant response in Caracas, where Foreign Minister Luis Gómez Ruiz issued a vehement denial that the regime was holding 2,000 political prisoners. He insisted that only 197 were in jail for political reasons, and that some thirty of these would face charges of misconduct in office, while others were accused of inciting sabotage and violence in the oil fields.[15] The matter did not rest there. On April 7, the Uruguayan ambassador to the UN, Dr. Alberto Domínguez Campora, asked Secretary-General Trygive Lie for further information about the alleged violations of human rights by the regime in Caracas.

If inquiries from the United Nations could not change the nature of the Military Junta, they at least brought results in the form of release of some of the political prisoners. On April 21, 1949, twenty-two such captives were permitted to leave the Cárcel Modelo in Caracas. Some of these, such as the former Minister of Communications Leonardo

Ruiz Pineda, ex-member of the Supreme Court Guillermo López Gallegos, AD organizer Dr. Raúl Nass, and a few others were accorded "unconditional liberty", *i.e.,* they were free to leave the country to go into exile. Many others, including physicians, dentists, teachers, and artists were instructed during a required post-release visit to the offices of the Seguridad Nacional to remain in their homes, or were assigned to certain areas of the interior of the country where they could be watched.[16]

It is clear that the activities of *adecos* in the United States, in combination with the clandestine operations of Acción Democrática within Venezuela, were causing the regime in Caracas to move in different directions at the same time. Like any ruling clique that has come to power by illegal means, the Military Junta was extremely sensitive to world opinion, and did not wish to be censured by the United Nations. It was for this reason that groups of political prisoners continued to be released and sent, or allowed to go, into exile during the spring and summer of 1949. At the same time, the Junta adopted a tough policy against internal resistance of any kind, for it knew that it must take seriously the threat posed by the AD underground to frustrate the government's plans by fomenting internal resistance. As early as January 27, 1949, Delgado Chalbaud, Pérez Jiménez, and Llovera Páez found it necessary to direct a joint communiqué to the Venezuelan Armed Forces to warn against the subtle and subversive propaganda emanating from the clandestine presses and radio broadcasting stations of Acción Democrática, already operating throughout the country.[17]

Such underground activities of the *adecos* had begun early in December, 1948, and were directed by Betancourt himself from his sanctuary in the Colombian embassy. The Junta complained in the Caracas press that the AD leader's conduct was a violation of the conditions of political refuge, but there was no formal protest to the Colombian government, for it was clear that Betancourt remained there only because the military regime refused to grant him safe-conduct out of the country. A small diplomatic quarrel also resulted from this situation when Chile, which had offered sanctuary to Betancourt, complained to the OAS about Venezuela's "negligence" in refusing to grant the desired safe-conduct. For this "unfriendly act", the Junta withdrew its diplomatic representatives from Santiago, and the Chilean government responded in kind.[18] It was immediately after this action that the AD leader was allowed to leave the country, and it soon became apparent that he and other exiles could direct the resistance effectively from abroad.

Agents of the Seguridad Nacional were kept busy attempting to locate the hidden *adeco* presses and radio transmitters, and the effort to find these sources of clandestine propaganda involved large numbers of police, house-to-house searches, interrogations of suspects, and the use of paid informers. When such AD centers were located, government agents confiscated the subversive propaganda and treated all apprehended persons with great severity. After all possible information had been extracted from them by beatings, electric shocks, ice treatments, and mutilations, prisoners were often sentenced to indefinite terms at hard labor in the Colonias Móviles de El Dorado, a prison colony located at the confluence of the Yuruari and Cuyuní Rivers in the hot and humid region of eastern Venezuela.

Although not comparable in hardships and hopelessness to the dreaded Guasina concentration camp, which we shall describe in a later chapter, a sentence to El Dorado involved a long period of enslavement in an unhealthful climate, amid insect pests, poisonous snakes, jungle fevers, poor and unsanitary food, and constant exhaustion. But it is a fact that most captured *adecos* withstood the interrogations and accepted sentences to the penal colony rather than buy freedom by betrayal of their cause.[19] Not only members of the AD underground were the victims of such punishment; unco-operative students, labor leaders, newspaper editors, teachers, artists, and professional people often received similar sentences.

The infamous conditions obtaining at El Dorado had long been common knowledge in Venezuela, but only the most confirmed and hardened criminals had ever been sent there. A sentence to that camp was usually considered definitive, for health hazards were so great that few prisoners served out their terms to return to civilization. There was general consternation and shock when, on October 8, 1949, two Caracas papers, the official *Ultimas Noticias* and the Communist *Tribuna Popular,* carried the announcement that 23 political prisoners had been shipped the day before to the Colonias Móviles de El Dorado. Both papers gave the names, ages, and occupations of the prisoners, nearly all of them adherents of Acción Democrática. The group included five university students, an engineer, an Air Force captain, and a chauffeur; the rest were members of labor unions.

On the following day, despite the censorship, the Copei's *El Gráfico* and the Catholic *La Religión,* as well as the right-wing *La Esfera,* condemned the sentence as unjustified, cruel, and morally indefensible. Newspaper editorials and intellectuals in many countries spoke out against this Nazi-like treatment of political opponents. In reply, the Military Junta inserted an official notice in Caracas papers on October 12, stating that the prisoners were, indeed, criminal persons, for some of them had scattered tacks on a highway, and others had written slogans on walls.[20]

There were, and are, prisons in all parts of Venezuela; but, during the period under consideration, five of these became infamous centers for the incarceration of political prisoners. In Caracas, the Cárcel Modelo and El Obispo Prison (the latter especially known for its dirty and unpalatable food) received persons apprehended in the Federal District and such nearby states as Miranda, Aragua, Carabobo, and Yaracuy.

Prisoners who had been interrogated by SN Chief Jorge Maldonado Parilli were often sent to one of the Caracas centers for later transfer to prisons in the interior, or to penal colonies in the east. San Juan de los Morros, in the north of Guárico State, was one of the largest of Venezuelan prisons; during the two-year period in question, more than 200 political prisoners, including ex-Cabinet ministers, professors, doctors, and labor leaders were crowded into the cells of that institution, where they were denied proper food, baths, or medical care.

The Public Prison of Trujillo, located in the state of that name, received persons detained in the Andean states of Mérida, Trujillo, and Táchira; conditions there were no better than in San Juan de los Morros. Prisoners taken in Zulia were locked in the Public Prison of Maracaibo, where they were under the direct control of the sadistic Miguel Sanz, SN chief for that region. So severe were the tortures and privations inflicted there that many victims attempted suicide, and others became mentally ill.[21]

On May 19, 1949, Miss Frances R. Grant, chairman of the Latin American Commission for the Rights of Man, announced that she would present at the United Nations the question of political prisoners in Venezuela. The Junta reacted by releasing additional small groups of former officials. On June 28, seventeen prisoners left the Cárcel Modelo with the announced intention of going to the United States. Only three of them were able to leave: AD petroleum expert Pérez Alfonso, former Development Minister Oropeza Castillo, and AD official García Arocha. All the rest were detained on "passport formalities". At the same time the government announced that *all* remaining political prisoners, of whatever standing, would be freed throughout the republic on July 5.[22] No such wholesale release was ever made.

During the years 1949 and 1950 the attention of the Military Junta was directed to the realization of three principal objectives: 1) the maintenance of absolute civil order through the imposition of armed force; 2) the winning of international respect and consideration, particularly among the industrially advanced nations; and 3) the attraction of more foreign capital for greater exploitation of Venezuela's natural resources. Fulfillment of the first of these objectives involved the establishment of a police state. The second caused the regime to release considerable numbers of political prisoners in order to gain international respect, and required the imposition of censorship so that other nations should not become too indignant at the extent of the tyranny. The third objective could be realized only by fulfillment of the first two: the creation and maintenance of safe conditions for the investment of foreign capital.

In the spring of 1949, Laureano Vallenilla Lanz became the principal economic consultant and adviser to the Military Junta. He continued to publish the Caracas daily, *El Heraldo,* of which he was co-owner and which had become a semi-official mouthpiece of the regime, and he prospered on the most profitable advertising available. Although Vallenilla looked upon Delgado Chalbaud with scepticism and distrust, and upon Llovera Páez with complete indifference, he apparently felt a deep admiration for the cold and crafty Pérez Jiménez. The latter responded by consulting Vallenilla about the financing of construction projects, the first of which was the super highway to be built between Caracas and the coastal city of La Guaira. In August of the same year the Junta repaid the helpful adviser by appointing him to the lucrative post of President of the Industrial Bank of Venezuela. He continued to aid the regime in establishing a favorable climate for foreign investment, while at the same time increasing his own personal fortune.

The new economic tendencies of the military government became apparent as early as May 9, 1949, when the Junta's Minister of Development Pedro Ignacio Aguerrevere held a press conference in Caracas which attracted much favorable attention in the United States. Aguerrevere announced that his government would give the petroleum companies a much better deal than they had received from the Gallegos regime. He made it clear that the Junta would lighten the tax load imposed by the AD government on the foreign-owned companies, and that it would revoke the rule of "no further oil concessions to private concerns", because it was "not logical to lock the door on a national treasure and throw away the key". The Minister also expressed disapproval of the insistence of the previous government that Venezuela must receive at least 50% of the oil revenues. United States investors were naturally delighted at the new economic attitude perceptible in Caracas, and correctly regarded it as an open invitation to invest more heavily in Venezuela's natural resources with the expectation of greater profits.[23]

In the United States, others were busy creating the desired attitude on the part of groups influential in finances and government. On September 27, 1949, at a meeting of the Export Managers Club held at the New York Statler Hotel, one of the speakers was Mr. Edward J. O'Brien, former manager of the Co-ordinator's Office of Inter-American Affairs at Caracas. He described Venezuela as an attractive place for investment, and for the setting up of factories and business enterprises. In the face of devaluations of currencies in other countries, and an expected 10% decrease of purchases of U.S. products, the bolivar had held firm at 3.35 to the dollar, and the prospect was that Venezuela would be an expanding market for this country's goods. The Iron Mines Company of Venezuela expected to start exporting iron ore very soon, and the Junta had also granted concessions to other United States steel companies.

All of this was true, but not necessarily unrelated to the fact that at the time of the New York meeting, Mr. O'Brien was engaged in the sale of construction materials and building equipment in Caracas. He advocated a U.S. government policy of long-term credits to stimulate exports to Venezuela.[24]

On February 15, 1950, Dr. Carlos Eduardo Stolk, chief delegate to the United Nations from the Military Junta, addressed the Venezuelan Chamber of Commerce of the United States. Stolk extolled the financial opportunities to be found in his country, and invited foreign capital to invest there, especially in oil. He assured American businessmen of "high and sure benefits", and stressed the fact that the Venezuelan income tax was a low 3.5%.[25] Less than a month later a Venezuelan trade mission to the United States announced that Bethlehem Steel would soon begin to export ore from its concession at El Pao, south of the Orinoco. The ore was to go by rail from open pits to river barges, and thence to the coast, there to be transferred to ore boats for shipment to the Bethlehem Steel plant at Barrows Point, Maryland. The trade mission also emphasized the low Venezuelan income tax, and stated that U.S. exports to that country amounted to one-half billion dollars in 1949.[26]

The Military Junta had undertaken to stimulate an economic boom in Venezuela, and the effort was successful. Many Americans, as well as Venezuelans, were engaged in the purchase of suburban real estate and house building as a speculative venture in Caracas, Los Teques, Maracay, Valencia, and elsewhere. According to Vallenilla Lanz, who transacted much business with them, the Americans made enormous profits.[27] Public works projects involved the purchase of much heavy equipment from the United States and the employment of American engineers. Building of the Caracas-La Guaira super highway, started by the AD regime, was continued by the Junta in 1950.

Other projects initiated by Acción Democrática which were finished by the Junta during the period of Delgado Chalbaud included the construction of public buildings and street renovations in downtown Caracas and in cities of the interior, and the building of various schools and hospitals. When these works were terminated, however, no similar projects were started. By the end of 1950 the over-all AD program for social improvement was largely abandoned. The military regime was not oriented toward long-term plans involving the development of a diversified national economy.

In 1950 the *de facto* government not only turned its back on the social betterment programs of the preceding regime, but undertook to nullify the judgments decreed by the courts of that period against those found guilty of financial corruption in past years. It will be recalled that former Presidents López Contreras and Medina Angarita, and many *gomecista* officials had been convicted of *peculado* and some of their ill-gotten gains returned to the public Treasury. The Attorney General for the Military Junta was none other than former Senator Antonio Pulido Villafañe, who had been censured and suspended by his colleagues in 1948 for attempting to incite the Armed Forces to rebellion against the Gallegos government. The 1946 judgments of the Jury of Civil and Administrative Responsibility having been declared null and void on September 16, 1949, by Junta Decree No. 270, Attorney General Pulido began, on March 23, 1950, to redistribute the sum of Bs. 240 million to the several dozen individuals who had been required to pay fines and indemnifications.[28]

The first half of 1950 was also marked by a renewed government drive against the AD underground, severe penalites against newspapers that violated the censorship rules, and a new wave of strikes by petroleum workers that seriously retarded production, particularly in Zulia State, source of most of the nation's crude oil.

On March 30, the SN Political Brigade raided a house in Caracas, where it confiscated a printing press and arrested one Enrique Castro Recio, a Dominican exile from the Trujillo dictatorship, who was found in possession of 5,000 copies of a paper called "Liberación", edited in Havana by AD activist Augusto Malavé Villalba. Several Venezuelans were taken into custoday, but the SN, according to its custom, gave no information about them.[29] On April 13, Machado's Communist *Tribuna Popular* was suspended indefinitely for having "repeatedly disregarded the orders of the Junta, and for publishing material of a political nature without permission of the Censor." On the same date, the Copei's *El Gráfico* received a three-day suspension for similar reasons.[30]

On April 21, *El Nacional* was suspended "until further notice" for having published an article "seriously disrespectful of the Supreme Authorities of the Republic". The newspaper in question, while giving an account of the dedication ceremonies of the new Olympic Stadium in Caracas, made a reference to the "three little pigs" of the nursery rhyme. The censor interpreted this as an allusion to the three members of the Junta; the paper's editor and several employees were arrested and jailed.[31]

On May 3, because of the regime's refusal to grant improvements in pay and working conditions, about half the working force in six principal oil fields around Lake Maracaibo began a slow-down and partial stoppage in production. Similar action was taken by workers at the Amuay Refinery in Falcón State, and in oil fields in Anzoátegui and Monagas. The Labor Ministry reiterated that there was no basis for negotiations of any sort because the Junta, in Decree No. 56, signed on February 25, 1949, had ruled that wages and working conditions then prevailing would be in effect for three years.[32]

Within two days the strike movement had spread to practically all oil fields in the country, and students at the Universidad Central in Caracas and at many secondary schools staged demonstrations in sympathy with the petroleum workers. The widespread nature of the movement made the government aware that centralized direction was involved, and this could come only from the AD underground or the Communist Party. The Ministry of Labor at first attempted to cope with the situation by halting all movement of persons, by car or on foot, in the oil fields, and by threatening the workers with permanent loss of all employment benefits unless they returned to work at once.

These methods did not produce an immediate end to the strike and, on May 6, the Junta Militar, in conjunction with the Council of Ministers, decreed the dissolution of 45 petroleum unions, which included all of them except a few controlled by the Black Communists. To cope with the supporting activities of students, Education Minister Augusto Mijares took to the radio to announce that all classes were suspended until further notice.[33]

On May 13, the Junta decreed the dissolution of the Communist Party of Venezuela, alleging that political agitators of that group had cooperated with AD agents to bring about all of the troubles in the oil fields and in the educational institutions.[34] This accusation was undoubtedly correct; both organizations fervently desired the overthrow of the military regime, although for very different reasons. The strike had failed to achieve its purpose, and Venezuela settled once again into an uneasy truce.

The rivalry that existed at the time of the *coup* of November 24, 1948, between Delgado Chalbaud and Pérez Jiménez intensified during the following two-year period. There is no doubt that the government of the Delgado Junta was much milder than the military rule of the later period; but there is no reason to believe that the rivalry between the two men was based on differences of ideology. Such differences, if they existed, would have been difficult to conceal over a period of two years. It is simpler and more logical to see their antagonism as based on personal ambition rather than on political considerations.

It is true that Delgado, during the summer and autumn of 1950, spoke amicably on more than one occasion with URD leader Jóvito Villalba and the Copei's Rafael Caldera of the desirability of holding democratic elections for a constituent assembly and the selection of a new President. This lip service to democratic processes has led some writers to conclude that he really intended to make good on the routine promises made to the U.S. State Department when the regime was seeking diplomatic recognition. Rómulo Betancourt did not give this interpretation to the words of the Junta President. Remembering the adroitness with which Delgado was able to manoeuver between President Gallegos and the Pérez Jiménez conspirators and to emerge unscathed by scandal, the AD leader considered it unlikely that Delgado intended to relinquish his power.[35]

As for the theory that the Junta President was toying with the possibility of offering himself as a candidate, it is well to remember that he never had been popular with the rank and file of the Venezuelan people, and he was too perceptive not to realize it. Indeed, Betancourt asserted that Delgado Chalbaud and Pérez Jiménez had two points in common, both of which disqualified them for leadership: "a total lack of scruples in political morality, and a certain irritated ill-will toward the people."[36] Nor was Delgado popular among the officers and men of the Armed Forces. The elegant and dignified graduate of Saint Cyr, who spoke correct French and affected European manners, was accepted among the aristocratic circles and "first families" of Caracas society, but he had little contact with the masses or with the men in uniform.

By contrast, Defense Minister Pérez Jiménez had won for himself a position of influence among officers of the Armed Forces. As previously noted, the tradition of the preëminence of Táchira in the political and military control of Venezuela, established by Cipriano Castro in 1898 and unbroken until the October Revolution of 1945, had remained very much alive among professional soldiers during the brief period of democratic rule. The military élite of that southern Andean region, known as the Grupo Uribante, had enjoyed a disproportionate representation in the officer corps throughout the country, and especially in the Defense Department. After the November *coup,* Pérez Jiménez, as a *tachirense,* seemed to represent the promise of a restoration of the predominance of Táchira.

The conflicting personal interests of the Junta President and the Defense Minister were a matter of common knowledge and much comment from the very moment of the November *cuartelazo.* The main reason that the Junta addressed a joint communiqué to the Armed Forces on January 27, 1949, was to counteract the declarations from the AD underground and the rumors among military personnel, that there was bitter enmity between the two military leaders. According to Vallenilla Lanz, who viewed Pérez Jiménez as the great man of the future, and clearly hoped that he would somehow oust his rival, there was open speculation in official circles as to how and when this would come about. Delgado was well aware of the hostility of members of the Defense Ministry, was inclined to be depressed by it, and occasionally expressed presentiments of disaster.[37]

All guessing about the outcome of the rivalry came to a sudden halt on November 13, 1950, with the assassination of Junta President Delgado Chalbaud.

Chapter VI

The Assassination
of Delgado Chalbaud

A special chapter is devoted here to the murder of the President of the Junta Militar for several reasons. It was the first assassination of a chief executive in the history of Venezuela, and it was an event of great complexity and mystery that has intrigued and baffled commentators for many years. Even more compelling is the fact that the violent death of the unpopular leader of an oppressive regime was able to engender such immense indignation and controversy throughout Latin America that it is still the subject of renewed interest and discussion whenever another national leader is killed anywhere in the world.

In order to present here an account of this matter that is as clear and impartial as possible, we set forth as follows: 1) the essential facts of the assassination itself, on which there is substantial agreement in all sources, 2) the identity of the principal parties related to the crime, their antecedents, and points of contact, 3) conflicting theories that attempt to explain motives and guilt, 4) evaluation of evidence, and 5) the conclusion of this study.

At about nine o'clock on the morning of November 13, 1950, Carlos Delgado Chalbaud left his house in the northeast suburb of Chapellín to go to his office in Miraflores Palace. Accompanied by his aide, Naval Lieut. Carlos Bacalao Lara, he occupied the rear seat in the chauffeur-driven presidential limousine, and set forth on the trip toward downtown Caracas, reading the morning paper and making casual conversation with his companion. His only escort was a single motorcyclist, Pablo Emilio Aponte, who followed the President's car. After proceeding a very short distance, the limousine came to a halt, its way blocked by another vehicle that had stopped crosswise in front of Delgado's car. Almost immediately there emerged from the roadside bushes a dozen or more men, led by one Rafael Simón Urbina, who was known to Delgado as a hot-headed ruffian and notorious veteran of many armed uprisings and unsavory exploits of the past. Urbina and nearly all of his followers were intoxicated, and all carried revolvers or pistols in both hands. They quickly disarmed Delgado, Bacalao Lara, and the motorcyclist Aponte, and ordered the presidential party to enter another vehicle. Four other cars had meanwhile closed in behind the limousine.

In answer to objections and remonstrances from the Junta President, Urbina and his men poured out a flood of insults and obscenities, with threats to kill Delgado on the spot if he did not obey instantly. In the kidnap vehicle, the President was placed in the rear seat with Rafael Simón Urbina on his left and Aponte on the right. There were four in the front seat, the car being driven by a Negro named Carlos Mijares, and on his right, Domingo J. Urbina, cousin and accomplice of Rafael, Bacalao Lara, and a gunman named Pedro Díaz. This car, followed by another filled with Urbina's henchmen, took off rapidly toward the southeast and entered the suburb of Las Mercedes where it came to a halt before an unfinished house that bore the name "Quinta Mariza". During this trip, Delgado had tried to reason with his kidnapers, pointing out the inevitable consequences of such an action, but they held their guns to his head and chest and appeared ready to murder him and his military aide from one moment to the next.

At the Quinta Mariza, Urbina ordered the four men in the front seat to get out first. While this was taking place, the pistol of Pedro Díaz fired accidentally, the .45 calibre bullet passing downward through the back of the front seat and lodging in Urbina's ankle. The latter had indicated that his plan, at least for the moment, was to hold Delgado as a prisoner in the vacant house, but with the pain of his crushed and bleeding ankle, he managed only to limp from the automobile and sit down on the front steps of the building. Delgado and Bacalao—to gain time in a dangerous situation, according to the latter—both pointed out the necessity of binding Urbina's ankle at once in order to preclude excessive bleeding. Under the guns of Domingo Urbina, Díaz, and Mijares, they occupied themselves for a few moments with a handkerchief bandage. They could see no way to escape, nor to disarm the the kidnapers. The three gunmen then ordered Delgado, his military aide, and the motorcyclist Aponte to enter the house. Aponte, who appeared very nervous and frightened, obeyed at once; Delgado and Bacalao backed slowly through the doorway.

The Junta leader shouted at the three men not to commit murder, and at this point Lieut. Bacalao attacked Díaz in an effort to wrest the gun from him; he was unable to do so, and received a bullet in the chest which passed through his right lung. At the same moment, Domingo Urbina and Carlos Mijares opened fire on Delgado Chalbaud, riddling him with bullets in the head, chest, stomach, and legs. The Junta President fell to the floor, and his two assailants then turned their attention upon the fight between Bacalao and Díaz. Both of them fired upon Delgado's aide, who was wounded in the thigh, shoulder, and head. As the latter fell to his knees, Domingo Urbina delivered a smashing blow upon his head with the butt of a revolver, leaving him unconscious.

No shots were fired at the motorcyclist, Aponte, who then helped the three gunmen to load the wounded Rafael Simón Urbina into the car. They drove to the house of a lawyer named Juan Francisco Franco Quijano, so that a doctor could be summoned there to treat Urbina's fractured ankle. Quijano, whose identity will be established presently, refused to permit the kidnaper to remain in his house. On the pretext that he might soon bleed to death, he urged the criminals to take the old man to a clinic at once. Helped again into the car, the now fainting and nearly exhausted Urbina decided that he would not risk immediate capture by going to a hospital. He ordered his men to take him to the embassy of Nicaragua, where he requested and received permission to enter. His wife, María Isabel Caldera de Urbina, and his children were already in the embassy, having preceded him there from the house of Franco Quijano, where they had awaited his return from the kidnaping. Urbina, accompanied by Aponte, remained on a cot in one of the back rooms of the building, while his three assistants drove away in the hope of hiding from the police.

Meanwhile, at the Quinta Mariza in Las Mercedes, Lieut. Bacalao Lara recovered consciousness to find that the kidnap-murderers had departed, leaving him alone with the body of Delgado Chalbaud. Scarcely able to stand, the wounded man crawled to a house in the neighborhood where he called Miraflores Palace to inform authorities of the crime, and to summon help. He was soon taken to a hospital by a radio-patrol car.

Urbina, although suffering frequent fainting spells, and so weak that he could not arise from his cot, nevertheless wrote and signed the following note:

> Commander Pérez Jiménez
> My very dear friend:
> At this moment I have the Venezuelan people up in arms. As I told you when I arrived in the country, I do not want anyone but you for President. Delgado Chalbaud was badly wounded, although I did not want them to kill him, as the motorcyclist knows. I hope you will back me up at the Embassy of Nicaragua where I am badly wounded.
>
> (Signed) Rafael Simón Urbina

Urbina handed this note to Aponte, with instructions to place it without fail in the hands of Pérez Jiménez himself. The motorcyclist set forth to do just that, but he stopped at the police station in the suburb of Chacao to telephone the Defense Ministry that he was on his way. Officers of the Seguridad Nacional who were present at the station, having informed themselves of the situation, took the compromising note from

Aponte. Its contents thereby came to the knowledge of many other people before it was finally placed in the hands of Pérez Jiménez.

Aponte was then taken by SN Chief Maldonado Parilli himself to Miraflores Palace, where he gave account of the morning's events to Presidency Secretary Miguel Moreno, Llovera Páez, Vallenilla Lanz, and others who were present. This group, after delays that seem astonishing under the circumstances, finally went together in a car to the Quinta Mariza where the body of Delgado Chalbaud still lay unattended. No ambulance was called, and no doctors were taken to the scene in case they could still be of assistance.

In the meantime, Delgado's wife, Lucía, had been notified that her husband's limousine had been found not far from his home, and that he had disappeared. After numerous telephone calls of inquiry, Sra. Delgado went to Miraflores Palace and was informed that her husband had been assassinated and that his body was in a *quinta* in Las Mercedes. Rushing there at once, she was appalled to find Llovera Páez and other officers chatting in the patio and the driveway, with no effort being made to see whether the Junta President was alive or dead. With some help, she managed to get Delgado into a car and to an emergency hospital. There she was told that he was still alive, but in a very critical condition from wounds and loss of blood. Despite transfusions and injections of adrenalin, Delgado died two hours later.

While the preceding events were taking place, Rafael Simón Urbina was also examined by two physicians at the Nicaraguan embassy; they informed him that he should go to a hospital at once for treatment. The Ambassador, Diego Manuel Sequeira, representative in Venezuela of Nicaraguan dictator Somoza, and long-time friend of Nicaraguan-born María Isabel Caldera de Urbina, was in a difficult position. He wished to help Urbina, if possible, but murder of a Chief of State is not recognized as an acceptable basis for requesting political asylum in a foreign embassy, and Sequeira was obliged to telephone the Venezuelan Foreign Ministry to admit to the presence of Urbina in his house. The office of the Federal District Prefect was notified, and two officers went unarmed to the embassy to persuade Urbina to leave voluntarily. The old warrior, too weak to protest, and in the hope of medical treatment, allowed himself to be carried to a car.

The officers, a Major Carlos Morales and one Hernán Gabaldón, did not take Urbina to a clinic, however, but to El Obispo Prison, where he was left under armed guards and without medical attention until late at night. He was then carried forth on a stretcher and placed in a prison truck to be transported to the Clinic of the Cárcel Modelo. Having arrived at that destination, and as he was being brought out of the truck on the stretcher, Rafael Simón Urbina was suddenly shot to death by guards of the Seguridad Nacional "while trying to escape." A casual and somewhat garbled account of this incident appeared in Caracas papers on November 15, but no hearing was ever held to establish the facts of the case, and no official report was ever filed by the competent authorities.

It was Defense Minister Marcos Pérez Jiménez who, in a brief radio broadcast delivered in a grief-stricken voice, announced to the nation the death of the President of the Junta Militar de Gobierno. He decreed a period of national mourning, as well as a state of emergency and curfew. He also promised that the perpetrators of the "unspeakable crime" would be brought to justice.

The Venezuelan public reacted with unprecedented anger and indignation. Great crowds lined the streets of the capital during the period that the body of the fallen leader lay in state, and immense throngs attended the funeral at which he was buried with full military honors, decorations, and posthumous promotion.

Then the investigation began. Within a few days, Domingo Urbina, Carlos Mijares, Pedro Díaz, and all others, including Urbina's wife, who had participated in the kidnaping and/or murder of Delgado Chalbaud were apprehended, indicted, and clapped into jail to await trial.

On the same day that the assassination occurred, legal machinery was set in motion for the hearings which would take place in the Federal District Court in Caracas. These actually began on December 15, 1950, and continued until July 15, 1951. The entire results of this long judicial procedure were published by the Oficina Nacional de Información y Publicaciones in September, 1951, under the title *Sumario del juicio seguido a las personas indiciadas de haber cometido el asesinato del Coronel Carlos Delgado Chalbaud, Presidente de la Junta Militar de Gobierno.*[1] This enormous volume, a kind of ponderous prototype of the Warren Commission Report, containing 665 pages, including maps, photographs of persons, weapons, and automobiles, as well as lists of bank-account withdrawals and old correspondence from the 1930s, is plagued by countless defects of all kinds. The testimony of the dozens of witnesses is presented on large pages in double columns of very fine print, recorded verbatim, with no attempt made to elicit meaningful answers to specific questions. It is therefore filled with such extraneous details as family illnesses, the purchase of automobiles, conditions of employment, gifts received, trips taken, and meals eaten. But, hidden in this mass of verbiage are important facts that have a bearing on the crime.

The court was under the domination and direction of the two surviving members of the Junta, and it is not surprising if the inquiring scholar has the impression that the *Sumario* was designed not so much to reveal the truth as to conceal it. The tiresome judicial procedure used has one important advantage: since witnesses were not restricted to answering the questions of counsel, but were permitted to choose their own words and to speak as long as they wished, they were free, if they so desired, to "tell the truth, the whole truth, and nothing but the truth". There is no doubt that some of them did just that. And so it is possible, by much sifting and comparing, to arrive at a basic residue of solid facts and a reasonable conclusion.

Unlike the assassination of President John F. Kennedy, there was, in the Delgado case, overwhelming evidence of conspiracy from the very outset. One person, Rafael Simón Urbina, could have provided the facts to clarify the entire case. But he, like Lee Harvey Oswald, had been silenced by bullets even before he could be interrogated. One person, Marcos Peréz Jiménez, was so strongly implicated as the hidden planner and ultimate beneficiary of the crime that there could be little hope of ever explaining away the evidence.

In addition to Rafael Simón Urbina, and the men hired to help him in the kidnaping of Delgado Chalbaud, others directly involved in the plot were: Antonio Aranguren, Juan Francisco Franco Quijano, and Antonio Rivero Vásquez. Following is a brief biographical sketch of each of these individuals, and his relationship to Delgado Chalbaud.

Rafael Simón Urbina was the descendant of an old and proud family of *hacendados* of the State of Falcón (formerly, Coro) in northern Venezuela. The men of his family, like feudal barons of medieval times, had been accustomed for generations to giving orders and being obeyed in the entire mountainous region surrounding Churuguara, in the southern part of Falcón. Rafael Simón, who seemed determined to prove himself as arrogant as any of his ancestors, became the leader, while still very young, of the kind of band known in Latin America as a *montonera, i.e.,* a gang of lawless horsemen who took what they wanted by force and had little regard for human life, obeying only the orders of their *cacique.* Urbina reached maturity in the early years of the dictatorship of Juan Vicente Gómez, and soon won local notoriety for the daring and brutality of his exploits, particularly in defying the orders of General León Jurado, appointed by Gómez to govern the State of Falcón. In 1929, he gained nation-wide fame when he led an expedition to invade the Dutch island of Curaçao in the hope of pirating sufficient armaments to invade Venezuela and overthrow the Gómez regime. Although he slaughtered many guards on the island, he did not find the desired munitions, and was forced to flee to Venezuela where he fought his way through *gomecista* forces, finally taking refuge in Colombia.

After the death of Gómez in 1935, Urbina returned to his country where he became a great favorite of President Eleazar López Contreras, who appointed him Governor of the Territory of Amazonas. In that post, he demonstrated his unscrupulous character by banking in his own name a large part of the territorial administrative funds received from the Federal Government. As a result, he was indicted by the AD Revolutionary Junta of Betancourt for *peculado* in office. Found guilty by the Tribunal of Administrative Responsibility, he was stripped of his illicit wealth and sent into exile. He spent part of the three-year period of democratic rule in Santo Domingo as a guest of Trujillo, then lived in Costa Rica on a pension supplied by his long-time benefactor, Venezuelan millionaire Antonio Aranguren. In 1947, Urbina moved to Barranquilla, Colombia, in order to be closer to the large numbers of right-wing Venezuelan expatriates who were plotting there the overthrow of the government of Acción Democrática. It was in Barranquilla that he met and formed a close friendship with Franco Quijano.

After the *coup d'état* of November, 1948, Urbina returned at once to Venezuela. He had maintained contact with Delgado Chalbaud through an emissary during his time of exile, and he was at first well received by the new Junta President upon his return. He also made the acquaintance of Pérez Jiménez, who presented Urbina with a revolver, gave him a permit to bear arms and an authorization to make arrests.

Antonio Aranguren, eighty-four years old at the time of the Delgado assassination, was a Venezuelan of humble beginnings but considerable business ability. Having begun a profitable but somewhat undignified career as manager of gambling houses and taverns for Dictator Juan Vicente Gómez, he received as a reward for various services a large tract of land near Maracaibo at a time when the importance of petroleum was only beginning to be recognized. Although Aranguren undertook to arrange contracts with American companies for Gómez, he chose to negotiate with the Anglo-Dutch concern, Royal Dutch-Shell, for the exploitation of his own oil rights. As it turned out, a fabulously rich well known as "La Rosa" was discovered on the Aranguren property, and he soon found himself the owner of many millions of pounds sterling in London banks.

While he lived abroad, investing in various enterprises, Aranguren's jealous enemies at home had turned the dictator against him, and he found that he dared not return to Venezuela. He therefore began to lend support to those who sought to overthrow the Gómez regime and, as noted in an earlier chapter, it was he who financed the disastrous expedition of the "Falke" in 1929, commanded by Román Delgado Chalbaud. In that same year, but somewhat earlier, Aranguren had read of the daring exploit of Rafael Simón Urbina against the island of Curaçao. He straightaway became the faithful friend and supporter of Urbina, and tried to persuade him to join the Román Delgado expedition. Instead, Rafael Simón used the funds sent to him by Aranguren to lead an equally unsuccessful invasion attempt from Mexico, in which he lost an unhappy crew of Mexicans, although he managed to save himself. Contained in the *Sumario* of the Delgado assassination are some two dozen letters written by Urbina to Aranguren between 1932 and 1947. Semi-literate, filled with earthy clichés and the picturesque expressions of northern rural Venezuela, they afford a clear insight into his temperament and background.

Dr. Juan Francisco Franco Quijano, 55 years of age in 1950, was a native of the Department of Cundinamarca, Colombia, who had fled his country because of some complicated legal difficulties. He settled in Venezuela during the Presidency of Eleazar López Contreras, and very soon became an indispensable tool of that regime, manipulating the fraudulent electoral procedures through which the *lopecistas* kept control of Venezuelan politics. After the October Revolution of 1945 and the coming to power of Acción Democrática, Quijano was *persona non grata* in Venezuela. He was forced to abandon his lucrative operations in Caracas and wait abroad for the return of more promising conditions. He settled in Barranquilla, Colombia, where he worked at first in a factory, but soon was able to supplement his income by putting his considerable legal and journalistic skills at the service of reactionary Venezuelan exiles. He not only met and befriended Urbina during this period, but wrote many anti-*adeco* articles for Colombian periodicals, some signed and others anonymous. With the overthrow of the Gallegos government in 1948, Quijano wrote another series of articles in favor of the *de facto* regime of the Junta Militar and worked in Bogota as a paid agent of Vallenilla Lanz to bring about Colombian recognition. Having succeeded in this, he returned to Caracas to reclaim his house and resume a profitable career.

Little is known about the origin or family of Antonio Rivero Vásquez. Middle-aged at the time of the Delgado murder, he was a well-known businessman engaged in the processing of various foods, particularly fish. He had been a protégé of President López Contreras, amassing a considerable fortune on tax credits and government loans for his several enterprises. After the October Revolution, Rivero Vásquez suffered a period of eclipse similar to those already described. He spent most of the period 1945-48 in Miami, where he worked very hard, according to his own testimony, with other right-wing elements to bring about the fall of the liberal AD government. After the *coup* of November, 1948, this man also was able to resume a satisfactory business career in Venezuela.

Rivero Vásquez and Aranguren, as well as Rafael Simón Urbina, had been at one time on very friendly terms with Delgado Chalbaud, but all three had come to hate him with great intensity. Franco Quijano, on the other hand, did not act from personal animus; he was simply lending his services to like-minded friends.

Urbina, while still in exile, had made every effort to persuade Delgado to intercede with the Gallegos administration for the restitution of some of the property confiscated from him as a result of the graft trials. It is probably true, as he claimed, that the money and real estate owned by his wife was taken unjustly. There is also reason to believe that Urbina was unfairly deprived of a dairy farm that he owned near Petare. Delgado made many promises to help bring about such restitution, but nothing was done in this direction. When Urbina returned from exile in December, 1948, he began formal proceedings to regain his property, and after a long wait received a very unsatisfactory settlement without the intervention of the Junta President.

Another cause of resentment on the part of Urbina was the social rejection that he suffered at the hands of Delgado. Not wishing to have his children baptised in exile, Rafael Simón had waited long years to choose Venezuelan godfathers for them. Both Aranguren and Quijano accepted invitations to be *padrinos* for two of Urbina's ten children, but Delgado did not even acknowledge this delicate request. Again, on the occasion of his oldest daughter's sixteenth birthday, Urbina sent party invitations to all three Junta members. Pérez Jiménez and Llovera Páez sent gifts and courteous excuses while Delgado ignored the matter.

The case of Antonio Aranguren goes back 21 years, to 1929. After the failure of the "Falke" expedition against Gómez, and the death of Román Delgado Chalbaud, Carlos returned to Europe where he was welcomed and protected by the financier who had supported the undertaking. Carlos Delgado became almost a member of Aranguren's family. He lived in the millionaire's home, shared the company of his sons and daughters, and was indebted to him for his education. When Delgado became President of the Junta, however, he turned away from his old benefactor and, according to testimony offered by Sra. Lucía Delgado, rejected the business deals that Aranguren proposed for mutual enrichment, scolding and condemning the financier as immoral.

The source of Rivero Vásquez' resentment was entirely monetary. Despite his sworn testimony that he considered Delgado a good friend, and had no grievance against him, it was well known that he was resentful because the Junta President had rejected his petitions for the same favored treatment that he had received from López Contreras. Indeed, Delgado's wife testified that her husband had expressed the belief, shortly before his death, that Rivero was a member of a plot to assassinate him.

All indications are that the plan to kidnap the Junta President was completely formed by the middle of October, 1950. It was then that Aranguren, who owned the luxurious home in which Urbina lived, offered the house to María Isabel de Urbina as a gift. All the monetary support that he had given to the family over the years had gone into her hands, as Urbina was "delicate" in such matters. They accepted the house, although, at the last minute, they decided to have the deed to the property registered in the name of María Isabel's aunt, who lived with them. Only a few days later, Aranguren bought "as a speculative venture" the Quinta Mariza, in Las Mercedes, where Delgado was to be slain.

As for the men who were selected to help Urbina in the kidnaping, testimony consistently reveals that he began to recruit them in the latter part of October, on the pretext of such small jobs as driving cars or carrying messages. Most of them were not hardened criminals or assassins, as the newspapers reported, but ordinary working-class Venezuelans. Urbina kept them in his comfortable home for many days, was generous with money, food, and especially alcoholic drinks. All but two of the men were totally unaware until the morning of November 13 that they were to take part in a crime. Rafael Simón's cousin, Domingo J. Urbina, was summoned from Falcón State in October, and knew of the whole plan from the beginning. Carlos Mijares was called into private conference with the two Urbinas on the evening of November 12 and informed of the details of the plot.

María Isabel was in the habit of following her husband's orders without question, and it is obvious from her testimony and that of other witnesses that she knew nothing of the conspiracy. During the period of preparations, Domingo Urbina made a plane trip to Punto Fijo, on the coast of Falcón, and brought back six *falconianos* to help in the enterprise. Rafael Simón bought ten camp cots which he set up in the Quinta Mariza to provide sleeping quarters for them; seven or eight others slept on the third floor of his house. During these days also, Urbina made several nocturnal visits to the Defense Ministry where he conferred for hours with Marcos Pérez Jiménez.

It is clear that if a simple sequestration and murder had been planned, no such numbers of men would have been needed. Urbina was preparing for a *coup d'état* which, he imagined, was meticulously co-ordinated with appropriate action at the highest level of the Ministry of Defense. Sly old *cacique* that he was, veteran of ruthless plots and treacherous intrigues, Urbina could not know that he was but an expendable pawn in the hands of the master conspirator, Pérez Jiménez. María Isabel, who had many lonely months in a prison cell to put the puzzle together, concluded that her husband had been "stupidly deceived."

On Sunday, November 12, Urbina brought the men and cots from the Quinta Mariza to his own house, where he kept them playing dominoes or visiting in his living room most of the day. He also had ample supplies of whisky, brandy, and champagne, and he plied them with drinks so constantly that they were in a state of semi-inebriation all of the time. On that same Sunday, he received visits from Aranguren (which was nothing unusual), from Franco Quijano (somewhat less common), and from the Ambassadors of both the Dominican Republic and Nicaragua, which was *very* unusual. In the afternoon Urbina, his cousin Domingo, and Carlos Mijares drove to Chapellín where Delgado lived. Rafael Simón pointed out details of the terrain, and explained to Mijares exactly what he was to do on the following morning. He also had Mijares practice the drive from Chapellín to the Quinta Mariza.

Returning home, Urbina finally told his wife that something important was to happen the next day, a "political and military matter". She was to prepare a number of suitcases, with two changes of clothing for herself, each of the children, and the servants, as he planned to send all of them on the following day to stay with Franco Quijano for a time. By her own account, María Isabel wept at this news, for she did not want her husband involved in revolutionary actions. However, she did his bidding, as always.

The evening meal was served by Urbina's wife because he had forbidden the servants to have any contact whatever with the men. It was then, and in their presence, that he said to his wife: "Tomorrow, on your way to Franco Quijano's, stop at the house of Rivero Vásquez and tell him that the man is under arrest, so that he can communicate this to Pérez Jiménez". When María Isabel inquired what man was under arrest, Urbina replied that one of the *corianos* (men from Falcón) had been driving in Caracas without a licence and had been arrested by the police. If she wondered why the Minister of Defense should be secretly informed of a minor traffic violation, she said nothing of it. That night, Urbina collected the keys to the four cars that were to be used the next day, then sent everyone to bed early.

On Monday morning, November 13, Rafael Simón roused his household at six o'clock, brought many cartons out of a locked closet, and distributed pistols, revolvers, and ammunition to his sleepy followers, many of whom were still feeling the effects of the previous day's drinking. Only then were they told that they were to take part in a "revolution", and several of them, including Pedro Díaz, who knew little or nothing of firearms and had no stomach for a fight, begged to be left at the house. Urbina, who had deliberately kept them ignorant of his plans, and their curiosity dulled by alcohol, brushed aside their objections and bullied them into following his orders. The oldest daughter was told to transport the children and servants, with suitcases, to the house of Franco Quijano. María Isabel drove her husband to a point near Delgado's house, where she was made to wait until the Junta President's limousine passed, so that Urbina could signal with the horn of her car to Mijares and Domingo Urbina, who waited just beyond a curve in the road. She was then sent quickly away.

There was much conversation between Urbina and Delgado as soon as the latter was accosted, and Rafael Simón's vociferations reveal his motives as well as the type of plan he imagined to have worked out with Pérez Jiménez. As testified by several witnesses, his first words were: "Now you are going to see, *carajo,* who Rafael Simón Urbina is." And after they were in the Mijares vehicle and en route to the Quinta Mariza, he said, "Four times I have offered you my friendship, *carajo,* and you have not accepted it. Now you are not going to be President any more." With that, Urbina tore the Presidential emblem from the left side of Delgado's coat. Domingo Urbina, sitting in the front seat, turned and ripped off the emblem from the right side. Rafael Simón then ordered Delgado to remove his coat, and when the latter refused, Urbina attempted to tear it off by force. With that the Junta President gave a great leap and struck out with both feet. Urbina then slapped him in the face, knocking off his glasses. These fell into the lap of Aponte, who put them into his pocket and later turned them over to SN Chief Maldonado Parilli. Rafael Simón, resisting the urging of Domingo to kill Delgado then and there, said: "We are going to a place where we can talk; Pérez Jiménez knows all about this". The President shouted: "Who says so? That's a lie!"

It is certain that Urbina's plan, as worked out with Pérez Jiménez, and possibly with other members of the high command, did not include the murder of Delgado. The remainder of the Defense Minster's scheme was never revealed, of course, because of the death of the Junta President and that of Urbina. But, in all probability, it provided for the sudden and forcible deportation of Delgado Chalbaud to France, or elsewhere.

No doubt this alternative would have been preferable to Pérez Jiménez because it involved less risk to himself; but there is no doubt that he also foresaw the strong possibility that Delgado might be assassinated in the course of the kidnaping. In that case, the plan was disposed in such a way that Urbina and his men would bear all of the blame and could be shot down by the police once they had served their purpose.

Testimony offered by Delgado's wife, Lucía, indicates that the President was aware that a plot existed and that he strongly suspected the intentions of several persons closely associated with the Junta, including Major Pulido Barreto, Junta Secretary Dr. Miguel Moreno, and retired Lieut.-Col. Julio César Vargas. He could hardly have imagined a planned kidnaping by such a man as Rafael Simón Urbina.

The loyalty of Delgado's aide, Bacalao Lara, appears beyond question. His severe and nearly fatal wounds alone go far to establish his innocence of any complicity in the plot. He also made a valiant attempt to save the President's life, and no one could have expected more of him in that situation. Bacalao's testimony is not contradicted by that of any other witness, except the story of Domingo Urbina, who obviously strayed far from the truth in an effort to minimize his own guilt. On the other hand, Aponte, who meekly obeyed the kidnapers and received not so much as a scratch, was almost certainly a member of the conspiracy. In fact, Rafael Simón told his wife at the Nicaraguan embassy that the motorcyclist was working for Pérez Jiménez.

The complicity of Antonio Aranguren is strongly indicated not only by his ownership of the Quinta Mariza, and the large amounts of money that he supplied to Urbina, but also by the fact that he appeared near that house shortly after the crime on the pretext that he was "checking to see whether the electricians had installed some lights" that he had ordered. Also, by seeming coincidence, he appeared at the Nicaraguan embassy while Urbina was awaiting medical attention. Besides, the old man perjured himself by declaring that he had not met any of the corianos who were at Urbina's house; the men themselves testified to the contrary.

The guilt of Franco Quijano is very obvious. His willingness to permit Urbina's wife and children to stay at his house for no apparent reason indicates that he knew of the business at hand, and expected it to succeed. His instant refusal to allow the wounded Rafael Simón to remain there shows his anxiety to disassociate himself from a criminal undertaking that had misfired. If more proof were needed, Quijano burned a large part of his records and correspondence on the night of November 12, a few hours before the crime was committed.

Although the foregoing people were involved in the conspiracy against Delgado Chalbaud, it is quite clear that none of them, not even Aponte, was privy to the Pérez Jiménez scheme to betray Urbina.

The case of Rivero Vásquez was decidedly different: he knew of the plot against Delgado, and was also aware of the treacherous intentions of the Defense Minister with respect to Urbina. The food merchant was taken into custody and required to testify for two reasons: first, many witnesses had remembered and repeated the indiscreet words of Rafael Simón in ordering his wife to stop at Rivero's house to give the message that "the man was under arrest" so that this news could be transmitted to Pérez Jiménez; and second, so great was the curiosity of Rivero Vásquez to ascertain the outcome of the doings at the Quinta Mariza (of which he supposedly had no knowledge) that he appeared near that place shortly after the arrival of the police. An officer had questioned him on the scene and later reported his presence there; so Rivero, as a civilian, had to be called to explain it. When finally brought to the witness stand on February 14, he said that he had gone there to take his children out of a school which they attended in that area because he had heard police sirens and thought that "something strange was going on".

The difference between Rivero's case and that of all other suspects is indicated by the contrasting treatment they received from the Seguridad Nacional. María Isabel and Domingo Urbina, as well as Mijares, Díaz, the *falconianos,* Quijano, and even the 84-year-old Aranguren were arrested immediately, thrown into dirty prison cells, served unpalatable food, and forced to sleep on a bare floor. Rivero Vásquez was never indicted at all, but only held temporarily for questioning. He was housed in a comfortable apartment at the Cárcel Modelo, treated with respect and consideration, and released immediately after signing his testimony.

Various theories have been advanced over the years to explain the murder of Carlos Delgado Chalbaud. Most, but not all of them, point to Marcos Pérez Jiménez as the "intellectual author" of the crime, though not always to the same degree or for the same reasons. The Communist explanation, offered by Juan Bautista Fuenmayor (*alias* Norman H. Dupray), which naturally claims to be the correct one, deduced "with the help of the positivist method of historical analysis", is that Delgado was about to hold national democratic elections in which he would support the candidacy of Dr. Arnaldo Gabaldón, the famous and respected malariologist, for President of Venezuela. According to this notion, the candidacy of Gabaldón was greatly favored by the petroleum companies and the State Department, as well as Nelson Rockefeller and and Rómulo Betancourt. He was a prestige candidate who would also be a pliable tool for all of these interests. It was to prevent this development, says the Marxist commentator, that Pérez Jiménez planned the assassination of Delgado. It is true that the Junta President had mentioned the possibility of a Gabaldón candidacy, but no electoral statute had yet been adopted, and the country was still a long way from presidential elections.

Another theory has it that Rafael Simón Urbina intended to take over the government of Venezuela himself, and that he kidnaped Delgado in order to use him as a decoy to entice the other two Junta members into a trap. He would thus be in a position to dictate his own

terms. This ingenious explanation fails to take into account the testimony
of many witnesses which shows that Urbina believed that he was working in concert with the Minister of Defense. It also fails to account for
the murder of Rafael Simón by the Seguridad Nacional. In all the
mountainous evidence presented in the *Sumario,* there is nothing to
suggest that Urbina contemplated a *coup d'état* through which he
would become dictator of the country, or that he imagined himself
capable of defeating the Venezuelan Armed Forces with a handful of
corianos.

As to the authorship of the conspiracy to eliminate Delgado from
the Junta, it would be naive to suppose that a man who had already
achieved two successful *cuarteladas* (October, 1945, and November,
1948) would hesitate to undertake a third one, provided he could do so
without great danger to himself. We have noted that in the first of these
coups, he used a combination of military and civilian forces (the UPM
and AD) to overthrow a Chief Executive who represented both of these
elements, President-General Medina Angarita. To bring down the
civilian government of democratic President Rómulo Gallegos, he
employed an exclusively military force; a political solution was neither
desirable nor possible. In the third case, the Chief of State who stood
in his way was the President of a Military Junta, and it was logical that
a civilian tool should be used. Any other course would have involved a
split in the Armed Forces and a bloody civil war with unforeseeable
consequences.

Pérez Jiménez preferred games in which he stood to gain much and
to lose almost nothing. In this case, the civilian to be used against Delgado must be carefully chosen. The ideal candidate for the role should
be a man who nursed a great resentment against the Junta President,
and who was also ambitious, vengeful, sly, arrogant, determined, not
overly intelligent, and utterly unscrupulous.

Unless Pérez Jiménez some day writes a candid autobiography—an
event not to be anticipated—, we shall never know how many possi-
bilities he considered and rejected before settling upon Rafael Simón
Urbina. Although the Defense Minister and his prospective ally came
from very different regions of Venezuela, the first being a *tachirense*
and the second a *falconiano,* their backgrounds in matters of political
power and social orientation were not essentially dissimilar. Pérez
Jiménez, though somewhat younger, had also reached maturity during
the *gomezalato.* The *montonera,* whether led by Cipriano Castro or
Gómez in Táchira, or by Urbina in Falcón, was part of the provincial
politico-military tradition; and alongside the glorification of the caudillo's brute force was the accompanying current of the means to attaining power and leadership: the carefully laid plot, the secret alliance, the
cuartelazo, and the sudden betrayal. The innumerable conspiracies
that existed during the Gómez period, the dramatic rise and sudden fall
of provincial leaders, were all part of the cultural inheritance of Pérez
Jiménez. It is clear that he understood Rafael Simón Urbina so com-

pletely that he could use him as an instrument for the realization of his own ambitions.

It should be noted that while similarities in background enabled the Defense Minister to perceive clearly the kind of man that Urbina was, there were differences in personal experience and temperament which gave him an even greater advantage. Pérez Jiménez had changed with the times. Having attended various military schools and risen through the ranks of the regular Armed Forces, he was a modern caudillo accustomed to the superficial norms and formalities that his calling demanded. Urbina, on the other hand, had not altered his *modus operandi* in any important way since his assault on Curaçao in 1929, an operation as primitive and undisciplined as any desert raid by Bedouins or Apaches. Although, in the years between that event and 1950, he had traveled to Europe and the United States, and had lived in many Latin American countries, he was so inadaptable to modern ways that he never learned to drive a car, knew nothing of legal contracts, and could not even bank his own money. The old customs of the *montonera* were clearly present on the morning of the Delgado kidnaping when Urbina supplied each carload of his men with one or two bottles of whisky. It is not surprising that the elegant and French-educated Junta President would reject the social advances of such a man, nor that the crafty Defense Minister would exploit the resulting discord to his own advantage.[2]

The guilt of Pérez Jiménez in the assassination of Delgado is at least as clear as that of many Nazi leaders tried and sentenced at Nuremberg for crimes planned and directed by them but committed by others. But, in calculating the odds, he had perceived that in the police state which Delgado himself had helped to establish, with a tightly censored press, an intimidated judiciary, and the fear of arrest and interrogation by the Seguridad Nacional, he would be able to ride out the wave of public indignation by maintaining official silence on the crime while consolidating his power. It is significant that no member of the government was ever called upon to testify in the case. SN Chief Maldonado Parilli was not required to explain the killing of the weak and wounded Urbina at the Cárcel Modelo. And despite the testimonial evidence that so strongly incriminated Pérez Jiménez himself, the new strong man did not find it necessary or desirable to make an explanatory statement to the Venezuelan people.

Nevertheless, the newspapers were pressured to continue publishing articles which tended to denigrate the memory of the slain Junta President, and to exonerate his colleagues of blame for his death. On December 4, 1951, more than a year after the event, *El Universal* ran an article entitled "La muerte de Delgado Chalbaud" which included the statement: "Whoever repeats a calumny is as vile as the one who invents it. Sensible and fair Venezuela knows that the blood spilled on November 13, 1950, did not spatter on any member of the government." The same article suggests the following sarcastic epitaph for Delgado's tombstone: "No one so unpopular as he in life! No one so popular as he . . . after he died!"[3]

A great many Venezuelans reasonably supposed that the power-hungry Pérez Jiménez would lose no time in moving into the Presidency of the Junta Militar after the death of Delgado. The expression: "Ya va a saltar el tachirense de la Planicie a Miraflores" was seen on walls in Caracas at the time. No doubt he was sorely tempted to do just that, but once again the cautious conspirator pulled back from the seizure of full power. The situation was not quite ripe; he could not bring himself to relinquish the Ministry of Defense to a rival who might do to him what he had done to Delgado Chalbaud. Besides, he had great financial plans for the future, plans that involved the granting of billions of dollars worth of oil concessions, contrary to the Petroleum Law then in effect, which was inherited from the fallen AD government of Gallegos. To bring about these changes, he needed a *legal* government rather than a *de facto* regime. But, since he controlled no political machinery of any sort, it was clear that an interim period was necessary to make the proper adjustments. Meanwhile, he would begin the appearance of transition toward legality by shifting from a Junta Militar to a Junta de Gobierno, headed by a puppet President who must be a well-known and eminently respectable nonpartisan civilian.

To the surprise of many people, the first name seriously proposed for the Presidency of the new Junta was that of Dr. Arnaldo Gabaldón, who had organized and directed the amazingly successful anti-malarial campaign during the rule of Acción Democrática. A scientist of inter-national repute, and a leader of proven organizational ability and un-questioned integrity, he had never been associated with any political party. His decision to accept was therefore almost as astonishing as the offer, for he could not be unaware of the kind of men with whom he would have to collaborate. His acceptance was formally tendered, and the matter appeared settled.

Before Dr. Gabaldón could be installed in office with the appropriate ceremonies, however, Pérez Jiménez began to have serious second thoughts. The scientist, it seemed, had two qualities that were anathema to the militarists and the businessmen who had been running the government for the last two years: he was utterly incorruptible, and he was his own man. After indicating his willingness to serve as Presi-dent, Dr. Gabaldón made known in Miraflores the changes that he would make in the composition of the Cabinet and the organization of the Presidency. He appeared to take for granted that his wishes would be carried out without question. The cronies of Pérez Jiménez raised a cry of anguish. Miguel Moreno was to be replaced by an honest and competent Secretary of the Junta; Vallenilla Lanz would lose his lucra-tive position as President of the Industrial Bank. Peculation and plotting would be at an end. Pérez Jiménez, seeing that he had made a serious blunder, quietly notified Gabaldón that the offer of the Presidency had been withdrawn.[4]

The next candidate to whom the Defense Minister offered the Presidency of the Junta was neither eminent nor respected. Dr. Germán Suárez Flamerich, Venezuelan Ambassador to Peru, was a dull and colorless figure, a complete non-entity in his own country, who gave promise of being the perfect puppet. Pérez Jiménez ordered him back to Caracas where, on November 27, just two weeks after the murder of Delgado Chalbaud, he went faithfully through the ceremonies that would make him the figurehead President of the Junta de Gobierno for the next two years.[5]

Chapter VII

The Junta
of Suárez Flamerich,
1950-1952

The new three-man Junta, which Rómulo Betancourt contemptuously labeled "a zero between two aces of spades", wished to begin on a positive note. On the day of the inauguration of the new cipher-President Suárez Flamerich, the ten-member URD National Committee was released from jail, where they had spent about a week because of unfriendly remarks they had made concerning the cancellation of the Gabaldón candidacy. Suárez Flamerich conveyed to the people the impression that Pérez Jiménez wished to give: that the "provisional and *de facto* government was in its last stages", elections would be held soon for the "restoration of a constitutional order", but first it was necessary to complete the national census which was then under way, in conformity with the resolution passed at the Conference of Bogotá in 1948.[1]

Pérez Jiménez took advantage of the Presidential inauguration to order a few Cabinet changes, the new Ministers being, without exception, obedient reactionaries who would carry out his wishes. Some of them were to become personal adherents of the new boss until the fall of the dictatorship in 1958. One member of this clique was Minister of Health and Social Welfare, Dr. Raúl Soulés Baldó, a specialist in the treatment of tuberculosis, who could have done much to mitigate the ravages of this national scourge. Instead, he neglected his post in favor of personal enrichment, flattery of the boss, and such pastimes as mandolin playing, and collecting water-colors of bullfighters.[2]

With the intention of establishing credibility in its democratic leanings, the Junta, on December 30, 1950, promulgated a decree which purported to restore some of the freedoms of Venezuelans. What was offered as a restitution of the inviolability of correspondence and of the home was carefully hedged with exceptions and, in any case, was not observed. The secret police continued to raid private homes in search of AD agents, open private letters, and confiscate citizens' automobiles.

But it is clear that Pérez Jiménez had embarked on a new tactical manoeuver: exclusively police-state methods were no longer sufficient for his purposes; he must find a way to the appearance of legality through the use of political machinery. He planted brief articles in the press on February 2, 1951, to the effect that "political circles" suggested the formation of an "independent national electoral organization" which would be non-partisan in the ordinary sense. Elections would not be held until early in 1952, but in the meantime a Supreme Electoral Council could be appointed which would promulgate an Electoral Statute to establish the time and conditions for the election of a Constituent Assembly.[3]

In conformity with this intention, the Junta promulgated, on April 18, the desired Electoral Statute, granting obligatory suffrage to all citizens of either sex over the age of 21, whether literate or not. The Constituent Assembly, once elected, would have no legislative functions, as in the past, but would limit itself to writing a Constitution and inspecting the record of the Junta government.[4]

On May 18, the required 30 days having elapsed, the Junta named the membership of the Supreme Electoral Council. The Copei and URD were represented with two members each, the Partido Socialista Venezolano with one member. To no one's surprise, the other ten members were "Independents", that is, adherents of the regime. If Rafael Caldera and Jóvito Villalba were not enchanted with the arrangement, they did not say so in public.[5] On the following day, the Junta's political activist, Pedro Gutiérrez Alfaro, coyly admitted to reporters that he was chairman of a committee to organize an "Independent Electoral Front" (FEI), to be composed of "responsible citizens who had no political commitments". The composition of the Council was sufficient to show that the Junta intended to maintain strict control of the electoral machinery, but the appearance of the Frente Electoral Independiente was the first indication that Peréz Jiménez had personal political ambitions.[6]

In late August, another political group, decidedly conservative but more democratic than the FEI, attempted to organize under the name Bloque Democrático Nacional (BDN). Organizer and president of the new party was one Dr. Carlos Morales who had taken seriously the regime's invitation for the formation of such political entities. The Junta found that it already had sufficient competition in the existing parties, the Copei, URD, and PSD. Legalization was permitted to the BDN only for the Federal District. To further protect the future prospects of the FEI, which was not a bona fide party and had no program other than the intentions of Pérez Jiménez, the Junta clamped severe restrictions on campaigning by Copei and URD. The political situation was to remain in this state of suspended animation until the spring of 1952.

The year 1951 was marked by increasing efforts of the AD underground to provoke greater popular discontent by fomenting strikes and publicizing the defects of the regime. Many of the AD leaders, including former state governors and members of the National Congress, who had been exiled or had left the country voluntarily after the fall of the Gallegos government, returned to Venezuela with false passports to direct the activities of the underground. In April, Dr. Luis Augusto Dubuc, a former secretary-general of Acción Democrática, and Dr. Domingo Alberto Rangel entered the country in this way. They and a dozen others were captured by the Seguridad Nacional in early May and locked in San Juan de los Morros Prison. On May 9 Dr. Alberto Carnevali, another AD secretary-general and former Governor of Mérida State, was captured together with Dr. Miguel Toro Alayón who had been Governor of Guárico.[7]

The capture of Alberto Carnevali was touted as a great victory for the regime, and an example of the efficient SN methods. On July 7, however, Carnevali suffered an "accidental" fall in his jail cell, and was transferred to a hospital for treatment. There, four other AD agents, dressed as orderlies, entered his room and forced his release at gun point. Other countries received this interesting bit of news through items filed by foreign correspondents, but Venezuelans saw nothing of it in their press, although they soon heard it over the clandestine radio and read it in the AD newsletter.[8]

A measure of the Junta's desperation in trying to combat the AD underground was the attempt made on the life of Rómulo Bentacourt in his Cuban exile on April 18, only one day before announcement of the new Electoral Statute. The AD leader was about to enter his car on a street in Havana when he was suddenly approached by a man who attempted to inject something into his arm with a hypodermic needle attached to a syringe. Betancourt, although slightly pricked by the needle, was able to avoid the injection, and knocked the apparatus from the assailant's hand. After the attacker fled, Betancourt retrieved the object from the grass. Chemical analysis revealed that the syringe contained cobra venom. Subsequent investigations by the Cuban Secret Police ascertained that three individuals had arrived from Tampa, Florida, shortly before this incident, and that one of them had made the attempt on Betancourt's life. They later returned to Florida, where one was assassinated by fellow gangsters, another was sentenced to 30 years in a Florida prison, and the third disappeared. The Venezuelan Junta de Gobierno reportedly had "contracted" to pay $150,000 for the murder of Rómulo Betancourt.[9]

The Censorship Office (Junta de Censura) which, since the *coup* of November, 1948, had been directed by Adolfo Salvi, was reorganized in the spring of 1951. Some positions in the regime, although powerful, did not offer great opportunities for personal enrichment; one such post was that of censor of the nation's press. In April the efficient Salvi was rewarded with the governorship of the State of Cojedes, where the possibility of graft was more promising. The name of the censorship office was then changed to Comisión de Examen de Prensa, and its new director was Vitelio Reyes, a *gomecista* functionary from Zulia State, who became an implacable and vindictive scourge of the Venezuelan press.[10]

The year 1951, like the preceding one, began with rosy prospects of greater profits for investors and for members of the regime. On January 3, an article in the New York *Times,* sent by Jules Lloyd Waldman, declared that Venezuela was "the most fortunate country in the world in 1950" because her dollar reserves remained high, oil production was the highest in her history, and she had "virtually no unemployment". The bolivar was strong, and Mr. Waldman saw very bright prospects for 1951. Bethlehem Steel planned to begin large-scale shipments of iron ore in January; its subsidiary, Iron Mines of Venezuela, expected to export two million tons in 1951, and U.S. Steel envisioned sending out ten million tons by 1955. These figures were only slightly inflated; the exportation of iron ore did begin on a large scale, and Venezuela broke all previous records in the extraction of crude oil in 1950 and again in 1951.

The greatly increased revenues were not enough, however, to meet the even greater expenditures incurred by the Junta de Gobierno. In the fiscal year 1947-48, the last full year of AD rule, the Gallegos government had an income of Bs. 1,562 million, and an expenditure of Bs. 1,437 million. Despite its many programs of social improvement, Venezuela could show a surplus of Bs. 125 million. In the fiscal year 1949-50, the first full year of Junta rule, despite an income of Bs. 1,896 million, the government had expenditures of Bs. 1,928 million, with a resulting deficit of Bs. 32 million. In the following year of 1950-51, although its revenues increased by Bs. 229 million over the previous year, the regime still ran a deficit of Bs. 26 million.[11]

What were Pérez Jiménez and his associates doing with these enormous and unprecedented revenues? It is true that the Caracas-La Guaira *autopista* was still under construction, other public works projects were under way, and the defense budget was markedly increased over previous times. But by 1951 the government was no longer continuing the projects begun by Acción Democrátia, such as the building of schools, hospitals, and service roads to rural areas. The discrepancy between the known income of the government and justifiable expenditures was so excessive that the charges of widespread graft and corruption made by the exiled liberals appear well founded.

According to the previously-cited *Libro negro de la dictadura,* Laureano Vallenilla Lanz used the funds of the Industrial Bank, of which he was president, to purchase for himself the Caracas suburb of La Mónica, which he developed, parceled, and sold again, realizing a profit of many millions of bolivars. Vallenilla himself, throughout his book *Escrito de memoria,* brags of this and other clever deals. It is certain that with any salary he may have earned at the bank, he could hardly have acquired the resorts that he owned on the coast and the many luxurious mansions in the capital. Similar or even greater *peculado* appears to have been practiced by Pérez Jiménez, Llovera Páez, Suárez

Flamerich, and members of their Cabinet, as well as high officials in all other branches of government.

In the history of nations, the names of a few men have come to be execrated as synonyms of pitiless and sadistic cruelty and moral degradation. Rome had its Nero, Spain her Torquemada, Germany a Himmler, and France a Robespierre. Some of the most degenerate cases have acquired special epithets; the dreadful Nazi butcher, Ilse Koch, will long be remembered as the "Bitch of Buchenwald". In Venezuela, "El Chacal de Güiria" (The Jackal of Güiria) was the term with which citizens commonly referred to Pedro Estrada, who became the new Chief of the Seguridad Nacional on August 31, 1951. The previous director, Jorge Maldonado Parilli, had been unable to cope with the activities of the AD underground to the satisfaction of Pérez Jiménez, who demanded the absolute annihilation of the *adecos*.

A native of the coastal town of Güiria, in the northeast, Estrada worked in various parts of the country during his youth, but his early career was relatively undistinguished. Near the end of the Gómez dictatorship, the future SN Chief served on a launch that regulated river traffic at Ciudad Bolívar. As a youth, he also worked for a time in a bicycle shop in Caracas. During the regime of López Contreras, Estrada found his true vocation when he joined a police force in the State of Aragua, a post from which he moved directly to a more responsible one in Caracas, under Federal District Governor Elbano Mibelli. Soon promoted to Assistant Chief of Police, he proved to be an efficient persecutor of liberal elements when López Contreras undertook his great purge of political dissenters in 1937. Estrada was instrumental in bringing about the expulsion from the country of Rómulo Betancourt, Raúl Leoni, and other future AD leaders, all of whom at that time were labeled Communists.

In the more liberal climate of the Medina administration, the reactionary Pedro Estrada was dismissed from his post in the Federal District Police, and obliged to accept a lesser position in one of the Caracas suburbs. With the October Revolution of 1945 and the advent of Acción Democrática, Estrada left for the United States where he learned to speak fluent English, and where he consorted with other right-wing Venezuelans who later joined the inner circle of the Pérez Jiménez regime. He also spent some time in the Dominican Republic, where he undertook special assignments for the secret police of Rafael Leonidas Trujillo. After the military *coup* of November 24, 1948, Estrada lost no time in returning to Venezuela, where he soon appeared at the office of speculator Laureano Vallenilla Lanz with the sum of $325,000 which he had somehow acquired on a trip to Brazil and which he wished to invest as profitably as possible. Vallenilla later recalled with pride that he was able to place this money at the usurious interest rate of 30%.[12]

As chief of a secret police organization, Estrada was by no means typical. He had nothing of the tight-lipped and gimlet-eyed attitude

often associated with men in such positions. Tall and handsome, with
large dark eyes and a flashing smile, he displayed a disarmingly affable
manner and a charming courtesy that belied the unbelievable cruelty of
which he was capable. Many political prisoners who survived the interrogations of the Seguridad Nacional expressed amazement that Estrada
was able to munch a sandwich and chat casually with guards while
watching a prisoner being beaten into unconsciousness, or hearing the
agonized screams of naked victims to whose genitals electric shocks
were applied.

Prior to the appointment of Pedro Estrada to SN leadership, the AD
underground had publicized the news that Dr. Leonardo Ruiz Pineda,
latest secretary-general of Acción Democrática, had re-entered the country to create further difficulties for the Junta. Pérez Jiménez was enraged; he ordered Llovera Páez, as Minister of the Interior, to open the
concentration camp of Guasina, a swampy island located in the delta
of the Orinoco. The Junta was in the process of preparing Guasina for
captured *adecos,* student demonstrators, and unco-operative labor
leaders at the time of Estrada's appointment. On this occasion, the new
SN chief held a press conference at which he announced that his only
commitment was "to defend the interests of the regime."[13]

To achieve more direct control of activities at the autonomous Universidad Central, the Junta also made changes in the University administration. A new rector, Dr. Eloy Dávila Celis, took over his new post
on August 30, 1951. He was a known political conservative, as was the
new vice-rector, Dr. Luis Eduardo Arocha, and the Junta hoped for
their co-operation in combatting the AD underground on the campus.
Throughout September, tensions ran high in all parts of Venezuela.
There were constant rumors that the Columbus Day celebrations of
October 12 would be disrupted by riots and bombings.

It is difficult to make a sound evaluation of the violent events of
October, 1951, or even correct attributions of the actions. Both sides
created incidents, and sought to use for propaganda purposes those that
occurred spontaneously. An example of such tactics was the confrontation, on October 6, between Dr. Dávila Celis and a group of students
who insulted and pushed him because they objected to his appointment as rector. The government asserted that their action was inspired
by members of the "dissolved party Acción Democrática, allied with
the Communists", while the underground labeled the Dávila appointment an attempt by the regime to undermine the University's autonomy.
The incident, though small, was a forerunner of more serious troubles
to come.[14]

The riots that began in Caracas on October 12 and quickly spread to
other parts of the country were the result of a combination of causes:
spontaneous acts of rebellion by an angry and resentful populace; incitement to revolt by AD underground agents; and an elaborate farce
staged by the Junta itself as a pretext for a crack-down by the police.

The Columbus Day turmoil started with the accidental explosion of a home-made bomb and the death of two men identified by the Junta as AD agents. They had allegedly intended to blow up the Avenida Bolívar tunnel during the celebrations. Then, during the ceremonies in the Plaza Colón, someone threw a bouquet of flowers onto the platform where the three Junta members were standing. Guards snatched the bouquet and found in it what appeared to be a bomb. Police and SN agents immediately charged the crowd, making numerous arrests. Fighting broke out, and a general riot ensued. More than 300 citizens were taken to jail.[15]

The government denounced the flower-throwing incident as an example of AD terror tactics, but many people had been quick to notice that the "bomb" concealed in the bouquet never did explode.[16] Nevertheless, on the night of October 12 and throughout the following day, the SN raided hundreds of private homes, jailing suspected AD collaborators and sympathizers. Armed uprisings of citizens occurred at widely separated points in Venezuela. In Puerto La Cruz, civilians armed with machetes, shotguns, rusty revolvers, and clubs attacked SN headquarters, held some of the agents captive for a time, and destroyed the office files of the organization.

Similar rebellions took place simultaneously in Río Caribe, Tunapuy, Tunapuicito, and Valencia. Noisy parades and vociferous rallies were held at Central University, where faculty and students denounced the Junta for its suppression of freedoms. On the evening of October 13, Llovera Páez made a radio broadcast to the nation reasserting the government's determination to stifle "the rebellious tendencies of the Venezuelan people" by whatever means were necessary, including the use of the Armed Forces.[17]

The last of this series of uprisings occurred on October 21, when armed civilians, led by AD agents, attempted to take over the Escuela de Cadetes of the National Guard in Caracas. The AD plan had provided for coordination between officers within the building and armed civilians on the outside, but timing was defective and the operation failed. According to the Junta, two attackers were killed and 40 taken prisoner. Betancourt asserts that many more were killed, and 14 cadets and several officers were tortured in the process of interrogation.[18]

Meanwhile demonstrations at the University brought from the Junta, on October 17, Decree No. 321, which removed the autonomy of the institution and subjected it to armed occupation by the government. An open letter to Junta President Suárez Flamerich, signed by almost the entire faculty, was published two days later, asking the government to rescind this harsh decree. After ten days, the figurehead President replied, refusing the request and complaining that the University had always co-operated with the *adeco* regime, but assumed a negative attitude toward the Junta de Gobierno.[19] Demonstrations continued on the campus, and on November 9 the Junta ordered the institution closed until further notice.

The University remained inactive until the end of January, 1952, when a Consejo de Reforma (Reform Council), for which provision had been made in the Junta's Decree 321, published an "Agreement of Provisional Arrangements" which set forth the conditions under which the institution might again function. The Consejo announced a list of nine students who were suspended for three years, and 128 others for the remainder of the year. Classes resumed for two weeks in February, 1952, but frictions were so great that normal functioning was impossible. The Consejo therefore declared that the institution would be closed for the rest of the year.[20]

Guasina, Venezuela's "Devil's Island", was now destined by Pérez Jiménez for political prisoners only, and particularly members and sympathizers of Acción Democrática. It had been opened originally by President López Contreras in 1939 as a safe place to hold a number of Nazi saboteurs who had landed to destroy oil installations. In 1943, after Dr. Arnaldo Gabaldón condemned use of the island for any purpose whatever because of its health hazards, the Medina government closed the camp.

The island of Guasina has been described as one of the most unhealthful places on earth. Its highest point is only a few feet above the normal level of the Orinoco which surrounds it, and when the river overflows after heavy rains, a large part of the island is inundated. When the waters recede again, there remains a thick residue of sticky mud in which millions of poisonous reptiles and insects proliferate. Humans are exposed there to great swarms of malaria-bearing mosquitos, the *golofa* fly whose painful bite causes ulcers and general swelling of the body, fleas that transmit typhus, the *chupón* bug that carries the virus of the incurable Chagas' disease, besides great numbers of crocodiles, rattlesnakes, and other crawling things. The temperature is constantly between 95 degrees F and 100 degrees F, and the humidity close to 100 per cent. Guasina is so remote from the nearest civilization that escape would be virtually impossible. It is good to report that shortly after the fall of the Pérez Jiménez regime, this frightful island began to sink below the surface of the Orinoco and has now become uninhabitable.

The first consignment of prisoners destined for Guasina consisted of 447 political offenders taken from the jail cells of Caracas, Barcelona, Cumaná, and Tucupita. Despite assertions of the Junta that no students were being sent to this concentration camp, there is documentary evidence to the contrary.[21] Many students who had participated in the Columbus Day demonstrations, or in the subsequent rally held at the Ciudad Universitaria, were on board the old steamer *Guárico* when it left harbor at La Guaira on November 3, 1951, for its eastward journey to the Orinoco Delta, stopping en route at Cumaná, Guanta, and Puerto La Cruz.

Arriving at Guasina on November 8, the prisoners were made to pass the first two days without food while they cut a path with machetes from the disembarkation point to the center of the island, a distance of several kilometers. The jungle grasses and vines were more than six feet tall, and the prisoners, most of whom had never held a machete before, were constantly insulted and beaten by the National Guard soldiers to spur them to greater efforts. The dilapidated buildings of the central compound of the island contained some two feet of sediment deposited by the torrrential rains of past years, and the prisoners were required to clean these sheds before unloading the cargo. The latter consited of several thousand bags of cement, lumber, zinc sheets, farm and carpentry tools, grain, and other supplies, all of which must be carried on heads and shoulders, since no other transportation was provided.

The following account, written by a prisoner who arrived in a later group and survived the horrors of Guasina, gives some idea of the conditions prevailing on board the ships which brought political prisoners to the camp:

On the steamer *Guayana,* an old vessel of the Venezuelan Navigation Company, 287 of us political prisoners from Caracas, Puerto Cabello and Valencia were embarked at La Guaira on April 16, 1952. All of us were without luggage and, like a carload of cattle on foot, we were cast into the hold of the ship, where we stayed for the eight days of the trip, breathing stale air and covered with cement powder and all kinds of filth. During the voyage, an epidemic of dysentery broke out, and there were many cases of infectious fevers. Since prisoners were not permitted to go up on deck for any reason whatever, the sick had to satisfy their overpowering physical necessities on the same floor where we slept and ate. The stench was unbearable, and great swarms of flies descended upon us. The heat was suffocating. The only food given us was noodles and "funche" (rich mush) for breakfast, plain beans for lunch, and rice and beans for dinner. Water was given out in minimal amounts. If anyone, burning up with thirst, dared to ask the guards for a sip of water, he was then beaten without mercy. Several prisoners were flogged with machetes for this reason during the trip, insulted, and obliged to perform frightful tasks. At Guanta and Puerto La Cruz new groups of prisoners were added, until we numbered 314. On the same ship with us were 2,800 sacks of cement which we had to unload as soon as we arrived at Guasina, then we carried them on our heads to the center of the island where other prisoners were busy piling them in a shed.[22]

From the account of another survivor, we transcribe the following:

Except for the shacks and the command post, there was nothing on Guasina. The shacks were covered with weeds and mud. The prisoners built everything. They rehabilitated the shacks, put up sheds, warehouses, sentry boxes, fences, bridges, and a little dock on the river. Juan Manuel Payares, Alfredo Martínez, director and assistant director of Guasina, accompanied by Lieut. Pedro Antonio Ramírez, chief of the National Guard, and an SN man named Toribio Alfonso Filibet, were in charge of work and punishments. They organized the prisoners into work squads. Squads for carts, bridges, fishing, farming, carpentry, cargo, chopping, poling, masonry. Every job imaginable. Two months after arriving in the island the prisoners were ragged and half naked. Consumed by dysentery and hunger. Lieut. Ramírez, from the command post sentry box was spying with binoculars, and when he saw a prisoner rest for a few seconds, he ordered the man beaten until he fainted. With the same binoculars he watched flies on the wall. Flies copulating. And he came out of the command post to order punishments. Some prisoners go out of their minds and take off across the work fields. The guards beat them to bring them back to their senses. They flogged Luis Aguirre all the way around the island until he fell senseless to the sand.[23]

José Vicente Abreu, author of this last account, was a member of Acción Democrática when he was arrested by the SN in May, 1952, at the age of 24. In the course of the following five years, he spent time in the jails of Tucupita and San Fernando de Apure, the Cárcel Modelo and the Obispo Prison in Caracas, worked as a forced laborer in Guasina and Sacupana, and was finally incarcerated in the infamous Political Prison of Ciudad Bolívar. He observed or experienced all of the sadistic tortures developed by the fertile imagination of Pedro Estrada to extract information.

Methods employed by the SN men went far beyond the use of bright lights and endless hours of interrogation, known in the United States as the "third degree". One technique was to force a prisoner to stand naked and motionless for many hours with his bare feet on the edges of an automobile tire rim; the slightest movement would bring an electric shock. This was known as the "ring". Another, used mostly at SN headquarters, was to place the victim upon a block of ice and leave him to the point of insensibility, followed by painful thawing and re-freezing until mental resistance was broken down. Equally horrendous tortures were used upon the wives and daughters of AD leaders. Many such women and girls, after being imprisoned with prostitutes and pickpockets, were violated by guards in prison corridors.

In short, the Venezuelan military dictatorship had embarked upon a campaign of terror against the civilian population, embracing practices used mainly by fascist and Communist regimes during World War II for the systematic destruction of millions of human beings. There was one notable difference: Nazi Germany and imperial Japan had practiced their barbarism principally upon prisoners of war and ethnic minorities; the Venezuelan Junta focused its terror upon the best and most democratic elements of its own country.

On February 27, 1952, as if to demonstrate its indifference to the recent riots and strikes, the Junta's Interior Minister Llovera Páez took to the radio to announce the beginning of registration of voters throughout the country for the fall election of a Constituent Assembly. The government would like to avoid the commotion of an election, he said, but "we must point out, in accordance with the doctrine of the Liberator, that the greatest good that a republic can dispense and enjoy at the same time is a popular government that can count on the support of the fundamental institutions of the nation, and is backed up by the votes of the majority."[24] The Junta and the Venezuelan people simply did not understand each other. Through some remarkable process of self-deception, the members of the regime had convinced themselves that what the rank and file of their countrymen really wanted was not democratic freedoms, but the strict controls of a police state.

The Venezuelan people, on the other hand, had no reason to believe that the government really intended to hold free and honest elections. All military regimes of the past had been notorious for electoral fraud, as well as graft, corruption, and general abuse of power. Most Venezuelans did not believe that the government really imagined itself to be popular or well liked. Faced with obligatory voting, they cynically anticipated a fraudulent election. In the following chapter, we shall study this phenomenon in greater detail.

On March 26, Llovera Páez, as Director of the Office of Special Studies of the Presidency, informed newsmen at a special conference that the government would spend Bs. 220 million in the construction of a steel industry at the confluence of the Orinoco and Caroní Rivers, near Puerto Ordaz in Bolívar State. A railroad would be constructed to connect the steel plant with the rich iron mines at Cerro Bolívar. The entire complex would be powered by a hydroelectric plant to be built at the falls of the Caroní, and a town of some 6,000 workers and families would develop there.

This ambitious undertaking included plans for the training abroad of some 400 Venezuelan technicians who would comprise 30% or 40% of the industry's technical personnel at the start of production. The plan envisioned an annual output of 120,000 tons of steel, and 51% of the company's stock would remain in possession of the government, the remainder being offered to Venezuelan as well as foreign investors.[25]

Considering the country's rich iron mines and abundant sources of power, there could be no doubt that a Venezuelan steel industry was entirely feasible. The project was, in fact, about to be realized by the Gallegos government at the time of the military *coup* of 1948. But the capacity of the Suárez Flamerich Junta to develop and administer such a complex undertaking, and its motives for announcing it in the election year of 1952, are subject to question.[26] The long delays, the vast expenditures of capital, and the technical blunders of the military government in carrying out the plan will be treated in a later chapter of this study.

It was during the pre-election period of 1952 that the Junta made a sustained effort to paint the AD underground as a terrorist organization in order to influence voter attitudes. Typical of this effort was an article

that appeared in *El Nacional* of Caracas on April 15, 1952, which began
as follows: "At 6 o'clock yesterday afternoon, Sr. Pedro Estrada, Director of the Seguridad Nacional, summoned representatives of the press
to give information about a plot against the life of Colonel Marcos Pérez
Jiménez, Member of the Junta de Gobierno and Minister of Defense,
and how he acted to frustrate it."

Illustrated with five photographs of alleged conspirators, bombs,
and the site where the assassination was supposed to take place, the
story gives details of an SN raid on a shack where 14 people were found
in possession of 280 bombs. All of them, according to Estrada, con-
fessed that they were *adecos* carrying out orders of Alberto Carnevali
and Leonardo Ruiz Pineda. As always, the SN found the captives
conveniently in possession of documents that incriminated the "dissolved party Acción Democrática of terroristic plans." Estrada also
said that the AD underground was responsible for a false fire alarm in a
church on the preceding Sunday, resulting in the death of 46 people,
mostly women and children.[27]

If the Junta had no difficulty in "proving" that Acción Democrática
was a terrorist group, the regime's censor also knew how to suppress
important news. In April, 1952, the Venezuelan ambassador to Washington, Dr. Antonio Martín Araujo, having heard many unofficial reports of the mistreatment of political prisoners, SN atrocities, and
persecution of labor leaders and students, made a visit to Venezuela to
ascertain the true state of affairs. To his dismay, he discovered that the
reports were only too well founded, and that he could no longer, in good
conscience, make official denial of the misdeeds of his government.
Shortly after his return to Washington, on May 5, Araujo submitted
his resignation. On the seventeenth, *El Nacional* published a brief
announcement of this event, including the false statement that the ambassador had "refused to explain the reasons for his resignation."

In a New York press interview, Araujo declared that he had found it
impossible to continue as representative of a regime that had established
a "reign of terror that included murder, torture, imprisonment and
exile." He stated that the opposition parties—Copei, URD, and the
Socialists—knew very well that they would be the "victims of fraud" in
the election of November 30 for delegates to the Constituent Assembly,
and that this body would hasten to do the bidding of Pérez Jiménez.[28]
Perhaps it is fair to note that, as early as April of that year, Herbert L.
Matthews, writing in the New York *Times,* expressed the unorthodox
but correct view that the Venezuelan Junta intended to hold an honest
election on November 30 because it really believed that it had gained
popular support and could win in a free and fair contest.[29]

It is clear that the public relations methods adopted by the Junta were
dictated by international as well as domestic considerations. Under the
conditions imposed by the regime, only a small sector of the Venezuelan
population could be favorably impressed by news of projected industrial enterprises. The average citizen had no money to invest in such

projects, but he might very well have a brother or other relative in jail or a concentration camp. As might be expected, the government's drive to publicize the investment opportunities deriving from its industrial development projects was much more successful in the United States than in Venezuela itself. Books and articles by American writers soon appeared, extolling the wonderful financial advantages to be found in Venezuela, "land of opportunity". The authors may have been aware of Guasina and the activities of Pedro Estrada, but they tended to overlook these details because the military had established the necessary conditions of *safety* for the attraction of foreign investment capital.[30]

Despite the resignation of Ambassador Araujo for the reasons indicated, diplomatic and commercial relations between Venezuela and the United States were, in general, marked by a spirit of cordiality and cooperation during the year 1952. Venezuela's average daily oil production was at an all-time high of 1,700,000 barrels, and its price in the world market was higher than in 1951 because of the Iranian oil crisis and the shut-down of the refining and shipping facilities in that country. With these vast revenues, great amounts of American heavy machinery and building materials were purchased for the Junta's works program, consisting mainly of new streets and highways in and around Caracas, sports stadiums and other public structures. New construction in the interior was notably lacking. Progress in the industrial sector was also minimal unless the industrialist concerned was somehow involved in the petrochemical or construction business on a large scale and had the blessing of the government.

Indicative of Venezuelan economic tendencies in 1952 was the reduced and weakened character of the Corporación de Fomento (Development Corporation). The organic statute under which the CVF was founded by the Betancourt Junta in 1946 provided for an annual appropriation of 2% to 10% of the national budget and the stipulation that a representative of the Federación de Cámaras de Comercio y Producción should participate in the management of the CVF. The military regime removed both of these clauses, so that the development budget was greatly reduced and its control limited to appointees of the Junta. The result of this removal of government support of the CVF was a marked decline in the production of goods most urgently needed by the Venezuelan people.

Some sectors of the food industry, such as milk, milk products, vegetable fats and sugar, continued to expand satisfactorily under the military regime because of the considerable government credits extended to producers during the period 1945-48. Such industries as meat and fish, however, were unable to continue expansion based on economic momentum imparted earlier, and production in these lines languished in the period 1948-52. The textile industry likewise showed a disastrous decline, producing in 1949 only 95.9% as much as in 1948, and in 1950 dropped to 84.3% of the 1948 figure. In 1952 Venezuela produced four times the amount of hides and skins as in 1948, but because of lack of support of the leather products industry, the production of shoes (another prime necessity) fell in 1952 to only 74.1% of the 1948 figure, and this despite an increase of nearly one million in the population of the country.[31]

On August 29, 1952, the Suárez Flamerich Junta announced ratification of a new commercial treaty with the United States. In reality, the new document was only a supplement to the already-existing Reciprocal Trade Treaty that had been signed between the United States and the López Contreras government of Venezuela in 1939. The modifications contained in the supplement provided for the relaxation of certain restrictions on the importation of U.S. goods into Venezuela, and the change was widely interpreted among businessmen and manufacturers as detrimental to native industry and an opportunity for certain circles to realize handsome profits. Despite the vehement declarations of Treasury Minister Aurelio Arreaza Arreaza that no massive importations of U.S. products in competition with similar Venezuelan goods would be permitted, public reaction to the agreement was strong and very negative.[32]

On September 29, Pérez Jiménez addressed a large group of officers at the Escuela Militar in Caracas on the subject of anti-government conspiracies among members of the Armed Forces. Since adverse criticism of the commercial treaty had been as prevalent in the Army barracks as elsewhere, he brought with him Foreign Minister Luis Emilio Gómez Ruiz to explain the details of that agreement to the officers in an effort to counteract the negative impression that had developed. The main purpose of the Defense Minister's visit, however, was to warn military personnel that he was aware of a current plot to overthrow his regime, and that he planned exceedingly strong repressive measures.

There was indeed such a conspiracy, as there had been many previous ones, and Pérez Jiménez was probably informed of most of its details. The Armed Forces were honeycombed with Pedro Estrada's spies, who often pretended to be AD agents or sympathizers bitterly opposed to the Junta and seeking to plan its overthrow. These agents often gained the confidence of real liberals and learned of the underground's intentions, then denounced them to the Defense Department. In this way, some 200 military men had been reported for subversive activities, interrogated by the SN, then sent to prison or to one of the concentration camps.[33]

As previously noted, the leaders of the November 24 *coup* never did enjoy the unanimous support of the Armed Forces. A great many officers and soldiers were admirers of Betancourt and Gallegos; *adecos* at heart, they yeared for a return to constitutional and representative government. One such officer was Captain Wilfrido Omaña, commander of the important Boca de Río Air Base in Aragua State. Informed of the threatening speech made at the Escuela Militar by Pérez Jiménez, and the latter's intention to place him under arrest, Omaña and a group of fellow officers acted within hours to start an armed insurrection by taking over the Air Base. This rebellion, like so many others, was overwhelmed by vastly superior forces sent to crush it, and Captain Omaña escaped to join the AD underground.

The uprising at Boca de Río caused immediate repercussions elsewhere. In Portuguesa State, at Villa Bruzual and at the farm colony of Turén, civilians armed with machetes and any other weapons at hand attacked the National Guard Prefecture. This insurrection was brutally crushed, not by soldiers, but by warplanes sent by the government to bomb and strafe the rebels. The armed forces that later arrived to restore order took no prisoners, but shot all those who surrendered.[34]

On the following day, at Maturín, capital of Monagas State, in eastern Venezuela, the José Gregorio Monagas Barracks rose in revolt. Led by Captain Juan Bautista Rojas and co-ordinated with AD underground leader Jorge Yibirín, this movement was able to occupy the offices of the Seguridad Nacional and the police, and controlled the city of Maturín for several hours. Through an accident, the rebel captain was killed in this action, and the AD activist seriously wounded. Deprived of its leadership, the insurrection failed.[35]

Undoubtedly the most painful and discouraging loss sustained by the AD underground in 1952 was not the failure of any particular uprising to spark a general revolution against the military regime, but the murder on October 21 of its most resourceful and respected leader, Dr. Leonardo Ruiz Pineda, known to his intimates by the code name "Alfredo". Often called "el Gran Leonardo" by his friends in Acción Democrática, and described by Rómulo Betancourt as "the soul, the nerve and the rudder of the resistance movement", Ruiz Pineda was an orator of renown and a fine writer who had served with distinction in the vanguard of liberal forces in the struggle for the triumph of democratic and representative government in Venezuela. One of the foremost supporters of election of the President by direct popular vote during the Medina period, Ruiz Pineda was named Governor of Táchira by the Betancourt Junta immediately after the October Revolution of 1945, a post from which he resigned in December, 1947, to become Minister of Communications in the Gallegos Cabinet.

After the military *coup* of November 24, 1948, Ruiz Pineda was jailed for a time, then exiled to the United States where he began at once to organize the AD underground. He soon managed to return to his country without the formality of a legal passport, making no secret of his presence there or the fact that he never carried a gun. Despite a standing order from Pérez Jiménez to the SN that the AD leader was not to be taken alive, but shot on sight, Ruiz Pineda was able to elude Pedro Estrada's agents for years while organizing and inspiring the resistance in all parts of the country.

On October 21, at about 7:30 p.m., the AD leader was ambushed by police and SN agents in a section of downtown Caracas known as San Agustín del Sur. Although unarmed, as always, he was instantly gunned down by officers who made no effort to place him under arrest. This event was totally falsified by newspapers, which showed photographs of the dead man clutching a .45 calibre revolver. When his widow, Aurelena de Ruiz Pineda, appeared at the Ministry of the Interior to claim her husband's body for burial, she was arrested and handed over to Pedro Estrada. Although interrogated and tortured by the Seguridad Nacional, she did not betray the AD underground.[36]

The murder of Leonardo Ruiz Pineda could only add to the anger and frustration of the Venezuelan people as the country prepared for the elections of November 30, 1952.

Chapter VIII

The Great Electoral Fraud of November 30 and the *Coup* of December 2, 1952

To the leaders of outlawed Acción Democrática, as well as to those of the Copei and URD, which still had legal status under the dictatorship, a government-perpetrated fraud in the election of November 30 was a foregone conclusion; their only problem was what position to adopt to make their opposition to the regime most effective.

As previously noted, the Electoral Statute promulgated by the Junta on April 18, 1951, made voting compulsory for all citizens of either sex over the age of 21, whether literate or not. The position adopted by the leaders in exile in the face of anticipated fraud was to advise massive defiance of the provision of obligatory suffrage and a general boycott of the election. For this purpose, a representative of Alberto Carnevali visited the leaders of the other opposition parties, and found many of them in agreement with the abstention policy advocated by Rómulo Betancourt. Mario Briceño Iragorri, prominent URD leader and former president of the Congress in the Medina administration, at first agreed with Betancourt that it would be a mistake to co-operate with the Junta by participation in the election. The rank and file of both the Copei and URD, however, were determined to present candidates and take part in the election, if only to register their opposition to the military regime.[1]

The Pérez Jiménez group that had announced the formation of the Frente Electoral Independiente (FEI) in May, 1951, was so sluggish and inept in any kind of political activity that the Junta found it necessary to forbid all campaigning for a whole year. On May 4, 1952, Jóvito Villalba, foremost figure of the URD, called the first meeting of the campaign in the Nuevo Circo in Caracas. The rally was unusual in several respects. It was attended not only by hundreds of *urredecos,* but by thousands of *adecos, copeyanos,* Communists, *medinistas,* and people of no party affiliation. The speakers were not only Villalba,

Briceño, Ignacio Luis Arcaya, and other leaders of URD, but Rafael Caldera, Pedro del Corral and many others who spoke for the Copei. There was no whistling, heckling, or interruptions of speakers, all of whom denounced the terroristic methods of the police state imposed by the military Junta.[2] It was clear that the government really had no political party and no program to offer the nation, but only a make-shift electoral apparatus by which it hoped to achieve a semblance of legality for its seizure of power.

The main instrument used by the dictatorship during the campaign was not a discussion of issues facing the nation, but a combination of bribery and threats. Interior Minister Llovera Páez sent large sums of money and instructions to the governors of states and other local authorities for the enrollment of citizens in the regional parties allied with the FEI. Much of the money was passed out in small amounts as direct bribes for votes; in other cases, farmers were given credits for the purchase of agricultural equipment, or were presented with clothing, powdered milk, and other small gifts. Priests in rural towns were bribed to speak from the pulpit in behalf of the FEI candidates, some of them allegedly advising the country folk to remember on election day that the regime's voting ticket was round "like the host in the Holy Sacra-ment".[3] The cynical Vallenilla Lanz was later to write in his memoirs of his own political ineptitude and that of other FEI candidates, none of whom could speak effectively nor devise any methods of campaigning except threats or bribery. Some, he recalled, even sent their elegantly dressed wives into the hillside slums of Caracas to distribute candy and clothing to the poor children and to urge the *rancho* dwellers to attend the Junta-sponsored rallies.[4]

In the months of July and August, 1952, Gutiérrez Alfaro, chosen by the Defense Minister to manage his campaign, was busily sending agents into the interior of Venezuela to push the candidacy of his boss for the Provisional Presidency prior to the election of November 30. On August 23 Llovera Páez revealed his lack of enthusiasm for the ambi-tions of his colleague by sending to state governors a coded circular telegram to the effect that such agents had no "authorization" to collect signatures for this purpose and that they should "obtain further infor-mation" before proceeding with this undertaking.[5]

In September, the URD and Copei issued position papers on the election. The Copei document, dated September 14, stressed the coercive atmosphere in which Venezuelans were *obliged* by the Electoral Law to vote for candidates to the new Constituent Assembly:

> The venerable halls of Central University have been closed. The Pedagogical Institute and other establishments of learning have similarly suffered the rigors of an iron-fisted government, and thousands of students have been torn from their homes. The peti-tion addressed to the Junta de Gobierno demanding the closing of the center for the confinement of political prisoners, known by

the name of Guasina, has elicited no other reply than a two-day detention of our entire National Committee.[6]

The URD position paper appeared on September 27, and pointed out that the outlawing of Acción Democrática had the effect of "confining vast sectors of opinion in a gigantic political leprosarium" and added that "those of us who enjoy the relative possibility of acting legally find ourselves persecuted at every moment, threatened, expelled, and spied upon." The URD document stressed the strong probability that the Junta was about to perpetrate an electoral fraud of unprecedented proportions:

> If fraud takes place, as now seems inevitable, the *de facto* state will continue in effect after the 30th of November. And it will continue with all of its baneful consequences for the political and economic life of the nation; with censorship of the press; with prisoners and exiles; with the shadow of violence, from the public or from the seat of power, threatening to fall upon the unity and peace of the nation. Fraud does not make right. Fraud is not the seedbed of peace or security.[7]

As noted earlier, the minority party called Bloque Democrático Nacional had been legalized only for the Federal District. Some of its leaders were in jail, and others had been forced into exile. Other splinter groups, such as the Partido Socialista Venezolano, could have similarly little impact on the electoral contest. The Red Communists of the PCV had, of course, been outlawed and exiled along with the *adecos*. Rodolfo Quintero's Black Communists had allied themselves, as was their custom, with the right-wing Junta de Gobierno.

Pérez Jiménez made an all-out effort during November to convince the public that the election would be scrupulously honest and that he enjoyed popular support. On November 20 his campaign manager arranged a meeting at the Instituto Escuela in which leaders of the captive teachers union, FVM, were photographed reading statements of "massive adhesion of union members to the Armed Forces and especially to Colonel Marcos Pérez Jiménez, candidate for the Provisional Presidency". Most Caracas newspapers carried pictures and accounts of this event the following day.[8]

On Wednesday evening, November 26, URD held its final rally in the Nuevo Circo. Orators Villalba and Briceño Iragorri were, according to report, "eloquent as never before", favoring re-adoption of the liberal Constitution of 1947. They predicted that if the election proved as honest as the government claimed, the people would have a great victory and Venezuela would return to civil rule.[9]

There were heavy rains in Caracas on election Sunday, November 30, but voters turned out in record numbers. Pérez Jiménez, supremely confident, spent the morning and part of the afternoon at his home in the company of Vallenilla Lanz, Gutiérrez Alfaro, and a few military friends. In mid afternoon he received news from the Defense Ministry that the first returns from various parts of the country were extremely unfavorable; URD appeared to have a strong lead in all precincts reporting. He and his supporters rushed at once to the Defense Ministry where they found a large gathering of officers, employees, and FEI candidates, all of them gloomy at the sudden prospect of an electoral defeat. Vallenilla Lanz, who was present and a major participant in the events that followed, has left a detailed account of the matter in his book, *Escrito de memoria*.[10] Since his story amounts to a shameless confession of fraud and swindle, there is no reason to doubt his veracity *on this occasion*.

At no point did Vallenilla and his military friends consider abiding by the results of the election unless these were favorable to their continuation in power. Their reiterated promises to respect the will of the people were based solely on the absurd assumption of a sweeping electoral victory by Pérez Jiménez and his FEI. At the first indication of a possible defeat, they were capable of the following dialogue, according to Vallenilla Lanz:

> Pérez Jiménez: "The news is not good, Dr. Laureano. The first returns examined in some of the eastern states show results favorable to URD. I consider it symptomatic. There is going to be a serious situation. At this moment the future of Venezuela is at stake. We must prepare for the worst."
> Vallenilla: "We are running a grave danger. We must inspire confidence and optimism."
> Col. Carlos Pulido Barreto: "That's right, boys. Things can be arranged. All is not lost. We have the power and the arms. We are not going to turn them over. This is treason by people who have sold out to the Communists!"
> Others in the group: "That's true! We are surrounded by traitors and bums!"
> Com. Oscar Tamayo Suárez: "The result of the election does not matter. What matters is that we stay united and disposed to retain command."
> Vallenilla: "The *civil* formula, the juridical solution, can be easily fabricated when we can count on the backing of *machetes*."[11]

During the remainder of election day and much of the following night, Vallenilla conferred with members of the Cabinet and military leaders. Of these, only Llovera Páez, who had always looked with disfavor upon the personalist ambitions of Pérez Jiménez, and Secretary of the Presidency Miguel Moreno appeared disposed to accept an unfavorable electoral verdict. All others, Chief of Staff Col. Félix Román Moreno, Col. Miguel Angel Leal, Minister of Health Dr. Raúl Soulés Baldó, and the Defense Minister's private secretary, Víctor José Cedillo eagerly accepted the Vallenilla proposal that the regime remain in power by force on one pretext or another.

In a long conversation with Pérez Jiménez, Vallenilla pointed out the probable consequences of respecting an electoral victory by the opposition. The Constituent Assembly, with a majority of URD delegates, would elect Ignacio Luis Arcaya as Provisional President, reserving Jóvito Villalba as a candidate for Constitutional President. Betancourt would then be permitted to return to Venezuela, and he would win the election, thereafter forming a coalition government with URD and the Copei. The military would be out of power and without influence. Junta members and the General Staff would find themselves in jail or in exile, and the oil revenues would once again be turned to social programs. Faced with such a perspective, said Vallenilla, Pérez Jiménez should not hesitate to seize the Presidency for himself.

Although in sympathy with the objectives of his advisers, Pérez Jiménez was filled with anxieties and doubts. Tireless schemer and meticulous plotter, he was invariably assailed with fears and misgivings when confronted by unanticipated situations demanding immediate and decisive action. He had successfully plotted the overthrow of Medina in 1945, but only to see the principal advantages reaped by Betancourt, who assumed the civil power, and Delgado Chalbaud, who became Defense Minister. Three years later, having brought about the *coup* against the Gallegos government, Pérez Jiménez saw his personal ambitions thwarted again as Delgado firmly took the Junta Presidency for himself. And even in 1950, when the conspiracy to oust Delgado ended in murder, Pérez Jiménez could not bring himself to seize the reins of power. He elected instead to operate through a figurehead with the illusion of somehow reaching the Presidency by way of the ballot box.

Now, in November, 1952, he was confronted with sobering realities. Perhaps his incredulous amazement at failing to achieve a landslide victory was no more absurd than the unfounded expectations of his supporters who had constantly assured him of his popularity. If he now hesitated to accept the advice of Vallenilla to disregard the will of the electorate, it was not out of moral considerations of right and wrong: he was simply unable to adopt at once a course of action that was not part of a well-meditated plan. He therefore replied that he must have some hours to reflect.

Meanwhile, the Supreme Electoral Council continued to receive returns from all parts of the country. On Monday morning, December 1, newspapers published the official results as of seven o'clock the previous evening. Representing only a fraction of the vote, these were, for the three leading parties: URD, 294,573; FEI, 147,528; Copei, 89,095. The three minor parties participating received less than 10,000 votes each.[12]

No further news was available until Monday evening. At that time the New York *Times* telephoned a private source in Caracas and learned that URD was still leading with a large majority of votes counted:

450,000. The Copei, in second place, had received 206,000. The government's FEI was said to be trailing in third place, but before the figure could be given, the communication was interrupted. The operator in Caracas then informed the New York *Times* that the line was "officially and indefinitely out of order".[13]

On the evening of election day, Pérez Jiménez had dispatched swift couriers to confer with the commanders of Army garrisons at Maracay, Mérida, and other points. He wished to know whether he could count on their support if he should decide to nullify the election. By Monday morning, he had arrived at a decision: he would prepare the groundwork for a take-over of power in case of electoral defeat. He instructed Vallenilla Lanz to prepare documents which would give at least a semblance of legality to what would be, in effect, another *coup d'état*.

Monday, December 1, was also a day of victory celebrations by URD leaders. They were determined that Venezuela should have the government that it had freely elected, and there was already much talk of the composition of the new Cabinet, and provisions of a new Constitution. There were also rumors that in case of a breakdown of civil authority, the poor people of the hillside *ranchos* were ready to sack and loot the homes of the rich.[14]

By that same evening Pérez Jiménez had made certain of two facts: 1) his FEI had truly suffered an overwhelming defeat at the polls; and, 2) he had the unconditional support of his hand-picked garrison commanders in all parts of the country. He thereupon ordered a blackout of all further election news.

The Defense Minister's intention to defraud the political opposition of its electoral victory was communicated to the URD leadership in a telegram dated December 2, 1952, at 3 o'clock a.m., and addressed to Ignacio Luis Arcaya and Jóvito Villalba:

> Your categorial denial of the serious deed attributed to you of accord with clandestine and anti-national parties is not sufficient to prove the good faith of your assertion. The ideas expounded by URD orators at different meetings and the voting by Communists and *acciondemocratistas* for the yellow ticket only corroborates the above-mentioned fact. The Armed Forces, so ill treated by you, are not disposed to permit the damaging, through vile agreements, of the prestige and progress of the nation, seriously compromised by the electoral triumph of Acción Democrática and the Communist Party, which URD has propitiated. Sincerely, Pérez Jiménez.[15]

In accusing URD of connivance with the outlawed parties and of receiving the votes of citizens who had previously voted for the candidates of those parties, Pérez Jiménez was grasping at straws. As we have seen, the Electoral Statute sponsored by his own regime made voting *obligatory,* and there was no stipulation concerning the previous political affiliation of any citizen. As for the influence of the *adecos* in determining the victory of URD, the Defense Minister was undoubtedly correct: indications are that a preponderance of *adecos* planned to boycott the election of November 30 in conformity with the directive issued by Betancourt in September. But when Leonardo Ruiz Pineda was murdered by SN agents on October 21, these same Venezuelans changed their minds and decided to vote against the government at any cost.[16]

On Tuesday morning, December 2, Vallenilla Lanz assured his boss that the date was auspicious for a *coup d'état*: Louis Napoleon had thwarted his enemies and seized power on December 2, 1851, while Napoleon the Great had won the Battle of Austerlitz on that date in 1803. Pérez Jiménez then dictated a decree naming the Ministers of his new Cabinet. Not surprisingly, Vallenilla was rewarded for his services with the Ministry of the Interior. For his management of the FEI campaign, Pedro Gutiérrez Alfaro was named Minister of Health. The previous occupant of the post, Raúl Soulés Baldó, was to become Secretary of the Presidency.

Tuesday passed amid rumors that URD would resist the Pérez Jiménez *coup* by calling a general strike and inciting the populace to rebellion. Pedro Estrada's agents reported finding tacks spread on certain streets and highways, and threatening crowds were said to be gathering in El Silencio. Another difficulty was that Dr. Vincente Grisanti, President of the Supreme Electoral Council and an honest political independent, was insisting on strict adherence to the provisions of the electoral Statute. He would refuse to certify the victory of FEI until all the votes had been counted according to the rules.[17]

Despite these inconveniences, the conspirators proceeded with the *coup*. At 8 p.m., December 2, military leaders gathered at Miraflores Palace with newly-named Cabinet members, radio and television technicians, and assorted witnesses. The Supreme Electoral Council was reported as having announced that early election returns indicated that FEI was leading with 570,000 votes; URD was credited with 463,708, and the Copei with 138,003. Although the FEI total was admittedly less than 30% of the expected national vote, no further counting of ballots was considered necessary. The Junta de Gobierno of Germán Suárez Flamerich thereupon submitted its resignation to the Armed Forces which, in turn, named Defense Minister Pérez Jiménez Provisional President. The remainder of the fraudulent ceremony consisted of the presentation of new Cabinet ministers, the signing of documents, and the broadcast of the Pérez Jiménez speech. The military *coup* was a *fait accompli*.[18]

To avoid possible complications with members of the previous Junta, it was announced that Suárez Flamerich was leaving for an extended vacation in Switzerland, while Llovera Páez would travel in the United States. Ignacio Luis Arcaya, President of URD, and known as a firebrand, had been arrested on December 1 and detained for two days, with his cousin, Dr. Mariano Arcaya, in a cell of the Caracas police building. Though released on December 3, both were under constant surveillance. They were marked for exile along with other leaders of the political opposition.[19]

On the morning of December 3, Interior Minister Vallenilla found on his desk the "irrevocable resignation" of Dr. Vicente Grisanti as President of the Supreme Electoral Council. Vallenilla, perceiving a danger to his falsification plan, attempted to summon the Council leader by telephone. But Grisanti, although so fearful for his life that he would not leave his house, was nevertheless intransigent: he would not certify the fraud perpetrated by the government. The Minister then summoned a more pliant member of the Electoral Council, Pablo Salas Castillo, who proved willing to substitute for Dr. Grisanti in the desired certification.[20]

At noon on the same day Vallenilla addressed the nation by radio, assuring Venezuelans, in the face of overwhelming evidence and general belief to the contrary, that "the FEI had really and truly won the election" and that no partisan uprisings or public disorder of any kind would be tolerated.[21]

The new regime's fears of adverse foreign press reaction proved well founded. In an editorial entitled "Democracy Loses in Venezuela", the New York *Times* of December 4 pointed out that what Pérez Jiménez did was not only an obvious fraud, but that he had broken the electoral law that his own government had sponsored: it provided that the new Constituent Assembly should elect the Provisional President on January 10, 1953; yet he had the Armed Forces proclaim him in this post on December 2 when results of the election were not yet complete. Bogotá's important *El Tiempo,* on December 3, and the *Times* of London, on December 6, also denounced the *coup*. On December 11, *The Economist* commented: "The outlook is serious. Colonel Pérez Jiménez has proved to be a clumsy politician, and his present lieutenants are either barbarians or weaklings. It is probable that his only method of countering the forthcoming outbursts of the opposition will be that of brutal repression against a people that feels more exasperated and infuriated than ever."[22]

In a brief article in the New York *Times* on December 5, commentator Walter H. Waggoner speculated that the grab of the Venezuelan Presidency by Pérez Jiménez would not cause any rupture of relations with the United States.[23] Pérez Jiménez was reportedly of the opinion that there should be no problem of recognition by Washington since "the regime was the same" as before; the executive power had simply ceased being collective and had become "unipersonal". And Vallenilla claimed to have assurances from the Apostolic Nuncio and American Ambassador Fletcher Warren that they shared this point of view.

On December 5 Vallenilla Lanz announced to the press that the FEI had won 49 seats in the election; URD was conceded 25 seats, the Copei 9, and one to Popular Republican Action. No mention was made of the number of votes counted. And it is not known just when, or by whose order, the ballot boxes in the states and territories were impounded and brought to Caracas. But a few days after the election all of the electoral evidence was in the hands of Vallenilla Lanz, and he was able to "juggle" the apportionment of seats at his own convenience. The numbers mentioned by the Interior Minister did not account for the full membership of the Constituent Assembly: of the total of 104 seats, 20 remained to be filled. In all probability, his "numbers game" was a ploy intended to attract the participation of the opposition parties.

It will be noted that if the unapportioned 20 seats were awarded to Caldera's party, the Copei would then have 29 seats, slightly more than URD. If they were given to Villalba's party, the URD would reach *near* parity with the regime's FEI. The participation of the opposition parties was necessary if the government hoped to maintain any appearance of legality.[24]

The Copei and URD leaders were not disposed to accept the minority participation offered. They were convinced that Pérez Jiménez was desperately in need of their help and that better terms could be extracted by adopting a tough and fearless attitude. A few days after Vallenilla's announcement of apportionment, Rafael Caldera paid a visit to the Interior Minister in the latter's home. According to Vallenilla, the *copeyano* proposed a deal: if the regime would guarantee his party three cabinet posts and the governorships of seven states, the Copei would co-operate in the work of the Assembly. Vallenilla replied that he would transmit this proposal to his boss. Meanwhile, Pérez Jiménez claimed to have evidence that URD's Villalba had contacted the commanders of military garrisons in an effort to organize an uprising against the regime. The Minister of the Interior was instructed to arrange for the arrest and exile of Jóvito Villalba.[25]

Vallenilla summoned the URD leader to the Ministry for 4 p.m. on December 16, and Villalba appeared with six co-partisans. His attitude, according to Vallenilla, was even more arrogant and demanding than that of Caldera. Villalba allegedly delivered a 24-hour ultimatum to the regime to rescind the falsified election returns and to make a new apportionment of seats in conformity with the Electoral Statute. Vallenilla was noncommittal, but outside his office all seven URD members were quietly arrested by SN agents. Jóvito and his friends were driven after dark to an airport where they were put aboard a plane for Panama without so much as a toothbrush, and with no opportunity even to telephone their families.[26]

On the following day *caraqueños* read in their morning papers that "Jóvito Villalba and six other leaders of the Unión Republicana Democrática have been invited to leave the country." The accompanying explanation by the Interior Minister was that the exiled men had been involved in conspiracies to foment public disorder. Vallenilla also announced once again that Guasina would soon be closed and that all political prisoners, except those whose cases were pending in court, would be released.[27]

Meanwhile, Mariano Arcaya and his brother Carlos had been exiled to the island of Curaçao and thence to the United States. Ignacio Luis Arcaya had taken refuge in the palace of the Papal Nuncio, and Mario Briceño Iragorri had found safety in the Colombian embasssy. Thus, in the period between the *coup d'état* and the convening of the Constituent Assembly, the Pérez Jiménez regime was able to free itself of all threats of political oppostion.

The new personal dictatorship now had the problem of forming a Constitutent Assembly that would "legalize" and ratify the decisions of a man who had been rejected by the great majority of his fellow citizens. Throughout the final days of 1952 and the first week of January, 1953, the Interior Ministry labored mightily to this end. As in the case of the November election, the regime found itself limited by rules that its own Electoral Council had formulated. One of these was the stipulation that an Assembly *quorum* must represent at least two thirds of the total membership of 104. Despite the deportation of Jóvito Villalba, and the refusal of Caldera to take part in the fraudulent Assembly, Vallenilla Lanz had coerced or bribed several members of URD and Copei into accepting seats in the gathering.

As the day for the first meeting drew near, the Minister was chagrined to find that all of the *urredecos* and *copeyanos* had withdrawn and refused to participate. Since it was necessary to have a *quorum* of at least 70 members, Vallenilla found that the 49 seats apportioned to FEI were not enough; it was necessary to discover an "error" in the original apportionment. Ten additional seats were accorded to FEI, giving that party a total of 59 places. Unhappily, even this bit of legerdemain did not solve the problem: nine of the regime's own FEI delegates refused to take part in the Assembly's activities. The latter, of course, were very soon in jail or in hiding along with the Electoral Council members who had opposed the government's fraud.[28]

Despite these troubles, the Constituent Assembly met, as scheduled, on January 9 in the Legislative Palace.[29] The Interior Minister found it expedient to hold the first meeting—accreditation and seating of delegates, traditionally open to the public—behind closed doors, with journalists and photographers barred. The reason: the 50 FEI delegates who finally appeared in the hall did not make up a *quorum,* and the government had placed among them 21 "alternates" who turned out to be policemen, clerks, and other civil functionaries.[30]

There was no question of electing a president of the Assembly: the regime had already appointed a Pérez aide to this post. The Armed Forces had also relieved the Assembly of the first responsibility assigned to it in the Electoral Law: the election of a Provisional President. The first function of the body, then, was to ratify the election of Peréz Jiménez, an act speedily performed without debate or objection.[31]

Although the Assembly continued its sessions for several months, its accomplishments were insignificant. The new Constitution of 1953—Venezuela's 22nd charter since 1811—, a mere patchwork prepared by

Vallenilla in the Interior Ministry, was capricious and contradictory. It changed the name of the country from "Estados Unidos de Venezuela" to "República de Venezuela", and made state governships appointive (by the President) rather than elective. The individual rights of citizens were enumerated and guaranteed in Title III of the Constitution, but their effect was totally nullified by one of the "Temporary Provisions" listed at the end of the document authorizing the President "to take whatever measures he may deem necessary for the preservation in every way of the security of the nation, the protection of social peace and the maintenance of public order."[32]

The Assembly not only failed to perform its proper functions, but exceeded its authority. *Time Magazine,* in its issue of April 8, 1953, began its coverage of Venezuelan news, under the title "A Mantle of Legality", with the following paragraph:

> Venezuelans found out one night last week that their country would soon have: 1) A new Congress, 2) A new Court of Justice, 3) A completely new collection of state and municipal legislatures, 4) A new Constitution, and 5) The same strongman as before for a period of 5 years. Voters would not have to worry about electing their officials. The whole team will be chosen in the next 9 days by the Constituent Assembly.[33]

On April 19 the new Constitution was promulgated, and Constitutional President Marcos Pérez Jiménez began a five-year term: 1953-58. On the following day Venezuelan papers carried full accounts, with photographic illustrations, of the inauguration ceremonies, the presidential ball, and other gala events.[34]

The slow but inexorable advance of Pérez Jiménez to the pinnacle of power during the four and one-half year period from November, 1948, to April, 1953, had cost the lives of hundreds of Venezuelans. Several thousand others languished in prisons or fought for survival in the pestilential swamps of Guasina and Sacupana. Still others, in hiding within Venezuela or in exile, continued their struggle against the tyranny through speeches, books, articles, and letters to the editors of the liberal press. The possibility had existed to avoid the total tyranny that developed as a result of the events from November, 1952, to April, 1953.

The principal forces—military, moral, economic, and political—which *could have* brought about a different situation may be identified as: 1) the Venezuelan Armed Forces; 2) the Venezuelan Catholic Church; and 3) the U.S. State Department. Let us examine how these entities could have acted, and why they were inoperative.

Perhaps it is true in any country that men who have chosen military careers as a way of life constitute the least democratic elements of society, and there is no reason to believe that the Venezuelan Armed Forces represented any exception to this rule. Military organization is, by nature, authoritarian and hierarchical rather than democratic. There is also the fact that, except for the period of rule by Acción Democrática, 1945-48, Venezuela's prior history is an almost unbroken series of military-dominated regimes.

There is persuasive evidence that Venezuela in 1945 was not only ready for an experiment in representative government, but that the following three-year period of AD rule was sufficient to establish, even in the Armed Forces, the beginnings of a democratic tradition among the most intelligent and liberal-minded officers. In no other way can we explain the many cases of uprisings in barracks throughout the country during this period, led by such men as Captain Wilfrido Omaña who demanded an end to the rule by a military clique and a return to representative government. Captain Omaña had co-operated with the AD underground since the abortive uprising of the Boca de Río Air Base in October, 1952. While in hiding thereafter he had sent a "Message to my Comrades in Arms and to the Venezuelan People" in which he explained that the "crime for which I am persecuted by an illegal government is the decision to fight beside my comrades in arms and the people against the dictatorship that oppresses the nation."[35]

Alberto Carnevali, secretary-general of Acción Democrática during the brief period between the assassination of Leonardo Ruiz Pineda and his own death (October, 1952-May, 1953), in a communiqué issued in December, 1952, in the name of the AD National Executive Committee, offers further evidence of disaffection in the Armed Forces and the tactics of emissaries sent by Pérez Jiménez to combat it in the barracks after the election of November 30:

> Some of these emissaries announced in a blunt and barefaced fashion to the officers gathered in the barracks for the purpose, that the government had lost the election. But they added the lie-story that the political parties planned to dissolve the Army and assassinate the officers' families, and that to avoid this chaos for the nation, Col. Pérez Jiménez was "sacrificing himself" by assuming the absolute control of power. In general, the officers were not consulted, but *notified* of this second crime against popular sovereignty, as if the Army were a flock of docile armed men who had neither judgment nor feelings to take into account. And in the few barracks in which a pretense of consultation was made, the chiefs were careful not to transmit "to the higher authorities" the real answer of the majority of officers, completely opposed to the ignoring of the electoral will.[36]

It is clear that not all of the officers and men of the Armed Forces were entirely subservient to the will of the Defense Minister, nor convinced that a personal dictatorship by him was the best possible arrangement for the country. The failure of the Armed Forces to oppose effectively the Pérez Jiménez power grab may be attributed to the following factors: 1) The military clique, aided by such civilian advisers as

Vallenilla Lanz and Víctor José Cedillo, used the Hitler and Göbbels "big-lie" technique to frighten the more naïve officers into acquiescence. 2) Although few members of the officer corps could have been deceived by the regime's false claims to victory in the November 30 elections, resistance to the *coup* of December 2 was rendered particularly difficult because Venezuelans no longer had a legally-elected President to whom they could pledge loyalty and support. 3) Most of the commanding officers of barracks, with the rank of colonel or major, were older men whose ideas had been formed before the advent of Acción Democrática; many of them were *tachirenses,* and they were inclined to identify their own interests with continued domination by the military. 4) The Armed Forces were honeycombed with the spies of Pérez Jiménez and Pedro Estrada, and it was dangerous to express ideas contrary to those of the General Staff; in December, 1952, many officers were arrested, jailed, transferred, demoted, or deported to frustrate any possibility of concerted resistance to the *coup.* 5) The tradition of personalist military rule was deeply rooted in the social fabric of Venezuela, and proved stronger in 1953 than the desire to return to representative government. But the fact that Pérez Jiménez finally fell from power in 1958 when his fellow officers withdrew their support shows that he could not have taken control of the country in 1953 without their help.

In considering the attitude of the Venezuelan Catholic Church toward the upheavals of the nation in the years following the *coup* of 1948, one is impressed particularly by its *lack* of any firm moral position with respect to the military regime's consistent disregard for basic human rights. Venezuelans are predominantly Catholic, and opinions expressed from the pulpit or in the widely-read Caracas daily *La Religión* are very influential in the thinking and attitudes of the people. The fact is that the record of the Church on questions of social justice in Venezuela prior to 1957 is dismal and reactionary. In general, the Catholic hierarchy was subservient to Juan Vicente Gómez and the other *tachirense* strongmen who ruled the country before 1945 and refrained from criticizing their tyrannical regimes. With the advent of Acción Democrática, this same clergy suddenly found it possible to express vociferous opposition, both orally and in print, to the mild provisions of the Constitution of 1947 which maintained separation of Church and State and sought to institute certain controls for the education of Venezuelan children in parochial schools.

After the fall of the Gallegos government in 1948 and the take-over by the military, the Church was once again in a relatively favorable position. State subsidies to religious schools, seminaries, and other Church-related enterprises, although never large in comparison to those in other Latin American countries, were once again more generous. Large numbers of clerical personnel, both priests and nuns, were imported from Spain to run the Venezuelan religious establishment. The Church eagerly accepted the friendliness and liberality of the Junta, and returned the favor by refraining from complaint when the regime began at once to suppress labor unions, destroy student organizations, muzzle the press, and dismantle the entire social-progress program begun by Acción Democrática.

It is not that the Church, either from the pulpit or through the columns of *La Religión,* praised the brutal activities of Pedro Estrada or condoned the atrocities committed in Guasina or in the torture chambers of the SN; it is simply that *it remained silent on these issues* while extolling the virtues of the regime for its maintenance of law and order, the blessings of prosperity deriving from the petroleum industry, and the continued peace and tranquillity of the Catholic community.

It may be that there were some isolated cases of protests against the dishonesty of the government on the occasion of the great electoral fraud of November 30, 1952. Perhaps such clerics, if there were any, were instantly arrested and punished for their temerity. This is not the type of news item that would be likely to appear either in the pages of the official Catholic paper or in the controlled commercial press, and no such case has come to light. The truth is that the Church maintained a safe and discreet silence in the face of the electoral fraud, the *coup* of December 2, and all of the official activities that led inevitably to the installation of Pérez Jiménez as Constitutional President of Venezuela.[37]

It is significant that Rómulo Betancourt, in his exhaustive work *Venezuela: política y petróleo,* touches only rarely and with great circumspection upon the delicate question of the moral responsibility of the Church for the tyranny that afflicted Venezuela during the decade 1948-1958. In Latin America, more than in most other parts of the world, it is a daring politician who will point out the moral shortcomings of the Catholic hierarchy and still hope to be elected to high office. Betancourt, a consummate politician, needed no instruction on these points. Although the present work is unimpeded by such considerations, the greatest possible care must be exercised in this matter, if only to render justice to a venerable institution that has, since 1957, demonstrated a much more laudable sense of social responsibility than was previously the case.

In a country like Venezuela, whose history of government has been predominantly personalist and authoritarian from the earliest times, it would be absurd to expect the representatives of the Catholic Church to exhibit a natural preference for a democratic form of government, this being so contrary to the structure and practices of the institution itself. Nevertheless, Catholicism's claim to worldwide moral authority surely carries with it some implication of moral responsibility and integrity on the part of Catholic officials in their relationships with civil authorities.

Anti-Communist writers, many of them Catholic theologians, have questioned whether it is possible to establish a truly moral society that is not only non-Christian but which does not recognize the validity of any religious ethic at all. Even more pertinently, we believe, it may be asked whether any Church hierarchy can be considered truly *Christian* which fails, for considerations of self-interest, to denounce flagrant dishonesty in elections, violations of basic human rights, and financial corruption in government.

The experience and reactions of the Catholic Church in dealing with right-wing dictatorships have been quite similar in the cases of the Hitler regime in Germany, the Perón government in Argentina, and the Pérez Jiménez military clique in Venezuela. Perón did not at first attack the Church, but sought instead to enlist its support by granting generous financial assistance to religious institutions and by announcing at the beginning of his rule in 1945 that his social policy would be "inspired by the Papal encyclicals".[38] The resulting *entente,* although very helpful to Perón in consolidating his power, brought a great loss of dignity and prestige to the Argentine clergy and a revival of anticlericalism. It was not until nine years later, in 1954, when Perón undertook a concerted campaign against the Church by arresting priests and closing Catholic newspapers that the Argentine hierarchy suddenly remembered its social responsibility and denounced the dictatorship for its immorality.[39]

An almost identical pattern developed in the relationship of the Venezuelan clergy to the Pérez Jiménez clique. It is true that in 1957, when the regime showed signs of anticlericalism and was the object of attack from several other sources, the Archbishop of Caracas labeled the government "anti-social and un-Christian". But in 1952 and 1953, when the illegal basis for the dictatorship was established, the response of the Catholic hierarchy was one of shameful acquiescence. Through concerted action in the pulpits and in the columns of *La Religión* it *could have* brought pressure to bear on the regime to abide by the results of the November 30 election, but chose instead an expedient course of short-term advantage. The Church must therefore bear its share of responsibility for the dictatorship of Pérez Jiménez.

A host of writers, both American and foreign, have stressed the overwhelming economic and political influence that the United States long wielded among other Hemisphere nations. No country whose economic well-being depended directly on U.S. markets controlled by import quotas determined in Washington could afford to ignore the admonitions of the U.S. State Department. This situation was self-evident and scarcely theoretical; it was rather a political and economic fact of life that was taken for granted in the United States and in the rest of the Hemisphere. The question at issue centered on the correctness or propriety of such influence in relation to the Latin American policy of the United States, and particularly to the matter of non-intervention in the internal or external affairs of other Hemisphere nations.

The United States, as a member of the Organization of American States (OAS) and a signatory to the Bogotá Charter of April, 1948, and documents of other Inter-American Conferences both before and after that time, is theoretically bound by certain "prnciples" of conduct in its relationships with other Hemisphere nations. Of all the principles set forth in these agreements and treaties, that of non-intervention has caused the greatest difficulty for the United States in the development of a viable policy toward Latin America. The following statement is found in the Charter of Bogotá, *Article 15:*

> No State or group of States has the right to intervene, directly or indirectly, for any reason whatever, in the internal or external affairs of any other State. The foregoing principle prohibits not only armed force but also any other form of interference or attempted threat against the personality of the State or against its political, economic and cultural elements.

This doctrine has received the enthusiastic support of some U.S. administrations, and has been regarded by others as a detestable handicap. In 1946, at the end of World War II, the United States supported an interventionist doctrine aimed at the overthrow of Perón. Assistant Secretary of State Spruille Braden pushed for OAS adoption of the anti-Perón "Larreta Doctrine", introduced by Uruguayan Foreign Minister Eduardo Rodríguez Larreta, who feared the expansionist aims of the Argentine dictator. This proposal was completely rejected by OAS member states.

Two years later, in 1948, the United States, having abandoned the Franklin D. Roosevelt policy of condemning fascist-type dictatorships and lending warm support to democratic governments, accepted the doctrine of non-intervention at Bogotá in the hope of forestalling some Latin American collective action against dictatorships.[40] It served for a time as a convenient pretext for the State Department in its refusal to take part in any action against right-wing regimes, which provided a high degree of social stability and safe conditions for the investment of American capital.

In May, 1954, in consideration of the alleged threat posed by the Moscow-oriented Arbenz government of Guatemala, the Eisenhower administration sought a way to circumvent the non-intervention doctrine of the OAS. There can be no doubt of the illegality of the subsequent actions of the U.S. government in air-lifting arms to Guatemalan rebels led by Castillo Armas on Nicaraguan and Honduran soil for an invasion of Guatemala. Those rebels soon carried out a successful attack, resulting in the overthrow of the Arbenz regime, while the State Department executed stalling manoeuvers at both the OAS and the United Nations until the *coup d'état* had become a *fait accompli.* The fact that the Arbenz government had expropriated some United Fruit Company land shortly before the U.S. intervention and the subsequent overthrow of the Guatemalan government was a lesson not lost on the Latin American mind.[41] And Venezuelans have asked: if Washington, despite agreements to the contrary, can intervene so openly to protect American investors by destroying a left-wing revolution, then why did the State Department find it so difficult to admonish a right-wing dictator that an electoral fraud would not be tolerated?

Was the U.S. government privy to the falsification of the election results before it happened? Probably not. Pérez Jiménez and his clique were practiced conspirators but inept politicians. The same arrogance that had alienated them from the people had also blinded them to the political realities, and all indications are that they really anticipated a landslide victory. It is unlikely that they would have conspired with the State Department for contingency action in the event of defeat.

But, on the evening of November 30, when loss of the election had become probable, and the following day when it became a certainty, did the Defense Minister and his advisers *then* seek the approval of an official U.S. representative for the ensuing fraud and the *coup* of December 2? Unfortunately this possibility cannot be discounted. Vallenilla Lanz, principal planner of the electoral swindle, recalls in his memoirs that he reassured Pérez Jiménez on December 2 that there was no reason to worry about any problem of recognition by other nations because the regime's "point of view" was shared by American Ambassador Fletcher Warren as well as the Pope's representative, Apostolic Nuncio Monsignor Armando Lombardi.[42] Ambassador Warren's tacit approval of the planned *coup* appears less improbable than we should like to believe, for it is known that he had a high regard for Pérez Jiménez and was a close friend of Security Chief Pedro Estrada. Both the American ambassador and the papal nuncio attended the Pérez Jiménez inaugural ball in the Legislative Palace on the evening of April 23, 1953.[43]

Early in December, 1952, and for many months thereafter, rumors were current in Venezuela that the State Department had not only given its wholehearted consent to the Pérez power grab, but had made clear to the regime that Washington would not recognize a Venezuelan government headed by URD's Jóvito Villalba. These reports were accepted at face value by many Venezuelans who would not forget that the State Department had made no effort to prevent the imposition upon them of an insufferable tyranny. More knowledgeable observers discounted the rumors as anti-American propaganda invented by the Communists, or a Pérez Jiménez ploy to convince doubtful military leaders that there was no alternative to the planned take-over.[44]

Washington's moral responsibility for the *coup*, like that of the Venezuelan military and of the Catholic Church, cannot be doubted. As noted by the New York *Times*: "It is an open secret that if the United States had expressed its displeasure at the robbery of the Venezuelan election by partisans of Col. Pérez Jiménez in November, 1952, the latter would have retreated, or at least would have come to an agreement with the opposition. By keeping ourselves strictly outside the conflict, and quickly recognizing the Pérez Jiménez regime, we, in a certain sense intervened."[45]

At the time of the electoral swindle, the Defense Minister could be certain that if Washington did not object to his intended fraud and seizure of power, he would have little to fear from the official reactions of other Latin American nations. The right-wing dictators of Argentina, Peru, Paraguay, Nicaragua, Cuba, and the Dominican Republic would be delighted. The indignation of the tiny democracies of Costa Rica and Uruguay could be safely ignored, and even the cold disapproval of Chile and Mexico would prove to be no deterrent.

Perez Jimenez had calculated correctly. The State Department recognized his regime with unseemly haste, and the other American States presently followed the lead of the great North American democracy.[46]

Chapter IX

Consolidation of the Tyranny (1953-54)

Mirage of Prosperity and Respectability

In the spring of 1953 the outlook for the Venezuelan economy was better than it had ever been. During the year 1952 the nation's petroleum industry had produced 660,400,000 barrels of crude oil, or a daily average of more than 1,500,000 barrels.[1] In the same period the country exported about $1.5 billion worth of products, nearly all of it petroleum or its derivatives. Imports came to less than half this figure, leaving the nation with a very favorable balance of trade. Investments by oil companies in Venezuela were also higher than in 1951. Royal Dutch-Shell finished a pipeline extension and built a plant for the manufacture of lubricants. Phillips Petroleum Company set up a new paraffin plant, while U.S. Steel made a great investment in facilities for the exportation of iron ore. Such U.S. firms as Sears, Roebuck and Co., General Motors, Celanese Corp., Proctor and Gamble, and several pharmaceutical concerns were planning expansion of operations in the country.[2] The regime's preliminary budget for the fiscal year 1952-53 had been Bs. 2,300 million, but its income amounted to Bs. 2,370 million. Expenditures during the same period were Bs. 2,377 million, leaving a deficit of Bs. 7 million.[3]

On taking office in April, 1953, as Constitutional President, Pérez Jiménez began almost at once to exhibit his marked predilection for impressive and showy accomplishments in the field of public works. Heading his list was completion of the Caracas-La Guaira *autopista.* The reason for the high priority of this project was no secret: the dictator was bidding insistently to play host to the Tenth Conference of the Organization of American States, scheduled to open on March 1, 1954. Pérez hoped to gain respectability for his government by bringing important Hemisphere figures to his capital; despite his tarnished reputation, most OAS members considered Caracas an agreeable site for the Conference. A proposed budget for the year 1953-54 had been set at Bs. 2,362 million, of which nearly one-third was marked for public works. About $300 million had been allocated for urban projects in Caracas, and several millions more for completion of the *autopista* linking the city to Maiquetía Airport at La Guaira.

The suitability of the Venezuelan capital as a site for the Conference then became a subject of controversy. In August, the New York *Times* published a letter from Rómulo Betancourt, then living in Costa Rica, stating that there was a strong movement by liberal governments and organized labor in Latin America against the choice of Caracas for the OAS meetings unless the regime released its political prisoners and re-established basic freedoms in that country.[4] Two weeks later a reply came from César González, Venezuelan Ambassador to the United States, attacking Betancourt, denying that there were any political prisoners in his country, and insisting that the Conference would indeed be held in Caracas the following March.[5] Vallenilla Lanz did his best to help by declaring solemnly that Guasina was closed and would never be reopened, and that political prisoners were a thing of the past. A short time later he destroyed whatever credibility remained to him by announcing that 400 political prisoners would be released under a "year-end amnesty".

The Pérez Jiménez *coup* of the previous December had brought a renewed effort from the AD underground to combat the dictatorship. In late January, 1953, Alberto Carnevali, latest secretary-general of Acción Democrática, was captured by Pedro Estrada's agents after a gun battle in downtown Caracas. The *adeco* leader was placed under heavy guard in San Juan de los Morros Prison where it was soon discovered that he suffered from an advanced case of stomach cancer. Many influential persons, including representatives of other Latin American nations, attempted to bring about the release of Carnevali for hospital treatment. Their efforts were in vain, and the AD leader died in his prison cell on May 21, 1953.[6]

On February 24 of the same year, Capt. Wilfrido Omaña, leader of the abortive military uprising at Boca de Río the previous October, was gunned down by SN agents in a shooting fray near Central University.[7] Santos Gómez, another AD militant, who drove the Omaña vehicle, was captured alive and sent to the SN torture chamber.[8]

Also lost to the AD cause was Antonio Pinto Salinas, 34, an economist from Mérida, who was captured by the police in an oil field in Anzoátegui State on the night of June 10. Wounded and manacled, he was loaded into a police car to be transported to prison. Before arriving there the agents, perhaps recalling the orders to "take no *adecos* alive", pushed the captive out of the car at 3:30 a.m. and shot him to death.[9]

Pérez had begun as early as January, 1953, to intensify his efforts on several fronts simultaneously, all tending toward the same objective: a situation which would appear totally anti-Communist and favorable to U.S. investors. The dictator had good reason to know that these two conditions were dear to the hearts of President Eisenhower and Secretary of State John Foster Dulles. He could scarcely have been more delighted when in late January Dr. Milton Eisenhower, on a "fact-finding tour for his brother, the President", appeared in Caracas, saw the sights of the capital, and had lunch with Pérez Jiménez and his wife.[10] The subject of their conversations cannot be known, but it is certain that the military regime thereafter redoubled its efforts to provide a tranquil anti-Communist atmosphere and a prosperous and democratic-appearing environment for the forthcoming Tenth Conference of the OAS.

The building program was accelerated and, to terminate the activities of the regime's enemies, Pedro Estrada was accorded an authority comparable only to that of Heinrich Himmler in Hitler's Germany or of Lavrenti Beria in Stalinist Russia; no ministry of government and no branch of the Armed Forces was exempt from his scrutiny. Although nominally under the direction of the Interior Ministry, Estrada in practice bypassed Vallenilla Lanz and reported directly to Pérez Jiménez every morning.[11] His men operated with impunity, invading and searching private homes without warrants, confiscating automobiles and other property, and jailing citizens for little or no reason and with no pretense of judicial process.[12]

By 1953, when Pérez Jiménez came to full power, organized labor was no longer a viable force in the country. All that remained of the previously flourishing movement was a small group of captive organizations totally dominated by the regime and kept in line by the secret police. But Venezuelans do not give up easily; on June 20, 1953, with full knowledge of the government's opposition, petroleum workers held a national convention of delegates from the seven principal petroleum regions of the country, representing 20 local unions. Their purpose was to form a single national petroleum union (Federación Unica de Trabajadores Petroleros de Venezuela) which would then be empowered to bargain collectively with the companies for a new contract. Delegates spoke candidly and forcefully of the necessity of wage increases; the cost of living had risen 12% in a single year. They demanded a 40-hour week, and company compliance with laws governing work on holidays. They pointed out the greatly increased profits of the companies, evident in the fact that 25,000 workers had been dismissed in the single year from April, 1951, to April, 1952, while oil production had doubled in that same period.[13]

Meanwhile the government was organizing its own national union which it named Movimiento Sindical Independiente (MOSIT), many of whose officers were SN agents in disguise. The regime provided luxurious offices and meeting halls for this captive organization in Caracas and other parts of the country. It was, of course, this group which arranged a new contract with the companies, including all wage rates, hours of work and other conditions. When the bargaining committee of the authentic labor union refused to accept this agreement, its leaders were summarily arrested and sent to prison or to Guasina.[14]

As for the eagerness of the Pérez Jiménez regime to continue its alliance with the foreign-owned petroleum companies to the detriment of

Venezuelan workers, the following figures published by the Banco Central de Venezuela in 1955 clearly show that the constant *increase* in oil production during this period was accompanied by an almost equally steady *decrease* in the number of employees, resulting in much greater profits for the companies as well as for the government:

Year	Employment, Petroleum Industry (Refineries not included)	Oil Production (In cubic meters)
1948	57,405	77,903,910
1949	41,812	76,679,805
1950	36,728	86,928,950
1951	38,674	98,921,500
1952	39,735	104,968,849
1953	38,519	102,423,435
1954	36,969	109,985,657

Source: *Memoria del Banco Central,* 1955   Cuadro El-I, Cuadro I-II

In the summer of 1953 Pérez Jiménez ordered Venezuelan consuls abroad to attract investment capital to the country by emphasizing the enormous profits, low taxes, and other advantages to be found there. On September 3, Consul General Delfín Enrique Páez held a reception in a New York hotel at which he spoke of the swift modernization of Venezuela, the need for diversification of its economy, and the splendid opportunities offered to U.S. investment capital. He mentioned, as an example, that American Can Co. was finishing a $2.5 million factory.[15] The very favorable business environment described by the consul was no exaggeration; *Time Magazine* in the same month offered the following comments:

> One place where U.S. businessmen abroad can still flourish in a climate of high-riding free enterprise is the oil-boom republic of Venezuela, on the north coast of South America. Since 1948, when the government and the foreign-owned companies—notably Standard Oil Co. (N.J.), Shell, Gulf, Socony—worked out a mutually satisfactory deal that calls, in effect, for a 50-50 split of all profits, production has shot up to 1,800,000 bbls. a day, flooding the sparsely-populated country with $700 million in oil income. The gratified government has thrown the door wide open to foreign enterprise, and the biggest colony of U.S. businessmen overseas is happily at work making money in one of the world's most profitable markets.
>
> Venezuelan law lets the foreigner operate freely, and U.S. firms, which own two-thirds of Venezuela's $2.3 billion foreign investment, take their profits out in dollars, with no red tape. *Yanquis* residing in Venezuela pay no U.S. income taxes, and the Venezuelan tax is downright benign. Not until a salary reaches a theoretical $8,400,000 a year would the government take the maximum bit of 28%; a man earning $60,000 a year pays only $1,800. There is no tax on stock dividends.[16]

Venezuela was, indeed, in the midst of a boom. But it was an economy artificially stimulated by two special processes: 1) the new wide-open season on the extraction of the country's natural resources, principally crude oil, and 2) the Pérez Jiménez building spree which, in turn, drew its revenues from the petroleum industry. The effects of the boom were not uniform throughout the country, but stimulated some sectors of the economy while depressing others. Venezuelans employed by the oil companies, although paid at much lower rates than Americans engaged in the same type of work, were nevertheless the most favored group of laborers in the country. Workers therefore earned more and spent more in the oil-producing regions than in other areas. Since the public works program was limited chiefly to Caracas and the *autopista* leading to La Guaira, wages paid to laborers were spent mainly in the capital and had the effect of stimulating the economy of the metropolitan area without raising production or income in the remainder of the nation.

The cement industry, begun during the period of AD rule, was greatly expanded to produce concrete and building blocks for walls, bridges, tunnels, street paving, and drainage ditches in the program of making Caracas a showplace. The boom in the nation's largest city attracted thousands of laborers from the farming areas of the interior, causing a decrease in the production of agricultural goods and a rise in the prices of staple foods. This disarticulation in the patterns of supply and demand necessarily brought about an increase in the importation of such basic foods as rice, wheat, milk (powdered), corn, and meat, as well as textiles, construction machinery, and manufactured products essential to the building program. Nearly all such imports came from the United States, and Venezuela was becoming the most profitable market for American exporters.[17]

As in the case of all booms, the one in question had some positive aspects. The high rate of trade between Venezuela and the United States maintained the convertibility of the bolivar, which remained at 3.35 to the dollar. And some people became excessively rich. Those who reaped the greatest rewards were, in descending order:

1) The foreign-owned petroleum companies, which managed to hold off import restrictions being urged in the United States by native producers, and derived the greatest benefits from their operations in Venezuela through the eager co-operation of the government of that country.

2) The entire hierarchy of the Pérez Jiménez power clique, all of whom were in a position to take handsome cuts on every construction project, business deal, and major item of imported equipment, in addition to enormous sums pilfered outright from the national Treasury. They were able to amass millions of dollars in personal bank accounts in Switzerland, New York, Miami, and Madrid against the day of their inevitable downfall.

3) The 23,000 to 25,000 U.S. citizens resident in Venezuela as employees of the exploiting concerns, who received high salaries, lived luxuriously in the American colony, belonged to private clubs, and paid

no income taxes to the U.S. government and very little to Venezuela.

4) The Venezuelans who were fortunate enough to be employed at a living wage, either by an oil company or in the public works program.

Clearly the total number of Venezuelans included in the above categories as beneficiaries of the Pérez Jiménez rule comprised only a tiny fraction of the population; the majority of citizens suffered all the negative effects of that situation. In 1953 and 1954, many American journalists, businessmen, and tourists returning from visits to Venezuela were euphoric in their descriptions of an orderly and prosperous nation. Their reports, appearing in such publications as the New York *Times,* the Christian Science *Monitor, Time Magazine, Business Week,* and *Coronet* were based on personal observations mostly limited to the city of Caracas and on conversations with members of the American colony, Venezuelan government officials, bankers, and prosperous businessmen. They heard from these sources only unstinting praise for the "efficiency, order, and progress" of the regime.

Those who inquired about the reported SN atrocities were assured that the police were simply maintaining order and preventing disruptions by leftist radicals and hoodlums. One American correspondent even interviewed Pedro Estrada himself in December, 1953, and reported that the police chief was "quiet, but tough and efficient", and that there was "no evidence of torture of political prisoners at the present time".[18] Obviously, the "evidence" existing in the concentration camps, the prisons, and Estrada's interrogation rooms would not be accessible to reporters. More visible and impressive to American eyes were the shops bulging with imported goods, the elegant clothes and expensive liquor found at cocktail parties, the new Cadillacs to be seen on the streets, and the luxurious new buildings going up on all sides. With so much evidence of material well-being, it was even possible to accept the businessman's remark that the "fabulous prosperity" was more important and desirable than all the democratic freedoms in the world.

The loss of such freedoms was not the principal burden suffered by the majority of Venezuelans who derived no benefit from the oil boom or the public works program. The most pressing problem was that the general population lived in grinding poverty, misery and neglect. The steadily worsening lot of the ordinary Venezuelan was a direct result of the years of military rule since the *coup d'état* of 1948. The amassing of private fortunes was the main concern of both civilian and military leaders, and the Pérez Jiménez mania for the creation of a gaudy and glittering capital city was motivated by the desire for prestige and self aggrandizement.

One of the commonest and most unpardonable aspects of dictatorships is the acquisition by the tyrant, or by people close to him, of a monopoly control of essential consumer goods. The Somoza family of Nicaragua not only owns more land and cattle than anyone else in the country, but controls the marketing of meat and milk and determines both their wholesale and retail prices. In the Dominican Republic, various members of the Trujillo family owned all pasteurization plants, sugar refineries, and candy factories. Under the domination of Juan Vicente Gómez, Venezuela's biggest cattle baron, the people became accustomed to the pernicious system of manipulation of the nation's meat and milk supply by government officials for private profit. With the exception of the three-year period of AD rule, the country was at the mercy of such manipulators until the fall of the last dictatorship in 1958. Pérez Jiménez and his intimate associates, with hundreds of millions of dollars in oil revenues available, never bothered with such small-time racketeering as "putting the squeeze on the commodities market". These opportunities for enrichment were awarded to lower-echelon servants of the regime.[19]

The serious deficiency of essential foods was one of the most harmful effects of military misgovernment. Many thousands of Venezuelans had migrated to the capital after the beginning of the oil boom and the public works program. This accretion, added to the natural increase of the Federal District population during the following years, amounted to an addition of many tens of thousands of persons to Caracas and the surrounding metropolitan area. Yet the government's own statistics show that, with the single exception of goats, there was no corresponding increase in the number of animals killed in the public slaughterhouses of the Federal District from 1948 to 1956:

Year	Cattle	Hogs	Goats	Total
1948	58,097	101,713	3,308	163,118
1949	66,415	105,501	7,942	179,858
1950	78,970	95,967	11,622	186,159
1951	102,692	85,209	10,388	198,289
1952	108,015	92,420	13,959	214,394
1953	55,451	28,058	15,101	98,610
1954	66,449	34,669	17,433	118,551
1955	64,818	23,487	14,077	102,382
1956	69,071	41,854	17,266	128,191

Source: Dirección General de Estadística, *Memoria del Banco Central de Venezuela.* 1956. Cuadros E3-III, E3-V, E3-VII Cuadro E3-XI

A similar reduction is noted in the amount of fish, another valuable source of animal protein, marketed during the same period. The following figures are for the entire republic and include both fresh and salted fish:

Year	In kilograms
1948	52,821,766
1949	44,440,406
1950	40,180,458
1951	44,137,233
1952	42,069,925
1953	42,975,667
1954	35,801,286
1955	49,513,179
1956	46,521,675

Source: Dirección General de Estadística, *Memoria del Banco Central de Venezuela,* 1956. Cuadro E3-XI

There is also evidence that the scarcity of milk at prices the general public could afford to pay resulted in serious malnutrition for thousands of school-age children. Underconsumption of this vital food prevailed not only in the Caracas area, but in cities and towns throughout the country. Most of the milk available was reconstituted from powder, of which 90% was imported from the United States, and there was only one liter per day for every five Venezuelans.[20]

Despite the indications of undernourishment owing to scarcity and high prices, there is no evidence that this situation was the result of a deliberate governmental policy. It was rather the natural outcome of ineptitude and indifference toward the welfare of the people. In 1951 the Suárez Flamerich Junta had abolished the Agriculture and Livestock Division (Departamento Agropecuario) of the Venezuelan Development Corporation, and transferred to the Bank of Agriculture the function of making loans to farmers; but long-term credits to cattle raisers were expressly forbidden, and only short-term loans would be approved. As previously noted, the improvement and expansion of beef and dairy herds, though paying handsome dividends in the long run, is a slow and costly process in its initial stages. The military regimes did not make this necessary investment.[21]

The manifestations of a disjointed economy during the early years of the Pérez Jiménez dictatorship were not limited to the contrast between the erection of luxurious but unnecessary buildings, on the one hand, and on the other, malnutrition of the general population. The government's *Boletín de Estadística* also revealed that in the period 1948-53, despite the increased population, there was a marked diminution in expenditures for cloth and shoes in the Federal District. At the same time, jewelry stores sold only Bs. 13 millions worth of merchandise in 1948, but their sales rose to Bs. 18 millions in 1953. Clearly this does not mean that poor people were buying jewelry when they could not afford clothing and shoes, but rather that another class of people, opulent as never before, could indulge their taste for costly baubles to go with their fine clothes.[22]

Suddenly announced by the government in late July, 1953, was Venezuela's withdrawal from its partnership with Colombia and Ecuador in the Grancolombiana Merchant Fleet. The joint communiqué issued by the three governments on July 23 dealt mostly with the terms of the settlement, and gave no clear explanation for Venezuela's decision to withdraw from the combined fleet. The Caracas press stated that "the initial objective sought in the creation of the fleet has been realized", that "circumstances existing at that time have changed", and that it was "indispensable to adopt solutions for the avoidance of frictions and misunderstandings".[23]

Betancourt, who had conceived the idea of the fleet and was proud of its success, saw the matter in another light. The enterprise, he noted, had been undertaken to avoid the excessively high freight rates imposed by the United States shipping interests of the "Caribbean Conference".

He saw his country's withdrawal as simply another instance of Pérez Jiménez' capitulation to the pressures of U.S. capitalists. Lending credibility to his assertion is the fact that the Flota Mercante Grancolombiana had consistently maintained rates 25% lower than those of the "Caribbean Conference"; but after withdrawal of its ships, Venezuela raised its rates to the level charged by U.S. companies.[24]

Of interest to Venezuelans at this time was the death of former President Isaías Medina Angarita on September 15, 1953. He had returned in ill health from his New York exile about one year earlier to spend his last days in Caracas. Many Venezuelans remembered him with affection and gratitude as a man of good intentions who had always desired the best for his country and who had avoided the extremes of partisan bitterness that afflicted the nation before and after his term. People turned out in great numbers for his state funeral, and they seemed sincerely to have forgiven him for whatever ill-gotten wealth he may have amassed during his years in power. Vallenilla Lanz, who paid a visit to Medina in his sick bed, reported years later in his memoirs that the ex-President had expressed a sense of anguish and mortification because of the great electoral fraud and the exiling of Jóvito Villalba.[25]

The reader will recall that after the fall of the Gallegos government, the Junta Militar had returned to Medina the wealth confiscated earlier by a special court under AD rule. After his death, the Caracas press referred to the corruption conviction of Medina as "the greatest juridical infamy in the memory of the nation." Perhaps it was. It is a fact, however, that after living seven years in an expensive New York apartment and another year in his mansion of "La Quebradita" in Caracas, the ex-President was still able to leave to his heirs an estate of more than two million bolivars.[26]

Not only did Pérez Jiménez maintain amicable relations with the United States during his first year as Constitutional President; he also cemented friendly relations with fellow dictators elsewhere in the Hemisphere. The President of Nicaragua, General Anastasio "Tacho" Somoza, pleased the Venezuelan military clique by stopping in Caracas in October, 1953, on his way home from a state visit to Argentina's Perón and Paraguay's Alfredo Stroessner. On the afternoon of October 20 he held a press conference at a luxurious *quinta* in the Caracas suburb of Campo Alegre. There, the Nicaraguan strongman, standing beside several important Venezuelan officials, including SN Chief Pedro Estrada, made sure of his accreditation with both Eisenhower and Pérez Jiménez by declaring himself a determined enemy of Communism and a supporter of the Monroe Doctrine. Nor did he forget to praise his host: Venezuela, he said, "led by Col. Marcos Pérez Jiménez, is marching with giant steps toward development and progress."[27]

By the end of the year 1953, the regime had established nearly all the conditions necessary for the opening of the Tenth Inter-American Conference in Caracas. The security police had assassinated or jailed all of the most active leaders of the AD underground; the exiled members of that party would need time to reform their ranks and to direct a new resistance within Venezuela.

The Caracas-La Guaira highway had been completed near the end of November, but the regime waited until December 2, anniversary of the *coup* of 1952, for the formal dedication and opening of the *autopista*, along with the official completion of several construction projects in the capital. One of the latter was the extraordinary complex located in eastern Caracas, called the Círculo de las Fuerzas Armadas, flanked by broad boulevards lined with palm trees and flower beds, decorated with enormous pools and fountains, impressive cement staircases, and marble statuary. All of this, however, was but a setting or background for the unbelievably extravagant and luxurious Officers Club, a calculated bid by Pérez Jiménez to gain and hold the loyalty of officers in all branches of the Armed Forces. *Time Magazine,* more than a year later, offered the following description:

> Nothing in Venezuela—or outside of it, for that matter—can compete with the palatial Círculo de las Fuerzas Armadas, the social club for military officers and top government officials. It has a hotel (television in every room), restaurants, bar, cocktail lounge, nightclub, two swimming pools, stable, gymnasium, fencing court, bowling alleys, library and theater. Some notably sumptuous touches: marble floors, blue Polaroid Windows, Gobelin tapestries, Sevres vases, Tiffany clocks, a glass-walled conservatory housing a living, blooming chunk of the Venezuelan jungle. To the grander dances at the club, some colonels' wives wear $1500 Balmain gowns.[28]

No observer acquainted with conditions in Venezuela could have seen the Club and failed to note the disparity between this conspicuous display of opulence and the unhappy lot of a population that lacked basic necessities.

More useful to the country's economy and needs was the Centro Simón Bolívar, a two-towered edifice in downtown Caracas designed to house most of the government ministries and to serve as a shopping center. Inaugurated on the same occasion were the Autopista del Este, another long section of excellent superhighway on the eastern side of Caracas, many newly paved streets in the capital, two hospitals, a school, several bridges and viaducts, and hotels to accommodate delegates to the Conference. Also timed for that event was completion of the 9-story library of the Ciudad Universitaria and the magnificent main auditorium, or Aula Magna, of that institution, equipped for simultaneous conversion of speeches into any one of the four official languages of the Hemisphere.

On December 30 Interior Minister Vallenilla Lanz announced that Pérez Jiménez had decided to grant freedom to 400 political prisoners of the regime, adding that this number constitutued 60% of the total of such confined persons. He also announced that Pérez Jiménez would offer amnesty to all political exiles still living abroad, and would invite them to return home without fear of persecution.[29] In a later chapter we shall note what happened to certain refugees who took the dictator at his word and returned to the country.

Throughout January and February of 1954 the controversy concerning Caracas as a site for the Conference continued. Only two nations had expressed an official position: the U.S. State Department was vehemently in favor of the Venezuelan capital, while Costa Rica had denounced the choice as incompatible with the principles of the Bogota Charter. The other countries maintained an official silence, but their attitudes were well known. Both houses of the Chilean Congress had voted against the Venezuelan locale, and many Uruguayan legislators had denounced it. Student organizations and organized labor throughout Latin America declared their opposition; and the liberal press of the Hemisphere expressed indignation that the OAS should choose to take a stand against Communist tyranny in a country dominated by a right-wing tyranny.

As set forth by Rómulo Betancourt in a special study devoted to this problem, the opposition was based on the following considerations:

1) Compliance by member states with the provisions of the Bogota Charter and the Declaration of the Right of Man is not optional, but obligatory. All member states of the OAS must maintain a system of democratic relations between government and citizenry.

2) The Pérez Jiménez government of Venezuela was totalitarian and anti-democratic. Its dishonest tactics and denial of democratic freedoms were a constant violation of the principles to which the Organization of American States is dedicated.

3) The moral credibility of the OAS would suffer irreparable damage if its Tenth Conference, called for the specific purpose of combatting the threat to democratic governments posed by Soviet Communism, were held in the capital of the anti-Communist *and equally anti-democratic* Pérez Jiménez regime.[30]

The principal objective of U.S. Secretary of State John Foster Dulles with respect to the Tenth Inter-American Conference was to obtain a strong anti-Communist declaration by the OAS including, if possible, a commitment to take overt action in the case of any infringement by the international Communist movement upon the sovereignty or political independence of any American state. The relentless and single-minded pursuit of this one objective, in seemingly blind disregard for the prestige of the Organization or the credibility of United States claims of protecting democracy, finds only a partial explanation in the obvious desire of the Eisenhower administration to obtain some kind of Hemispheric approval in advance for its intention to bring about the overthrow of the Arbenz regime in Guatemala.

We must recall that in the 1953-54 period, Americans in general were still very much affected by the peculiar hysteria known as McCarthyism. The horrors of the Korean War were fresh in the public memory. The names of Alger Hiss, Whittaker Chambers, and Owen Lattimore were household words; and the John Birch Society's Robert Welch could publicly denounce Dwight Eisenhower as "a conscious tool of the Communist conspiracy." So overpowering, in fact, was the State Department's dread of Communist contamination of Western Hemisphere nations that it forgot that Communism has thus far been known to sprout and thrive only in an environment of extreme material and cultural deprivation and tyranny, never in a free and prosperous democracy unless forced upon a nation from without, as in the case of Czechoslovakia.

In this context, it is apparent that the policy of Secretary Dulles in supporting the Pérez Jiménez capital as the site of the Conference did nothing to strengthen the Hemispheric defenses against Communism, if only because the choice was contrary to the interests of freedom and democracy. By contrast, the words of President José Figueres, of Costa Rica, in explaining his nation's decision to boycott the Conference, seem the essence of wisdom and courage:

> The Council of Government has believed it appropriate, after prolonged consideration, for Costa Rica to abstain from participation in the Conference.
>
> We wish our absence to be the expression of a current of American thought opposed to the holding of the Conference in Caracas, as long as conditions existing there with respect to human rights do not change.
>
> That opinion would be silenced by the unanimous attendance of all the States. That considerable current of opinion holds that two struggles are taking place simultaneously in America: one, the global action against outside aggression; the other, the internal conflict between democracy and dictatorship.
>
> Costa Rica considers that while other American States, by their attendance in Caracas, are paying attention to the general needs of Panamericanism and of Hemispheric defense, it is appropriate that some country make clear by its absence in the present circumstances the anguish of peoples sacrificed in the struggle against America's own totalitarianisms.
>
> Thus we shall contribute to paying attention to both struggles at the same time, the global and the internal.[31]

The secretary-general of the OAS, Alberto Lleras Camargo, later to be President of Colombia, assumed no particular position for or against Caracas as the site of the Conference, but simply acceded to the apparent desire of the majority of States to follow the preference of the United States. The Tenth Conference, held in the Venezuelan capital as planned, became a fact of history, as did the vain appeals for understanding expressed there by Guatemalan Foreign Minister Guillermo Toriello, who denied that his government was Communist oriented, and asserted that his country was embarked on a true social revolution and could not be the satellite of either the United States or the Soviet Union.

Although Toriello reportedly received "the warmest ovation of the Conference", the power wielded by the United States in the form of foreign aid, military aid, and import quotas proved decisive, and the American Secretary of State had his way. The correctness of the prediction that the OAS would lose prestige and moral credibility by meeting in the capital of a dictatorship was to be fully demonstrated barely two months later by the sorry role forced upon that organization by John Foster Dulles as a result of the State Department's Guatemalan adventure of mid-May, 1954, to which we have alluded in the last chapter.

As for any change in the standing of Pérez Jiménez as a result of the Inter-American Conference held in his country, there is little doubt that the loss of prestige suffered by the OAS represented a corresponding gain for the Venezuelan President. If other Latin American nations had been sceptical of his apparent position as reigning favorite of the Eisenhower-Nixon government, they doubted no longer. And, much to the surprise of many Americans, Venezuelans would not forget this fact when Vice President Nixon visited their country on a "good will" tour some four years later.

So self-assured was Pérez Jiménez by the summer of 1954 that he undertook to punish Costa Rican President José Figueres for his boycott of the Conference and, at the same time, to humiliate Rómulo Betancourt, then residing in Costa Rica. On June 22 a Venezuelan military plane flew over Costa Rica, scattering thousands of leaflets containing obscenities directed against Figueres and Betancourt, alleging that both men were sexual perverts. Far from achieving its objective, this attack was counterproductive. The indignant Costa Rican press instantly rejected the anonymous aspersions made against their President, and papers in other parts of the Hemisphere likewise deplored the manoeuver of the Venezuelan dictator.[32]

Meanwhile the great public works program continued at an ever-expanding rate. Many of the cement and steel structures erected during this gigantic effort to "bring about a rational transformation of the physical environment" were useful additions to the material wealth of the country. But to perceive the effect of the undertaking in terms of public needs and the general welfare, one must consider the nature and extent of expenditures as between the Federal District and the remainder of the republic (the twenty states and two territories) in relation to population and other factors.

	1953	1954
	Bolivars	Bolivars
Federal District	449,660,407.75	669,053,411.45
States and Territories	435,477,324.88	859,227,227.99
Totals	885,137,732.63	1,528,280,639.44

Source: *Venezuela bajo el Nuevo Ideal Nacional*, Imprenta Nacional, 1956, p. 235.

Considering that the population of Venezuela in the years 1953 and 1954 was roughly six million, and that of the Federal District about one million, the first disparity becomes immediately evident. In 1953 the regime spent more on the building program in the area of the capital than in all the rest of the republic together. The disproportion noted in 1954 is somewhat less, but still considerable, with the Federal District accounting for more than 40% of the total cost. These figures reveal only the extent of the disparity in terms of money expended; a much greater inequity is seen in the nature of the works provided. In the two-year period under consideration, far more public buildings, parks, plazas, sewers, bridges, and viaducts were lavished upon Caracas than any other comparable area of the country. Capital residents also derived benefit from a vast amount of expensive construction intended to improve their living conditions, both culturally and physically. Included in this category were: a new hospital on the Central University campus (Bs. 100 million); science buildings with classrooms, auditoriums, and laboratories at the same location; more than a dozen huge apartment buildings, called "super-blocks", to provide housing for workers formerly living in the *ranchos* of the hillside slums; and a great many medium-income dwellings in various parts of the city.

Expenditures on public works in the states and territories were extremely uneven, ranging, in 1953, from Bs. 147,128.45 for a park in the Amazonas Territory to many millions for varied projects elsewhere. The only state to receive more than Bs. 100 million that year was Lara (Bs. 119,862,131.26), and two-thirds of that amount was spent on highway construction. In 1954 three states (Aragua, Miranda, and Zulia) had public works budgets exceeding Bs. 100 million, and in all of these cases a very disproportionate amount went for road building, the paving of airports, barracks, control towers, officers' homes, and penitentiaries. In all of the states without exception, the amounts expended on school construction were exceedingly small, as were the sums spent on irrigation works for farmers, or anything else that might improve the living standards or education of the people.[33]

The failure of the Pérez Jiménez regime to solve the housing crisis in Caracas by the building of super-blocks for low-income families was owing largely to difficulties which are inherent in any large-scale undertaking that is not based on a detailed and competent analysis of the problem and a co-ordinated plan to solve it. It was, in part, the abandonment of agrarian reform and the cessation of government aid to farmers that brought discouraged rural workers and their families flocking to the capital in search of some means of subsistence. The regime's planners never understood this problem, nor thought of solving it by rendering effective aid to agricultural workers and cattle raisers to induce them to remain in their own communities. Apparently it did not occur to the government that no conceivable number of super-blocks in the capital could possibly solve a nation-wide economic and social problem.

The burgeoning population of Caracas was rapidly turning Venezuela into a macrocephalic nation, but without the industrial structure that might justify such a development.[34] Mexico City, São Paulo, and other Latin American cities have undergone similar periods of rapid expansion, but in those cases there has always been a parallel development in the industrial sector which, in fact, caused the growth of population and was able to support it. The Venezuelan phenomenon did not make sense, for the only important new industry was that of cement, which depended principally on the public works program for its market, and was therefore tied directly to the country's petroleum revenues. It should have been apparent that unless the capital's building spree went on forever, or the government should undertake to sponsor the development of a genuine industrial base—which was not to happen until after the fall of the dictatorship—, the situation of Caracas would have something in common with the boom towns of gold rush days.

As if the basic fallacy underlying the super-block concept were not enough, yet another factor militated against the success of the project and contributed to the frustrations of both the government as patron and landlord, and the workers as tenants and alleged beneficiaries. This had to do with the background and way of life of the people, as well as their method of dealing with one another. The typical Venezuelan *campesino,* whether *andino, llanero,* or *costeño,* is neither meek nor timid. He was probably born in a dirt-floored thatch-roofed hut without electricity, running water, or sanitary facilities, and is accustomed to privations and the constant struggle against poverty.

Those multitudes of rural families who came to the capital during the early years of the Pérez Jiménez dictatorship were fleeing, like the American Okies of the 1930s, from intolerable conditions in their native localities and hoping for a share in the prosperity resulting from the great building boom. Although mostly illiterate and ignorant of the world at large, they could observe the great contrast between their own poverty and the affluence of those who used the Officers Club and other luxurious facilities of the capital. They, as well as more fortunate Venezuelans, were owners of the nation's mineral wealth, yet they derived no benefit from it. These *rancho* dwellers on the Caracas hillsides were neither particularly humble nor markedly grateful when they heard that the government was going to provide them with housing. Moreover, the arrogant methods used by the regime in this project were such as to inspire anger and resistance rather than pleasure and co-operation.

Pérez Jiménez did not take into consideration the housing preferences of the people, nor did he devise any fair procedure for preëmpting the land on which the slum dwellers had built their shacks. He simply decided that these rural people, who had always lived close to the earth, would now move into high-rise apartment buildings, turning over to Pedro Estrada the responsibility of clearing people out of any area selected for a super-block. The SN agents then moved in suddenly, armed with machetes and rifles, and unceremoniously drove the people out of their *ranchos* barely ahead of the bull-dozers.

On June 16, 1954, the Venezuelan President received another boost to his ego when he was awarded the Panamerican Highway Prize for having "stimulated in an unprecedented way" the building of highways, particularly that section which comprised part of the Panamerican system.[35] Barely a month later, the Armed Forces, not to be outdone in honoring their boss, recommended to the Congress the promotion of Col. Marcos Pérez Jiménez to the rank of Brigadier-General. The Senate hastened to comply with this request, and the dictator received the desired promotion.[36]

The two events mentioned in the preceding paragraph, both of which occurred in recognition of alleged merits on the part of the dictator, were of little importance in themselves. The prize for highway building and the promotion in military rank were items of local interest only. Although released to the United Press and the Associated Press, these news services did not pick them up. But when the Caracas press, radio, and television announced with great fanfare on October 22, 1954, that President Dwight D. Eisenhower had decided to confer upon Pérez Jiménez the medal of the Legion of Merit in the degree of Commander in Chief, an immediate shock wave was noted in the press. The release from Washington was as follows:

> The President of the United States of America, authorized by the Act of Congress of July 20, 1942, has conferred the Legion of Merit, in the degree of Commander in Chief, upon His Excellency Colonel Marcos Pérez Jiménez, President of the Republic of Venezuela, for his exceptionally meritorious conduct in the discharge of high responsibilities. His Excellency Colonel Marcos Pérez Jiménez, in his position as President of the Republic of Venezuela and also previously, has made evident his spirit of collaboration and friendship toward the United States. His wholesome policy in economic and financial matters has facilitated the expansion of foreign investments, his Administration thus contributing to the greater well-being of the country and the rapid development of its immense natural resources.
>
> This policy, carefully combined with a public works program of vast dimensions, has achieved notable improvements in education, health, transportation, housing and other important basic necessities. This whole combination of achievements has raised the general well-being of the Venezuelan people. Also his indefatigable energy and his firmness of purpose have greatly increased the capacity of the Armed Forces of Venezuela to participate in the collective defense of the Western Hemisphere. The measures taken under his direction in preparing for the Tenth Inter-American Conference in Caracas constituted a decisive factor in guaranteeing its success. His constant concern toward the problem of Communist

infiltration has kept his government alert to repel the threat existing against his country and the rest of the Americas, and moreover his recognition of the similarity of interests of the United States and Venezuela has made the traditionally cordial relations between the two countries better than ever today.—Dwight D. Eisenhower (The White House)[37]

The ecstatic journalistic reactions of such papers as *El Nacional, El Universal,* and *La Esfera* were no more spontaneous than the tiresomely extravagant praises formerly heaped upon Stalin every day in *Pravda, Izvestia,* and the rest of the Communist press. Víctor José Cedillo, chief of the regime's censorship board, not only told editors what *not* to print; he also gave them specific orders as to what they *must* print, and the rejoicing on this occasion was a command performance. Less excusable was the coverage offered by the supposedly independent and moralistic *La Religión,* official mouthpiece of the Roman Catholic Church in Caracas, which on the following day (Saturday, October 23, 1954), ran a most enthusiastic front-page article featuring an interview with Ambassador Fletcher Warren in the American embassy. Most of the praiseful Eisenhower citation was repeated, and the State Department representative announced that Pérez Jiménez would receive the coveted decoration in a formal ceremony on November 12.

In the wake of the Eisenhower announcement of October 22, Venezuela's real friends also expressed their views on the great honor conferred by the democracy of North America upon a fascist dictator of South America. On November 8 the New York *Times* published a letter from Prof. Robert J. Alexander, of Rutgers University, who took the American President to task for conferring the Legion of Merit decoration upon "one of the two-bit dictators of the Caribbean". Alexander also pointed out that Eisenhower's eulogy of the tyrant's "anti-communism" was ill-placed, since the Pérez Jiménez "regime is larded with 'ex-communists' whose status as 'ex' is highly doubtful."[38]

Four days later the same paper published a rejoinder from Venezuelan Ambassador César González who, although not denying that the Pérez Jiménez regime was a fascist-type dictatorship which ruled against the will of the people, nevertheless attempted to prove by means of facts and figures on housing, birth and death rates, schools, highways, and national per capital income, that his government was indeed doing excellent things for Venezuela.[39] The New York *Times* was not impartial in the matter, and in a later editorial also deplored Eisenhower's granting of the Legion of Merit to the dictator in Caracas, alleging that the "incident shocked democrats and liberals throughout Latin America more than any single action by the United States in recent months", and condemned it as a "major error of policy".[40] Rómulo Betancourt contributed a letter pointing out that Pérez Jiménez had taken full advantage of the Eisenhower action with a sustained publicity campaign, and even had the Venezuelan Congress strike off a gold medal to cele-

brate the occasion of the honor received from the United States, contributing to the impression that he was backed in all things by the power
and prestige of the U.S. government.[41]

Another perceptive Venezuelan commentator, Dr. Rodolfo Luzardo,
previously cited in this work, after referring to the pitiless slaughter by
the dictatorship of such liberals as Leonardo Ruiz Pineda, Alberto
Carnevali, and Antonio Pinto Salinas, refers to the Eisenhower action
in the following terms:

> While these atrocities had Venezuela in a state of mourning,
> General Eisenhower, President of the United States, granted to
> Pérez Jiménez . . . the highest decoration that it was within his
> power to give: the Medal of the Legion of Merit—no doubt because
> the dictator was an implacable enemy of the Communists. But the
> American President forgot that Pérez Jiménez was also the enemy
> of democracy in all of its shapes and forms, and he did not notice
> that by doing this, he was sowing new fears among the Latin
> American people with respect to the good and sincere relations
> of the United States.[42]

Let us look more closely at the alleged or probable motives of President
Eisenhower in performing an act which made dictators rejoice, but
which brought only sorrow and anger to democratic elements throughout Latin America. In the first place, did the President really *forget* that
Pérez Jiménez was the enemy of democracy? Or did he perhaps *never
know* it? Or perhaps he simply did not think about it. We must note that
the word *democracy* is not mentioned even once in the extravagant terms
of the Eisenhower citation, nor is there so much as an indirect allusion
to this form of government in relation to the dictator's "exceptionally
meritorious conduct". Surely it is pertinent to inquire how it is possible
for the President of a nation whose government is "of the people, by the
people, and for the people" to consider that the brutal suppression of
representative government constitutes "meritorious conduct".

A careful reading of the Eisenhower citation indicates that the award
was based on a rationale consisting of three main points: 1) the spirit of
collaboration and friendliness of Pérez Jiménez toward the United
States, indicated by a financial policy which encouraged the expansion
of foreign investments; 2) his alleged contributions to the progress of
Venezuela through the public works program and other endeavors; and
3) the dictator's pronounced anti-Communism.

To consider the last point first, we may point out that the findings of
this study, as well as many other recent works by competent investigators,
indicate strong support for the belief that the best defense against Communist take-over in any country is not patronage and support for a
ruthless right-wing dictatorship, but the encouragement by every means
possible of true representative government. Many examples of the
validity of this contention come readily to mind, including the sudden

and disastrous results of the Batista tyranny in Cuba, coddled for years by American investors and the U.S. State Department. And *if* there was any significant movement towad Communism in the Dominican Republic in 1965, we may be sure that it was not caused by the brief period of liberal government under President Juan Bosch, but was rather a reaction to the prolonged Trujillo dictatorship which preceded it. This point of the Eisenhower citation was clearly ill-considered and without reasonable foundation.

As for the alleged "notable improvements in education, health and housing", mentioned in the Eisenhower statement, the statistical and other evidence set forth in the preceding chapters of the present study indicate clearly that the general well-being of the Venezuelan people suffered a decline rather than an advance under the Pérez Jiménez government. These refutations leave, as the only logical excuse for the award, the extreme friendliness of the dictator's financial policy toward the United States, and here indeed the American President was on very firm ground.

Not only were the great petroleum and steel companies predominantly American; Venezuela was also the best customer of hundreds of U.S. manufacturers and distributors, so that the enormous revenues paid for Venezuelan crude oil returned in large measure to the United States in the form of trade. And Americans who invested their capital directly in Venezuelan enterprises could be assured of extremely high profits under the most lenient tax laws to be found anywhere.

How, then, shall we evaluate the Eisenhower citation? Obviously the medal of the Legion of Merit and the generous but mostly erroneous words that accompanied it were of no importance in themselves; but as symbols of the official attitude of the world's best-known democracy toward a most repressive dictatorship, they assumed a very special significance. The truth is that President Eisenhower, who had spent almost all of his adult life building a distinguished career in military service, was no student of Latin American affairs nor, by all indications, was he much interested in that part of the world. His "crusade"—a virtuous Christ-oriented word of his own choosing—had taken place in Europe.

But President Eisenhower's sincerity cannot be doubted. He wished to be kind and generous; and though a warrior, he considered himself a man of peace. In all probability he sincerely believed that he was performing a generous and admirable act in conferring the Order of Merit upon Pérez Jiménez, one which should be pleasing to the poor and backward Latin Americans. In this, of course, he was most sincerely mistaken. But, considering his knowledge and interests, it is almost a certainty that he neither thought of this gesture himself nor had any part in composing the citation. His principal advisers in matters concerning Venezuela were: his brother Dr. Milton Eisenhower, Secretary Dulles, Ambassador Fletcher Warren (all friends of Pérez Jiménez), and a number of people whom he called "leaders of the American business community", in this case probably directors of the petroleum industry.

It was a foregone conclusion that the flood of indignant objections from democratic elements throughout the Hemisphere, following the Eisenhower announcement of October 22, would have no effect whatever on the State Department's plans to award the medal, and it would have been difficult indeed to have second thoughts at that point. On Friday evening, November 12, the impressive ceremony of pinning the Order of Merit upon the dictator took place in the presence of some 250 invited guests in the Caracas residence of American Ambassador Fletcher Warren. Newsmen and cameramen were present, and the occasion was enlivened by the music of a military band. The assembled guests also sang some church hymns. On the following day, the official Church paper, *La Religión,* ran a front-page spread of photographs of the ceremony. An article on an inside page was devoted to a detailed account of the entire event, including a minute description of the medal and its significance.[43]

Another Venezuelan also received some flattering attention from American officials during that same month of November, 1954, when he visited Washington. SN Chief Pedro Estrada was entertained by Secretary of State Dulles, Assistant Secretary of State for American Regional Affairs Henry Holland, and FBI Director J. Edgar Hoover. The Estrada visit to the U.S. capital on this occasion was apparently not announced by the State Department or any other source, and passed unnoticed by the American news media. But shortly after the fall of the Pérez Jiménez dictatorship, the Venezuelan Communist paper *Tribuna Popular,* in an obvious effort to increase popular resentment against Washington's Latin American policy, published in its issue of March 1, 1958, a series of pictures, taken by some unnamed photographer, on the occasion of Estrada's 1954 visit to the U.S. capital. One such photo shows him in a State Department automobile in the company of various U.S. officials; another shot reveals the "Jackal of Güiria" in friendly conversation with Secretary Dulles, and a third picture shows him in the doorway of the office of Assistant Secretary Henry Holland. An accompanying article avers that the "Venezuelan torturer and executioner" was feted in Washington by John Foster Dulles and especially by FBI boss J. Edgar Hoover.[44]

By December of 1954 the Venezuelan ruler had every reason to feel safe, successful, happy, and honored as never before. By the constant and relentless application of police-state methods, he had all but annihilated the AD underground, jailed or exiled the milder elements of political opposition, and created a mirage of national prosperity and well-being while maintaining the population in subjection, all this with the public approval of the United States government. The apparent triumph of Pérez Jiménez did not inspire in him an attitude of magnanimity toward his defeated and exiled opponents. The period in question was marked by a series of vicious and cowardly attacks by hired thugs on previous political rivals or critics of the regime, comparable to the axe-killing of the exiled Trotsky in Mexico or the kid-naping of Jesús de Galíndez by Trujillo agents in a New York subway.

One case involved a young Venezuelan military officer, Lieut. León Droz Blanco, who had been arrested for conspiring with the AD under-ground, then escaped and fled to exile in Barranquilla, Colombia. He was assassinated by SN agents in that city on June 10, 1954. Mario Briceño Iragorri, in exile in Madrid since the electoral fraud of Pérez Jiménez deprived him of the congressional seat he had won in the elec-tion of November 30, 1952, was attacked and savagely beaten with a club as he was entering a church on the morning of December 9 of the same year. In two other cases the victims were, ironically, supporters of the regime who were attacked by mistake and left senseless on the streets of Caracas. They turned out to be friends of Vallenilla Lanz who, by his own account, was so infuriated that he offered his resignation, which Pérez Jiménez refused to accept.[45]

Chapter X

Venezuela under the "New National Ideal" 1955-1957

So successful was Pérez Jiménez in his bid to hold the Tenth Inter-American Conference at Caracas, in defiance of widespread liberal opposition, that he decided to undertake a similar effort in the case of the International Petroleum Conference scheduled to take place in April, 1955. Delegates to this important meeting represented many governments as well as management, organized labor, and a branch of the International Labor Office (ILO), a specialized agency of the United Nations, with headquarters in Geneva.

Determined opposition to the Venezuelan site was a foregone conclusion; labor unions throughout the Hemisphere had denounced the anti-labor policies of the Caracas military regimes since shortly after the fall of the Gallegos government in 1948. In January, 1952, Matthew Woll, vice-president of the AFL and Jacob S. Potofsky, chairman of the CIO's Committee on Latin America, representing the International Confederation of Free Labor Unions (ICFLU), presented to the Economic and Social Council of the UN a formal complaint against the Venezuelan dictatorship's constant violation of UN Charter provisions with respect to human rights and organized labor. The resulting inquiries and admonishments addressed to the regime were, of course, unavailing.[1]

Two years later, vigorous representation by the ICFLU at the International Labor Office brought an initial rejection of the Caracas government's invitation. This decision was reversed at a subsequent meeting of the executive board of the ILO at which representatives of governments and management were present; a majority of board members voted in favor of Caracas. The rebuff did not cause the international labor movement to abandon its opposition. Shortly thereafter the Inter-American Regional Labor Organization, based in Mexico City, appealed to unions throughout the Hemisphere to boycott the Caracas meeting in protest against the crushing of the labor movement in that country. The bid from Mexico was well received. In mid-March, 1955, the AFL's George Meany and CIO President Walter Reuther issued a joint declaration that they would send no representatives to any meeting in Caracas while Venezuelan labor leaders were held in jail. One after another, the unions of Mexico, Canada, and Colombia followed suit; they would support the boycott, which was also endorsed by the International Federation of Petroleum Workers.[2]

Nevertheless, the meeting opened on April 25, 1955, as Pérez Jiménez had planned, in the Aula Magna of the Universidad Central in Caracas. Some 70 nations were represented there, as well as a great many free labor unions of Europe and Asia, and the ILO executive board from Geneva. According to report, the Venezuelan ruler sat in a fur-trimmed golden chair, his uniform loaded with shining decorations, including the Order of Merit recently received from President Eisenhower. To all appearances the occasion was to be another signal victory of tyranny over freedom, and dictatorship over democracy. But this time the meeting was not to follow a script prepared in advance by John Foster Dulles and Vallenilla Lanz.

After some innocuous introductory speeches, the Dutch labor leader, Adrianus Vermeulen, a labor representative of the ILO administrative board, rose to address the conference. It was expected that Vermeulen, a prudent negotiator and well-known moderate, would adopt a mild tone and perhaps seek to pour oil on any waters that seemed troubled. Instead, he delivered a stinging rebuke to the dictatorship, declaring that the ILO had for six years been receiving complaints of the violation of the principle of free unionism in Venezuela. Reading off a list of some of the Venezuelan labor leaders known to be still in prison, he asserted that they had never been brought to trial nor even accused of any crimes.

Vermeulen admitted that the International Confederation of Free Labor Unions had received "a great many telegrams signed in the names of Venezuelan unions, giving assurance that union freedom exists in Venezuela", but, he said, all the telegrams were so much alike that it was obvious they all had a common source of inspiration. "We call that", he said, "a very well prepared spontaneous movement". The ILO representative ended his address with three demands directed to the Pérez Jiménez government:

1) Free all union leaders not accused of any criminal acts, and permit them to leave the country if they wished.

2) Bring promptly to trial any such leaders accused of criminal acts.

3) Declare that it will develop and stimulate a movement of genuine free unionism, by legislative measures, and in accordance with the postulates of the International Labor Agreement on this matter.[3]

Pérez Jiménez, enraged and embarrassed, gave orders at once to prevent any recurrence of such revelations and demands. A few moments after delivering his speech, Adrianus Vermeulen was taken into custody by SN Chief Pedro Estrada, rushed to Maiquetía Airport and unceremoniously shipped to the Dutch island of Curaçao. There the labor leader dispatched an urgent cable to ILO Director-General David A. Morse in Geneva: "I have been declared, by the Security Police, *persona non grata,* having to leave the country immediately. I have been forbidden to talk with anyone. I vigorously protest this violation of International Rights".

On April 27, Mr. Morse sent a cable to Pérez Jiménez, the second half of which is reproduced as follows:

> You will appreciate that complete freedom of speech in meetings of Official International Organizations and the independence of representatives at such meetings is a matter to which the General Assembly of the United Nations has given a great deal of importance. The subject under discussion is of such a character that there will necessarily be worldwide repercussions and I therefore appeal to you that Mr. Vermeulen, who is presently in Curaçao, be permitted to resume his post at the Caracas meeting, with the honors requisite to a representative of the Executive of the International Labor Office, in which 20 governments are represented and which, designating Mr. Vermeulen as one of its representatives at the meeting, has acted in the name of 70 sovereign states which are members of the International Labor Organization. An immediate reply will be greatly appreciated because the members of the ILO executive board are meeting to consider the situation, of which I am also keeping the Secretary General of the United Nations informed. I am, Mr. President, with great sincerity and respect, your obedient servant, David A. Morse.[4]

On the same date of April 27, the Venezuelan President replied to Mr. Morse with the following telegram:

> In reply to your radiogram of today, I point out to you the following: it is a principle on which the sovereignty of our Nation is founded that questions concerning its internal policy belong exclusively to the jurisdiction of Venezuelans. Therefore it is impossible, without violating this principle, to have citizens of other countries mixing into matters of our internal policy. In the inaugural session of the Fifth Meeting of the Industrial Committee for the Petroleum Industry, Mr. Vermeulen read a speech containing disrespectful concepts concerning the internal policy of Venezuela. Mr. Vermeulen's attitude, which was also contrary to the "mutual respect" to which you allude, caused Venezuela, in the exercise of its legal rights, to declare the said gentleman *persona non grata* and to require his immediate departure from the country. I assure you that this measure, adopted exclusively as a result of the personal attitude assumed by Mr. Vermeulen, does not imply any lack of respect on the part of the Venezuelan government toward the international institution that you so worthily direct. With respect to your request, I can say

that the government of Venezuela is disposed to permit Mr. Vermeulen to return to Caracas and rejoin the meeting, if he rectifies the concepts expressed in his address and promises not to interfere again in the internal affairs of Venezuela. Sincerely yours, Marcos Pérez Jiménez, President of the Republic of Venezuela.[5]

As indicated by this cabled reply, the dictator sought some way to save face for his regime without causing an open and permanent rupture with the International Labor Office: Mr. Vermeulen could "mend his ways" and return to the Conference, or he could remain outside Venezuela.

In reality, there existed a precedent for this attitude, and Pérez Jiménez had some reason to imagine that it might be successful again. In 1953, on the occasion of the Panamerican Congress of Otolaryngology, held in Caracas, the eminent Uruguayan specialist, Dr. Justo Alonso, delivered an address in which he expressed the opinion that democracy, freedom, and human dignity were worth more to mankind than the construction of luxurious public buildings. On that occasion also the Security Police intervened, giving Dr. Alonso a choice of leaving Venezuela at once, or not attending any more sessions of the Congress. After a tense 48-hour impasse, the Uruguayan physician found his position untenable and opted to leave the country for home.[6]

The similarity of the Uruguayan's case with that of Adrianus Vermeulen was more apparent than real. As soon as the other conference members learned of the sudden arrest and deportation of the Dutch labor leader, they suspended their deliberations and were prepared to adjourn entirely unless the expelled member were returned to his seat in the assembly hall. Representatives of the regime then appealed to the other two members of the ILO executive committee present at the meeting, Mr. Ghulam Ali Allana, of Pakistan and Sir Guillaume Nyrddin-Evans, of the United Kingdom, to intercede with Mr. Vermeulen to "be reasonable". Mr. Nyrddin-Evans agreed to try, and was forthwith flown to Curaçao for this purpose. The Dutch official, however, proved adamant; he insisted that everything he had said was true, and he would not "change a single comma" of his address. At this, the great petroleum conference adjourned *sine die,* and all delegates departed.

Confronted with the complete failure of his policy toward the conference, and his inability to dictate the words and attitudes permissible to the delegates of other countries, Pérez Jiménez could save what face remained to him only by complete withdrawal from the organizations represented at the meeting. On May 2, 1955, Venezuelan Foreign Minister Aureliano Otáñez sent a cable to ILO Director David Morse announcing his country's resignation from membership in the International Labor Organization.[7]

It was shortly after the fiasco of the petroleum conference that spokesmen for the regime, principally Pérez Jiménez himself, began to develop and propagandize a number of materialistic concepts which came to be known as the "New National Ideal". This slogan or catchphrase, comparable to such U.S. political designations as "New Deal", "Fair Deal", "New Frontier", "Great Society", and "New Federalism", was first mentioned specifically and with capital letters in an address that the dictator delivered on October 18, 1955, tenth anniversary of the October Revolution. Some of the basic notions comprising the "ideal" had appeared in earlier speeches, such as the somewhat labored "rational transformation of the physical environment", to which was later added, as an after thought, "and the moral, intellectual and material betterment of the inhabitants of the country".

On July 6, 1955, at a ceremony involving military promotions, Pérez Jiménez sought to characterize what he claimed to envision as the "new Venezuelan nationalism" or "new national conscience". Although many of the expressions used on that occasion, such as "higher spiritual values", the "enthronement of mediocrity", and "cultural leveling" appear borrowed directly from José Enrique Rodó's essay, *Ariel,* they are applied in a totally different sense: what came to be known as *perez-jimenismo* could not possibly be confused with *arielismo.* It is clear, for example, that when he spoke of "the mediocrity of inept and incompetent political theorizers", he was referring to the democratic movement initiated by the exiled liberals. His "new nationalism" meant loyalty and support for the Armed Forces and specifically for the dictator himself. His notion of "spiritual values" had nothing to do with free intellectual speculation involving concepts of religion, philosophy, social morality, or human dignity, but rather with the building of grandiose public works as convincing physical evidence of alleged superiority. The following sentence is typical of his oratorical style as well as his social concepts: "A clear demonstration of our national conscience is the materialization of the abstract concept of the Fatherland in works of great scope, whose importance will be self-evident, in contrast to the atmosphere of sordidness, which some have even praised as an example of what is typical, in which the conjunction of negative factors can never be favorable to the prospering of human dignity".[8]

Pérez Jiménez was known to be a great admirer of the Romans, not for their contributions in the fields of literature and education, nor even as the foremost law-givers of ancient times, but for their remarkable ability as builders of roads, aqueducts, bridges, city walls, and amphitheaters, and as the world's most efficient maintainers of law and order. He clearly wished to emulate them within his own country.

In the autumn of 1955, not content with piecemeal efforts to propagandize his program to achieve greatness for Venezuela, Pérez Jiménez arranged for the publication of a new book with the impressively legalistic title of *Fundamento jurídico del Nuevo Ideal Nacional.* The author, Dr. Luis Cova García, was an adviser to Vallenilla Lanz in penal matters and one of the most faithful sycophants of the dictatorship. The title is wildly inappropriate, for the work does not establish anything like a "juridical foundation" for the so-called political doctrine that it expounds. The overriding concern of the author was to flatter the dictator, whose name occurs in nearly every paragraph of the book. Every chapter begins and ends with a passage of unstinting praise, such as the following:

This great citizen, this great civilizer, has set in motion a strong idea, an idea that is involving the country more every day, infiltrating the soul of the people, and is the idea that will bring Venezuela out of the swamp and the lack of initiative in which our First Magistrate found it. We applaud this great citizen for the transformation that he has brought about in the nation. And this great citizen's name is General Marcos Pérez Jiménez.[9]

Pervading the entire work is the *perezjimenista* concept of "democracy" which, within the doctrine of the New National Ideal, must be taken to mean the prosperity and prestige of the nation. Democracy in the political sense, involving freedom of speech and press, and the formation of political parties competing for the power to govern, is specifically excluded as prejudicial to the national interests. It is neither possible nor desirable, says Cova García, for the people to manage the nation's affairs; they lack self-restraint and have no sense of direction. When granted complete freedom of expression, they fall at once into the evils of "verborrhea" which gives the "illusion that words are deeds and progress, and that nothing more need be done". Political and economic power, he says, belongs rightfully to him who as the strength to grasp it, keep it, and wield it effectively. The Cova García book is, in short, the clumsy attempt of a paid propagandist to lend an air of legality to an illegal regime.

The economic outlook at the beginning of 1955 could hardly have been more promising for Pérez Jiménez. His country's record-high dollar income for the preceding year was nearly one billion dollars, about 80% of it from petroleum royalties. With the threat of nationalization of oil fields in the Middle East, particularly in Iran, the oil companies were exceedingly auxious to remain on good terms with Venezuela and even to acquire new concessions. In March, 1955, the Inter-American Investment Conference, held in New Orleans, ended with the announcement that fifteen new industrial plants would soon be established in Venezuela by U.S. companies, the reasons given being stable conditions, low taxes, low labor costs, and the free convertibility of currency.[10]

Although there remained a threat of restrictions on the importation of Venezuelan oil into the U.S. market, the Caracas government appeared to recognize it as a lever to bring about the granting of new concessions. In his budget message of May 3 to the Senate, Pérez Jiménez declared that if the United States imposed such a restriction, Venezuela would respond with an equivalent reduction in the purchase of U.S. products. He also asserted that his government had ample cash reserves and that he did not hesitate to announce a budget of Bs. 2,550,000,000 for the fiscal year 1955-56. Of this amount, the biggest single item, Bs. 734,000,000, was allotted for public works.[11] No restrictions were imposed during the Pérez Jiménez regime, and great new concessions were sold to the foreign-owned companies early in 1956. Crude oil production, national income and expenditures, and international reserves resulting mainly from the sale of new concessions were:

Year	Crude Oil Production Millions of Bbls.	National Income Millions of Bs.	Expenditures Millions of Bs.	International Reserves: gold and cash U.S. $ Millions
1955	787.5	2,992.08	2,983.16	496
1956	898.8	4,374.65	3,349.98	869
1957	1,014.5	5,396.61	4,360.99	1,354

Sources: *Memoria del Banco Central*, 1958, pp. 18 and 248; and Lieuwen, p. 140.

Despite the continued predominance of petroleum as the principal source of national income, other sectors of the economy made substantial gains during this period. The great iron mine of Cerro Bolívar exported increasing quantities of high-grade ore to the smelters at Barrows Point, Maryland. Increased income also came from the mining of aluminum, silver, gold, asbestos, and industrial diamonds in the Andes and in the Guayana region.

Importers did a thriving business, especially in U.S. products. Government credits to farmers, cattle raisers, and commercial fishermen, on the other hand, had declined every year since 1950, and there were equally steady increases in the importation of meat, dairy products, corn, wheat, and fish.[12]

Manufacturing in Venezuela increased spectacularly during this period, stimulated by massive infusions of foreign investment capital, which more than tripled between 1951 and 1957. Although more than thirty countries were represented in these investments, U.S. capital accounted for more than two-thirds of the total.[13] More than half of the foreign capital was invested in electric power production, chemicals, and metals, with lesser amounts in tobacco, textiles, cement, and cosmetics. No foreign investment was made in cattle raising nor in the production of cereals.[14]

In February, 1956, the Pérez Jiménez regime undertook the building of a vast hydroelectric plant and steel mill near Puerto Ordaz in Bolívar State. This enterprise, involving Italian engineers and technicians, Venezuelan laborers, and enormous amounts of capital, presented the usual opportunities for peculation. Despite the fact that Venezuela was well endowed by nature for the development of heavy industry, the project was poorly planned and ill-managed from the beginning and was not to come to fruition until after the fall of the Pérez Jiménez regime.[15]

Prior to the granting of the new oil concessions of 1956, exiled liberals pointed out that the proven reserves of Venezuela were equivalent to 15 times the current annual production, as compared to a ratio of only 12:1 obtaining in the oil industry of the United States. Even more impressive as an argument against further concessions was the fact that the total oil-field area in actual production constituted only 2.8% of areas already held by the companies.[16] Nevertheless, the petroleum interests prevailed, and in January, 1956, the regime conceded great new areas of public domain for exploration and exploitation. The new concessions of 301,214 hectares (745,233 acres) comprised more than 5% of the total oil-field areas then held by the petroleum companies.[17]

Within months of this development, events in the Middle East were to have a profound effect upon world petroleum prices, emphasizing the good fortune of the oil companies in their new acquisitions in Venezuela and the importance of their relations with the Pérez Jiménez regime. In October of that year Egyptian Premier Gamal Abdel Nasser seized control of the Suez Canal from the British, nationalized it to the exclusion of the Israelis, and promptly suffered bombing attacks from the combined air forces of Britain, France, and Israel, causing obstruction of the canal by sunken ships. The resulting shortage of oil in Europe and elsewhere soon brought about increases in the price of Venezuelan crude oil that ranged from 4 cents to 28 cents per barrel, depending on grade.[18]

In the year 1956, Venezuela's income from petroleum, comprising 97.4% of her revenues from exports of all kinds, was $1,307.11 million, by far the highest in her history. Of this amount, $982.58 million (75.2%) was derived from taxes paid by the oil companies, and the remainder from the sale of the new concessions and from royalties.[19] Similar figures for the year 1957 included a total petroleum income of $1,679.66 million, of which $1,256.41 million (74.8%) was received as taxes, and the remainder from royalties and continued payments on the new concessions.[20]

Comparing the nature and extent of the Pérez Jiménez spending program during the period of the New National Ideal with that of the earlier phase of the dictatorship, it is clear that the differences noted are not of kind but only of degree. Agriculture, cattle raising, the fishing industry, native small business and manufacturing, education, public health, and all other matters of general interest were increasingly neglected in favor of an all-out effort to create an appearance of wealth and luxury.

With no abatement in the construction program in and near Caracas, the regime undertook to erect a series of luxury hotels in the pleasantest and most scenic parts of the country, from San Cristóbal, near the Colombian border, to the Island of Margarita in the Caribbean. Three of these, built in 1955, include the Hotel Miranda, in Coro, the Hotel Aguas Calientes, in Ureña, and the splendid Hotel Bella Vista, on the Island of Margarita. The latter, built at a cost of Bs. 7,300,000, is a 10-story edifice of 49 rooms and seven spacious suites, boasting a covered penthouse terrace and bar commanding a view of the sea. A government release revealed its purpose with these words: "The construction of this modern hotel will contribute decidedly to the development of tourism in Venezuela".[21]

A more extravagant enterprise undertaken in 1955 as an added tourist attraction was a complex structure called the *Teleférico,* a system of 12 cable cars, each with a capacity of 28 passengers, to carry sightseers from a station located in the Caracas suburb of Maripérez to the top of Mount Avila, a towering peak north of the capital. Once there, as the government propaganda claimed, the traveler could enter the observation tower and contemplate the Valley of Caracas on the south and the port of La Guaira and the Caribbean on the north.

For tourists who might wish to stay longer on Mt. Avila the regime began work on a 20-story luxury hotel, a project finished at enormous cost in 1957. Featuring a dance pavillion, swimming pool, barber shop, game rooms, bars, dining halls, and even an ice-skating rink, this expensive monster proved a complete failure as a money-making venture. After the fall of the dictatorship, occasional groups of visitors were to take the guided tour through its empty halls and to stare in amazement at the ornate details of an enterprise whose only use had been to provide fat commissions for the insiders of the Pérez Jiménez regime.

Even more bizarre was a project begun in 1956 in downtown Caracas, allegedly to facilitate both shopping and entertainment. Called the *Helicoide*, this gigantic structure consisted of a series of spiraling concrete ramps on which shops, restaurants, and places of entertainment were to be located. A novel feature of the complex was to be a movie theater located at the top, arranged in such a way that a patron might enter at almost any hour of the day or night and see the film from the very beginning. When the dictatorship crumbled early in 1958, only the ramps and parking areas had been completed, and the subsequent democratic government left the fantastic structure as an ironic monument to the New National Ideal, whose motto had been "the rational transformation of the physical environment".[22]

A principal objective of the regime was the strengthening of ties with like-minded governments in the Hemisphere in order to enhance the Pérez Jiménez image. Carried out at great expense and with a flamboyance never equalled by any subsequent effort, was the state visit of the Venezuelan President in June, 1955, to Lima, Peru, where he spent a week with fellow dictator, General Manuel A. Odría, who had also come to power by means of a military *coup d'état*.

The saturation coverage of this event by the news media of both countries indicated that Odría's objectives were similar to those of his guest, but it was the Venezuelan who exploited the occasion to the fullest. A short time after the trip, the Venezuelan Ministry of Foreign Affairs published a glossy 271-page book, *La visita al Perú del Presidente de Venezuela,* containing a detailed itinerary of the visit, illustrated with nearly 200 photographs of banquets, receptions, dances, and military parades. Much publicized was the ceremony at which Pérez Jiménez presented to Odría a $3,000 jewel-encrusted replica of the sword given to Liberator Simón Bolívar by a grateful Peru more than a century before.[23]

So charmed was Pérez Jiménez with the results of his image-building that he invited the Peruvian to pay a return visit to Caracas in August.

Odría arrived on schedule, spent several days admiring the splendid buildings and modern highways, accepted an honorary appointment as General of the Venezuelan Armed Forces and, according to the Caracas press, was cheered endlessly by thousands of Venezuelans waving Peruvian flags.[24]

In July, 1956, Pérez Jiménez attended the meeting of Hemisphere presidents and chiefs of state held in Panama. Despite rumors that an interview would be arranged between Pérez Jiménez and President José Figueres of Costa Rica "in order to normalize relations" between their two countries, the Venezuelan was not greeted by Figueres. He was, however, warmly received by fellow dictators from Cuba, the Dominican Republic, Nicaragua, and Paraguay. Most gratifying of all for the Venezuelan was the splendidly cordial attitude of the U.S. delegation, headed by his friend and admirer, President Dwight D. Eisenhower. Other members of the party from Washington were: presidential assistant Sherman Adams; Dr. Milton Eisenhower, who had been the dictator's guest in Caracas; and his two staunchest supporters from the State Department, Secretary John Foster Dulles and Assistant Secretary Henry Holland.[25]

At one of the Panama meetings Pérez Jiménez presented a proposal originally made by Venezuela to the OAS more than a year earlier: the creation of an Inter-American Economic Fund from which needy nations could borrow. Because of her great oil revenues, Venezuela had offered to contribute to the creation of this fund, and Pérez Jiménez indicated that he wished to revive the proposal for the consideration of the delegates gathered there. According to the Caracas press, seven member states, including Colombia, Ecuador, and Paraguay wished to consider formation of the economic fund without delay. Four other nations were noncommittal. Nine, however, voted to turn the Venezuelan plan over to a committee, and to pass to other matters on the agenda.

Understandably, Pérez Jiménez was offended and angered by the casual rebuff of his offer and perhaps for this reason the Venezuelan press gave very limited coverage to the matter at the time. He later revealed the results of the voting at Panama, stating that he would make no further effort in support of the proposed fund, but would make no formal withdrawal of the offer. He also denied rumors, "current among foreign circles" at Panama, that he had made his proposal in a "haughty and arrogant fashion" that offended other chiefs of state.[26]

At the beginning of 1957 Pérez Jiménez renewed his program of cementing relations with other dictators. He arranged to meet the Colombian tyrant, Gustavo Rojas Pinilla, on February 22, at the center of the Bolivar Bridge that links Colombian territory with the Venezuelan state of Táchira. The two men talked privately there for several hours, after which Pérez Jiménez announced that he had accepted an invitation to visit Colombia in May and that he had, in turn, invited Rojas Pinilla to come to Caracas in July for the Venezuelan national independence week, Semana de la Patria.

Events in Colombia were destined to frustrate these plans for neighborly visits. Early in May, just when the Venezuelan ruler was completing plans for his trip to Bogota, a paralyzing general strike in Colombia forced the military leaders of that country to solve the crisis by placing Rojas Pinilla on a plane and shipping him into exile.

Meanwhile Pérez Jiménez had become involved in developments concerning another ex-dictator and the nation that he had ruled. Juan Domingo Perón, ousted from his command of Argentina's destiny in September, 1955, had first taken refuge with his friend Alfredo Stroessner, of Paraguay, then had stayed for some months in Panama. In late 1956 the former Argentinian boss accepted an invitation from Caracas to reside for a time in that city.

The reader may recall that in 1948, when Pérez Jiménez occupied the post of Chief of Staff of the Armed Forces in the Gallegos administration, he made a prolonged visit to Buenos Aires. Since that time he had made no secret of his admiration for the tactics of *peronismo*, and he was proud and flattered to have the Argentinian as his guest and adviser in Caracas. The Aramburu government in Argentina, having pressured Paraguay's Stroessner into denying further hospitality to Perón, was irritated when Venezuela extended a cordial invitation to the ex-dictator to live in Caracas. Perón had already shown that he still had great influence over his *descamisados* at home and was capable of much mischief. The inevitable result of his presence in the Venezuelan capital was the growth of mistrust and hostility between the Pérez Jiménez administration and the Argentine embassy in Caracas.

On Saturday morning, February 25, 1957, an Opel sedan belonging to Perón was partially destroyed by the explosion of a time-bomb that had been planted under the hood. Some windows were shattered and a few pedestrians were struck by bits of metal, but Perón was conveniently inside his house and out of danger. Although the incident was inconsequential in its effects, it received front-page coverage for several days in the Caracas press, with photographs of SN Chief Pedro Estrada, who appeared at a press conference to announce that he had undertaken an "intensive investigation" of the matter. No arrests were made and no one was accused of complicity in the act, but official news releases left the impression that the Argentine embassy was somehow involved. Perhaps it was; but it is also possible that Perón himself arranged the event, in concert with Pérez Jiménez and Pedro Estrada, in order to create an appearance of criminality on the part of the Argentine ambassador, and to provoke a rupture of diplomatic relations.[27]

In June Pérez Jiménez invited Alfredo Stroessner to accompany him and Perón in the celebrations and parades of Venezuelan independence week. The Paraguayan arrived on June 28, had words of praise for his host, and was the constant companion of Pérez Jiménez and Perón in the activities of the Semana de la Patria. In consideration of these arrangements, the Argentine ambassador, General Carlos Toranzo Montero, opted to remain in his embassy and took no part in the celebration. The outcome was a minor triumph for Perón: Pérez Jiménez, having created an untenable situation for the Argentine government, declared the ambassador of that country *persona non grata* in Caracas and demanded his recall to Buenos Aires, at the same time summoning the Venezuelan ambassador, Atilano Carnevali, to return home. Diplomatic relations between the two countries remained severed until the fall of the Pérez Jiménez regime in 1958.[28]

One aspect of the dictator's program to create a favorable image of his administration outside Venezuela was the effort to counteract the effects of an increasingly bad press in the United States. In mid-1955 such papers as the *New York Mirror, Journal American, New York Enquirer,* and *World Telegram* began to publish articles seriously exposing the nature of the Caracas regime. It was obvious that some very knowledgeable Venezuelan was providing accurate and damaging information to such popular columnists as Dorothy Kilgallen, Walter Winchell, Cholly Knickerbocker, and Lee Mortimer; but these writers had the habit of protecting their sources, and the dictator's propagandists in Caracas continued for some months in a state of frustration.

The informant in this case was indeed a Venezuelan exiled by the dictatorship and living in New York: Dr. Mariano Arcaya, a 39-year-old international lawyer who held degrees from George Washington University, Columbia, and Princeton, and was associated with a law firm in New York. He had been expelled from Venezuela at the order of Vallenilla Lanz, with his brother Carlos Arcaya, because of their opposition to the *coup* of December 2, 1952, and because they were cousins of Ignacio Luis Arcaya, president of URD and the real winner of the November 30 election. Mariano Arcaya's systematic supplying of information to the New York columnists was an attempt to expose and discredit the dictatorship, and he did so anonymously in order to protect his parents, who still lived in Caracas.

In December, 1955, Arcaya published in a magazine called *Whisper* an article entitled "Operation Orgy", a satirical exposé of the alleged sexual debaucheries of Pérez Jiménez and his friends. First published in English under the psyeudonym "Peter Amoros", it created a sensation, selling more than 1,800,000 copies. It was reproduced in Spanish on December 6, 1955, on the front page of *El Espectador* in Santiago, Chile, then reprinted by Accion Democratica for clandestine distribution in Venezuela. The piece carried the subtitle: "Love that comes down from Heaven for President Pérez Jiménez of Venezuela. Stupendous girls board shining planes in Havana to land in Caracas by moonlight. Then come parties that an emperor would envy!" Below a photograph showing the dictator standing on La Carlota Airport awaiting the landing of the four-motored plane was the following explanation:

> The American Eagle, Symbol of Liberty and Democracy, flutters lovingly over Venezuela as if protecting a golden egg. And, in reality, it is, for Venezuela pours out two and one-half million barrels of oil every day, most of it flowing toward the United States. Consequent-

ly, with some three billion dollars invested in Venezuela, it is not at all extraordinary that President Eisenhower, the Department of State, the Congress, and all the giants of the petroleum industry should be sweet and amiable toward President Marcos Pérez Jiménez of Venezuela. President Eisenhower even granted him the Legion of Merit, in the degree of Commander in Chief, the highest award that the United States can grant to a foreigner. But here, told for the first time, is the truth about Pérez Jiménez, the truth that even Ike doesn't know!

There follows a verbal caricature of the weekly system dedicated to the "satisfaction of the hormonal hunger of Dictator Pérez Jiménez". The planes embarked regularly with an "appetizing cargo" from Havana, and on landing in Caracas, the girls were greeted by the "Sex Minister of the dictator of Venezuela", an unmistakable reference to one Fortunato Herrera, also known as "El Platinado", a handsome silver-haired man of exquisite manners and impeccable dress who arranged secret parties for his boss, both in Caracas and on the Caribbean Island of Orchila, on which the tyrant had reputedly lavished millions of bolivars in the construction of pleasure houses.[29]

According to Arcaya's satire, Herrera was always accompanied on these occasions by "Pedro Estrada (The Executioner), chief of the secret police, official torturer and principal killer of the Pérez Jiménez regime. He behaves courteously and enchantingly when he receives the girls. None of them would believe that this attentive and hand-kissing official could make the streets of Caracas run red with blood". And then there was the "chubby little dictator with owlish eyes, his stomach tucked into an immaculate white uniform covered with gold braid and medals". Each one of the pretty strumpets, says Arcaya, received at least $1,000 for such a trip to Caracas to enliven the days of Perez Jimenez.[30]

If the Arcaya article was a source of pleasure to the enemies of the Caracas regime, it was the cause of no little rage to the dictator and his friends. According to Arcaya, the Venezuelan Consul in New York, Mr. Delfín E. Páez, soon received instructions to engage a detective agency to discover the identity of the author, and this was done at a cost of $30,000 in January, 1956.

The first reaction of the Venezuelan government after learning the identity of the enemy was as inept, childish, and unrealistic as the decision to build a 20-story tourist hotel on the top of cold and forbidding Mt. Avila. With an affectation of bland benevolence, Pérez Jiménez called a news conference on February 3 and made the astonishing announcement that he had instructed Venezuelan consuls abroad to issue passports and visas to any and all political exiles who wished to return to their country. To make this offer convincing and inclusive, he stated that even Betancourt and Gallegos were welcome to come home and that they could do so in safety, adding that he had ordered the release of political prisoners in Venezuela, including even those whose cases had not been tried. A similar statement emanated from the Venezuelan consulate in New York.

On the following day Rómulo Betancourt, questioned by newsmen in San Juan, Puerto Rico, rejected the offer for himself and Gallegos. He said that although a few exiles had been repatriated, many other citizens were being arrested for political reasons or were on their way from jail to the airport, bound for exile.[31]

Within days Mariano Arcaya received a courteous telephone call from Venezuelan Consul Delfín Páez, who invited him to the Consulate where he had a "pleasant surprise" for him. Arriving there, Arcaya was smilingly offered a passport and the necessary visa to return to Caracas with the "personal word of honor of Pérez Jiménez" for his safety. The exile did not accept the bait, but declared that he would never return to Venezuela until the fall of the dictatorship. Others were less cautious: Mariano's brother Carlos and his sister Ana Arcaya arrived in New York from Spain and, despite warnings from Mariano, announced their intention of accepting the amnesty offer. Ana departed first as a test case, and was permitted to proceed to her home without difficulty. Carlos Arcaya then left for Caracas, arriving at Maiquetía Airport on February 19. There, he was arrested by Pedro Estrada's agents and taken to Obispo Prison where he remained for more than three months.

The treachery of Pérez Jiménez in this case was counterproductive: Carlos Arcaya was a non-political figure who had done nothing to discredit the regime; Mariano, who had landed the telling blows, was still free to carry on his campaign. *Time Magazine,* which had not previously taken notice of the controversy, published in its issue of March 5, 1956, a detailed account of the conduct of the dictatorship in the Arcaya affair and denounced the amnesty offer as a trap for unwary political exiles. The New York *Times* also published a letter from Mariano Arcaya setting forth the facts of the case.[32]

In the last week of February, 1956, there were riots by highschool students in Caracas. Although the disturbances were in protest against academic requirements, the government declared that the students were members of the Communist Youth League, and the police suppressed their activities with great severity. Despite official denials of any student deaths, travelers arriving in Puerto Rico reported that many were slain by police and great numbers seriously injured. The New York press, now fully alerted to events in Venezuela, devoted an unusual amount of space to these developments. The New York *Times* even added the detail that "much of this information was obtained by Dr. Mariano Arcaya, consultant in Latin American law, with offices at 270 Park Avenue".[33]

The Pérez Jiménez regime, fearing the deterioration of its image in the United States, and perceiving Mariano Arcaya as the principal cause of its trouble, now adopted a new tactic. Vallenilla Lanz, self-admitted principal instigator of the electoral fraud of 1952, used his official position and his peculiar talents in an effort to impugn the personal integrity and veracity of Arcaya, and to discredit him with the very newspapers that had accepted his information.

As part owner of the Caracas daily *El Heraldo,* and constant contributor to that mouthpiece of the regime, Vallenilla published on March 2, 1956, a defamatory article entitled "Mariano Arcaya, Informer of the New York *Times*", alleging that the exile had given false information to American newspapers and magazines in an effort to "avenge himself against a regime that found it necessary to dismiss him because of incompetence and lack of scruples, from his post as informer to the Seguridad Nacional". The same article declared that "in New York, Dr. Arcaya is an assiduous visitor to the editorial rooms of newspapers and at night he is often seen in a cabaret called El Morocco, in company with a well-known homosexual by the name of Oleg Cassini who, under the pseudonym of 'Knickerbocker', writes a scandal column in the *Daily News*". As pointed out by Arcaya, the editorial in *El Heraldo* was not only libelous but mistaken, since it confused Oleg Cassini (Jacqueline Kennedy's dress designer, at the time) with his brother Gigi Cassini, who wrote a column for the *Journal American,* not the *Daily News.*

Vallenilla Lanz, in conjunction with Pedro Estrada, next fabricated documents carrying the forged signatures of Mariano Arcaya and purporting to prove that he had been a paid informer for the secret police. Photostatic copies of the bogus papers, together with copies of the editorial, were then sent to Consul Delfín Páez in New York with instructions to offer them for publication.

To the dismay of the conspirators, no New York paper would publish the documents, even at a high fee, for fear of a libel suit, unless the originals were presented as proof of their authenticity. Since this quality was totally lacking, the consul was unable to bring about the desired result. Vallenilla Lanz then published the spurious documents in *El Heraldo* on March 7, and sent nearly 5,000 copies of the paper to New York, most of them to Consul Delfín Páez. Although Arcaya saw his position jeopardized by these tactics, he was aware that he had no legal redress against libelous materials published in Caracas and then sent to New York.

At this point, Consul Páez committed the indiscretion of posting copies of the defamatory materials in a conspicuous place at the entrace to the Venezuelan consulate, together with a new editorial diatribe from *El Heraldo* containing the following: "The publications in the United States that have accepted as true the unfounded accusations of Arcaya can now judge the veracity of the informer and the origin of his resentment. Having failed in this country as an urban developer, as a lawyer, and as a secret agent, it is possible that he may also fail abroad in his new profession as blackmailer".

Mariano Arcaya, considering that the public display of these materials constituted libel, immediately instituted legal action for recovery of damages in the amount of $300,000 in the United States District Court, Southern District of New York. Because of the circumstances, the action could not be brought against the government of Venezuela, nor any member of the Pérez Jiménez clique in that country. The defendant named in the suit was Mr. Delfín E. Páez. Arcaya, as plaintiff, demanded presentation in court of the original documents or payment of damages for defamation of character. If Páez really believed that such originals existed, he must have been sorely perplexed that his government did not send them for his defense.

The Fifth Avenue law firm of Reuben B. Shemitz, engaged by the regime to defend the consul, replied to the summons on March 20 with a request for a postponement of the preliminary hearing in order to prepare a defense. A delay was granted, and appearance was set for May 10, 1956. The request was understandable: although Delfín Páez was technically the defendant, it was clear that if the court action went forward, the corruption of the Pérez Jiménez dictatorship would inevitably be aired in an American court, with the most unfavorable publicity imaginable in the very country in which it was most essential to retain an acceptable image. The conspirators in Caracas were in a serious dilemma; continued adverse publicity could lead to an investigation by a Senate committee, and it was not to be expected that friends in the State Department would compromise themselves in a shoddy affair involving falsified evidence.

The first attempted solution, probably proposed by Pedro Estrada rather than Vallenilla Lanz, was the one that promised to be the cheapest and most definitive. Two assassins were hired to murder the troublesome exile in his New York apartment on March 10, 1956. According to Arcaya, the New York Police Department discovered all pertinent details of the case: a Venezuelan radio-telegrapher in the employ of Estrada and stationed in New York was paid $10,000 to hire an "expert gun" to carry out the assassination. The agent, however, proved to be greedy, keeping $9,000 of this amount, and spending only $1,000 on two bumbling operatives who were unable to carry out their assignment.[34]

The next effort to avoid exposure of the regime involved the cooperation of the Venezuelan Minister of Foreign Affairs, Dr. José L. Arismendi, who instructed the Venezuelan ambassador in Washington, César González, to intercede with the State Department to have Arcaya's case dismissed. Such an appeal from a representative of a foreign government, requesting a U.S. Cabinet member to interfere in the Federal Judiciary System, was practically unprecedented.

Secretary Dulles, however much he may have wished to do a favor for Pérez Jiménez, could not openly intervene in a judicial matter. He did, however, have the ambassador's letter sent through intermediaries to Federal Judge Edward J. Dimock in New York. The ambassador's request was that Dulles should "suggest" to the Court that the case against Paez be dropped in consideration of American-Venezuelan friendship. It should be noted that although Dulles included with it no message of his own, the very act of sending the ambassador's letter to the Court constituted something of a "suggestion", and tended to warn the Court that extra-legal considerations were involved in the case.

On May 17, 1956, a counsel for the defense, Mr. Ernest A. Gross, asked the Court to dismiss the charges against Páez on the grounds that the Consul General of Venezuela enjoyed immunity from prosecution. When this motion was denied, Mr. Gross presented evidence that the defendant had been appointed Venezuelan Minister to the United Nations and was duly accredited in this status by the State Department on May 3, 1956, thus acquiring diplomatic immunity.

On June 21, Arcaya presented the testimony of a handwriting expert who proved that the documents published by *El Heraldo* were indeed forgeries. Despite this evidence of dishonesty and libel on the part of the Pérez Jiménez regime, disposition of the case was again postponed.

On October 15, Judge Dimock ruled to suspend further action for as long as Delfín Páez held his diplomatic position at the United Nations. Páez therefore enjoyed immunity until the fall of the dictatorship in January, 1958. Arcaya then reopened the case, and Mr. Páez settled out of court by signing a statement recognizing the falsity of the accusations and paying the sum of $5,000 and court costs.[35]

Although Mariano Arcaya was able to clear his name in 1956, and won a complete moral victory over Páez in 1958, the resources available to Pérez Jiménez, and certain peculiarities of the American judicial system, had enabled him to avoid exposure of his regime in American courts.

The oft-repeated "principle" of the New National Ideal was that political activity of any sort was the enemy of progress. For this reason, there could be no question of political parties or opposition programs. There was only the shadowy FEI headed by Pérez Jiménez. Since the election of November 30, 1952, Venezuelans had lived in a political vacuum. Newspapers were forbidden to speculate on the possibility of future elections unless so ordered by the government. The only former political leader not in exile or in prison was Dr. Rafael Caldera, and he was a close friend and protégé of Archbishop Arias Blanco. The last public rally attempted by Copei was on January 30, 1955, and all *copeyanos* who attended it, with the exception of Caldera, had been in prison since that time.

On October 25, 1956, Pérez Jiménez announced that "in conformity with the provisions of the Constitution", presidential elections would be held in the year 1957. He gave no hint as to whether he planned to be a candidate, nor did he indicate whether opposition parties would be permitted. Newspapers were ordered to print the announcement without comment, and there the matter stood for many months. Venezuelans could only be certain that the government would not let Pérez Jiménez lose in any electoral contest.[36] And when he announced on December 29 that construction of a new presidential palace would begin in 1957, it could hardly have occurred to anyone that the dictator was making such plans for a possible successor.

The fall from power of Colombia's Rojas Pinilla in May, 1957, marked the beginning of renewed hope among Venezuelans that their own dictator could not rule them forever. Despite the friendliness of Latin America's remaining military bosses, and the benevolent attitude of President Eisenhower and the State Department, political exiles began to insist more loudly that it was time for a change in Venezuela.

Even the Catholic hierarchy of Caracas, which for more than eight years of police-state terror, had shown only enthusiasm and approval of the dictatorship, now suddenly perceived that the Pérez Jiménez regime left something to be desired. In May, Archbishop Arias Blanco issued a pastoral letter deploring the poverty of the masses, and declared that "the great majority of the people live in sub-human conditions". He was promptly summoned by Interior Minister Vallenilla Lanz, who denounced the statement as an "unfriendly act", but the prelate would not retract his opinion, nor would he promise to refrain from further criticism of the government.[37]

Another important development, probably owing its inception more to the new attitude of the Venezuelan Catholic Church than to the fall of Rojas Pinilla, was the formation of a clandestine organization called the Junta Patriótica (J.P.). Fabricio Ojeda, a reporter for *El Nacional* and a member of URD, invited to his home on June 11 two other *urredecos* and a Communist named Guillermo García Ponce. Ojeda believed that the time was ripe to found a secret multipartisan organization to force a free and honest election in conformity with provisions of the Constitution. The group agreed to invite members of Copei and AD to join them, and to publish a manifesto proclaiming their objectives. They used the only clandestine press remaining in Venezuela: that of the Communist PCV, on which *Tribuna Popular* had been printed until the previous January.

The Junta Patriótica was soon joined by representatives of Copei and AD, and on June 29, at the beginning of the Semana de la Patria, distributed 200,000 copies of a flyer calling for Venezuelans to unite against the re-election of Pérez Jiménez. Soon thereafter branches of the Junta were formed in Maracay and Puerto la Cruz, and on July 10 the organization published an "Informative Bulletin", copies of which were sent to all newspapers in the country and to foreign correspondents.

On August 1 the J.P. published its "Manifesto No. 1", and thereafter, with amazing speed and boldness the group showered the country with hundreds of thousands of leaflets every week denouncing the government, demanding free elections, and publishing copies of Article 104 of the Constitution, which provided the rules for the election of a President. Estrada's agents scoured Caracas in a vain attempt to locate the hidden press and arrested dozens of suspects, but the activities of the J.P. continued.

July and August were disagreeable months for the Caracas regime. The exiled Jóvito Villalba sent the dictator an open letter, widely publicized in the Hemisphere, demanding political amnesty and general elections. The New York *Times* ran a series of articles exposing conditions in the country, and these were answered by a half-page ad from Consul Delfín Páez in the same paper attempting to refute the criticism, and accusing the *Times* of interfering in the affairs of a sovereign republic. He also repeated the assertion of Vallenilla Lanz that "Venezuela is a backward and ignorant country, in no way ready for democracy".

No word of this controversy appeared in the Venezuelan news media, but the regime's nervousness was revealed by the sudden arrest and imprisonment of Rafael Caldera on August 27. Three days later, with the Copei leader safely behind bars, Pérez Jiménez announced that the Congress would enact an electoral law in September and that the election for President would be held on December 15. He gave no information concerning possible political parties or candidates.[38]

Congress convened on October 31, but accomplished nothing until November 4 when the dictator interrupted the proceedings to announce that there would be a plebiscite rather than an election on December 15. There would be a single slate of candidates, one for each post in the government and for each seat in Congress. All Venezuelans above the age of 18 and all foreigners with two years or more of residence in the country were eligible to vote. No registration was necessary, and each voter would receive two cards, one blue and one red, to indicate approval or disapproval of the regime. In the weeks remaining before the plebiscite, no compaigning would be permitted, nor would the government tolerate any public expression of approval or disapproval of the plebiscite itself.[39] Pérez Jiménez did not indicate what would happen if a majority of voters disapproved of his regime.

It is said that an impending volcanic eruption is often preceded by such telltale signs as earth tremors and increased temperatures near the site of the forthcoming disaster. The weeks immediately preceding and following the plebiscite of December 15 was a pre-eruption period, and the usual symptoms were not lacking. The free press of the Hemisphere jeered that the dictator did not even dare to face a rigged election, and condemned him for keeping Caldera in prison while arranging to succeed himself for another five years.[40]

During the second half of November, nearly half of the students of Central University boycotted classes in protest against the plebiscite, while highschool students in the capital rioted, overturned and burned taxis bearing the likeness of Pérez Jiménez, hanged effigies of the dictator, and burned copies of El Heraldo on school grounds and in public squares. Pedro Estrada's agents attacked the demonstrators with clubs, machetes, and tear gas, and many students were injured and hospitalized.

Another incident arising from the same circumstances involved a Chilean citizen. Jorge Basulto, an attaché of his country's embassy, was arrested by SN agents and jailed for four days, during which time he was interrogated, threatened, and mistreated. According to the Caracas government, Basulto had been detained by mistake and released as soon as the error was discovered.[41] The truth was that Basulto had told the Canadian ambassador that there would soon be an uprising, and that the Pérez Jiménez dictatorship was about to fall. The ambassador's coded telegram to Ottawa, containing this information and mentioning Basulto as the source, was monitored and decoded by SN agents, who promptly took the Chilean into custody. Despite tardy and superficial regrets expressed by Caracas, President Carlos Ibáñez of Chile ordered an immediate severing of diplomatic relations with the Venezuelan regime.[42]

The symptom that most clearly indicated the impending distintegration of the tyranny was the extreme nervousness of the business community during the last quarter of 1957. Not that unethical financial practices on the part of the government were a new phenomenon: it had long been a matter of common knowledge that members of the regime siphoned off hundreds of millions of bolivars from the public works program, and that these embezzled funds were deposited in foreign banks under their own names.

As early as the beginning of 1955, although oil revenues were constantly increasing, the managers of the New National Ideal had adopted the practice of not paying their debts to construction companies promptly and in cash. Such delinquencies were permitted to go for three or four weeks, constituting forced interest-free loans to the government.

In most countries, government-guaranteed debt can be turned over to banks for cash at full value, but the Pérez Jiménez regime issued notes to settle their debts to contractors, and hard-pressed firms in need of cash were forced to sell such notes at a discount.[43]

By the second half of 1957 the practice of deliberate non-payment of debts, with ever-longer delinquencies, had become an established tactic of the regime in its dealings with companies, both foreign and domestic, and constituted an unfunded public debt of vast but unknown proportions. So scandalous was the situation that even members of the dictator's own Cabinet were alarmed. Interior Minister Vallenilla Lanz recalled in his memoirs that despite the ominous rumblings of discontent among bankers and businessmen, Pérez Jiménez "rubbed his hands together gloatingly over the Treasury surplus of Bs. 2,500,000,000" (about $746 million) and adamantly refused to authorize Treasury Minister Pedro Guzmán to pay the government's debts.[44]

In November, 1957, shortly after the announcement that there would be a plebiscite rather than an election, the dictator delivered a luncheon address at the Officers Club before a large audience of military personnel. Although the meeting had been billed as "an informal chat with brother officers", the stiff and self-conscious Pérez Jiménez read his message in his usual peremptory fashion, then asked whether there were any questions. When one officer inquired whether it was true that the government had enormous debts that were not being paid, the dictator hesitated a moment, then replied: "They are not debts, but obligations". This fantastic assertion, causing anger and consternation among the officers, has been variously commented by many Venezuelan writers. Even Vallenilla Lanz, who could usually find something admirable in the most inept of his master's remarks, had to confess that on this occasion the boss had made a "poor impression on his audience".[45] After the fall of the dictatorship, the provisional government was to discover that the unfunded debt left by that regime came to a staggering $1.4 billion.[46]

It would be difficult to overemphasize the excellent support tendered by the Venezuelan clergy to the cause of the Junta Patriótica. The great majority of Venezuelans, like most other Latin Americans, are Catholics, and the moral power of the priest speaking to his parishoners from the pulpit is enormous. As previously noted, it was the Pastoral Letter of Archbishop Arias Blanco, read by his order in all the pulpits of Venezuela on May 1, 1957, that served to notify the entire clergy that there had been an abrupt change in Church policy toward the dictatorship. Priests throughout the nation accepted that change with enthusiasm, and preached sermon after sermon pointing out the injustices and iniquities of the regime. In Caracas, Father Jesús Hernández Chapellín, director of *La Religión,* began to write editorials criticizing and contradicting the social theories and assertions of Vallenilla Lanz whose column appeared regularly in *El Heraldo,* signed with the initials *R. H.*[47]

On August 14, after a particularly sharp article in *La Religión,* entitled "Orientaciones a *R. H.*", the Interior Minister summoned Hernández Chapellín to his office and demanded that he moderate his tone. The Catholic editor, in no way intimidated, denounced the dictatorship and flatly refused to abandon his criticism.[48]

Shortly after that interview, Father Hernández received a visit from Fabricio Ojeda, who reportedly said: "Father, I come to tell you something as if it were a confession: I am the president of the Junta Patriótica". From that time on, the director of *La Religión* was not only an editor and a priest, but a conspirator. Many of the leaflets and flyers of the J. P. were printed on the Cathedral press.[49]

All members of the dictator's Cabinet were naturally aware of the new hostility shown by the religious community, but perhaps only Vallenilla Lanz understood it perfectly. As Minister of the Interior he had nominal jurisdiction over Pedro Estrada's Seguridad Nacional, but when his authorization was sought to proceed forcefully to suppress the clergy, he counseled for a time against it. Always a realist, and perhaps remembering the disastrous anti-clerical campaign of Perón in Argentina, he replied: "The Church is eternal and wise. It does not associate itself with lost causes." Vallenilla, like the Archbishop, had seen the handwriting on the wall.[50]

Chapter XI

The Fall
of the Dictatorship

The response of the Pérez Jiménez regime to the enmity of the Church and the disruptive activities of the Junta Patriótica was very much like its reaction in previous times of stress. Pedro Estrada sought to distract Venezuelans from the real issues of the moment with the invention of a new *adeco* plot against the life of the dictator. This time the story related to newsmen by SN Inspector-General Luis Rafael Castro was that five AD agents had crossed from the island of Aruba to Venezuela's north coast. One of them, Rafael Thielen Cortez, was alleged to have been captured. *El Nacional* and other Caracas papers obediently published on December 6, 1957, photographs and descriptions of the other four: Alberto Pinto Salinas, Luis Augusto Dubuc, Antonio Leidenz, and Alirio Llamosa, all well-known members of Acción Democrática. The fact that the New York *Times* and other papers outside Venezuela quickly reported that all of these men were known to be in Costa Rica and other parts of Latin America would be no embarrassment to the regime: such facts would not appear in the Venezuelan press.

By way of further distraction, Vallenilla Lanz published in his official mouthpiece, *El Heraldo,* on December 10, photographs of Rómulo Betancourt, Rafael Caldera, Jóvito Villalba, and Gustavo Machado, with the startling announcement that these four opposition leaders had just met together in Mexico to form a coalition against the Pérez Jiménez regime. The Interior Minister seemed in no way inhibited by the fact that Dr. Caldera was at that moment locked in one of Estrada's jail cells at the Seguridad Nacional, Betancourt was in Puerto Rico, and Gustavo Machado in Europe.[1]

Rules governing the plebiscite, as established by the Consejo Electoral at the specific orders of Vallenilla Lanz, were: voting would take place on December 15 at the various precincts from 7 a.m. to 5 p.m. Any identification offered by voters would be accepted at the polls. A blue card and a red one, with an evelope, would be issued to each voter, who would then step behind a screen for privacy, where he would seal one card in the envelope and discard the other in a wastebasket. After depositing the enlope in the box, one finger would be stained with indelible ink to show that he had voted. Despite these rules, it soon became known that all government offices and many private businesses had been instructed to inform their employees that if they wished to keep their jobs, they should appear at work on Monday, December 16, with the red card to prove that they had voted for the dictatorship.[2]

It was clear that Pérez Jiménez was taking no chances even in a voting operation in which he could not lose. Since it was a plebiscite rather than an election, he had no competitors and the voters had no choice. Even if the ballot boxes turned out to contain nothing but red cards of repudiation, Vallenilla Lanz had already shown his ability and willingness to falsify the results to whatever extent he deemed necessary.

On Sunday, December 15, as people in Caracas and elsewhere throughout the country (mostly government employees, policemen, and a few hundred foreigners) formed lines at the polling places, an air of quiet expectancy prevailed. No disturbances marred the prescribed and mechanical procedure of voting. There was no partisan shouting, nor indeed any parties to shout about. Well-armed security police stood guard over the precincts, and if Venezuelans confined their expressions to whispers and covert glances, it was because in eight years of living under a tyrannical regime they had learned that individual public protest was worse than useless. If the act of enforced voting for a dictator was carried out with fear and anger, many citizens were also resentful of the fact that great numbers of foreigners, especially Italians, were granted the right of suffrage on this occasion.

Informed Venezuelans were also aware that the plebiscite itself was illegal, since it violated Article 104 of the Constitution which set forth clearly the conditions under which a President could be elected. In any case, since the outcome of the charade was never in doubt, public interest centered on the size of the turn-out and on the reaction to it in the Armed Forces, the Church hierarchy, and the new Junta Patriótica.

The official announcement of returns held no surprises. On Monday, December 16, Vallenilla declared that the Federal District had voted 487,000 in favor of the regime, with 98,000 against, and there had been 53,000 voided ballots. He said that he expected an 85% affirmative vote for the nation as a whole and added once again that Pérez Jiménez intended to free all political prisoners and permit the return of all exiles, since it was clear that he enjoyed the support of the people and had nothing to fear from his "weak and disorganized opposition".

On December 19, the government announced an absurdly exaggerated final tally of the plebiscite: 2,353,935 votes in favor of Pérez, of a total of 2,900,543 ballots cast. The dictator was forthwith proclaimed President for the following five-year period 1958-63. He would be inaugurated on April 19, 1958. Vallenilla's *El Heraldo,* on December 21, happily declared that the good news "caused enormous enthusiasm in the public, which demonstrated at the headquarters of the Electoral Council and at Miraflores Palace".

The eleven remaining days of 1957 were quiet ones in Venezuela. It was not that the people had forgotten or forgiven the insult of the plebiscite. But it was Christmas time. Citizens went quietly to mass, or gathered with their families to eat their *hallacas,* and kept their own counsel.

The first strong indication of conspiracy in the military occurred on December 31, when the dictator ordered the arrest of General Hugo Fuentes, Colonel Jesús María Castro León, and several officers of lower rank. On the following morning, New Year's Day, before the arrested men could be questioned, Pérez Jiménez leanred that the important Army garrison at Maracay was in revolt against the regime. Almost at the same time, several planes from that base appeared over Caracas and began to make strafing runs on Miraflores Palace. Although a doorman was killed and several policemen were wounded, the dictator found safe refuge in the underground quarters of the Cuartel Miraflores, located just across the street. There he was joined by Chief of Staff General Rómulo Fernández, Vallenilla Lanz, and several other ministers and advisers. The anti-aircraft batteries at Miraflores fired constantly at the attacking planes, but scored no hit, providing an interesting spectacle for a fascinated populace. The planes also cast six bombs at the building of the Seguridad Nacional in an effort to knock out Pedro Estrada's headquarters, but only one of the bombs exploded, and that fell several blocks away from the target, causing little damage. It soon developed that officers commanding the Urdaneta Barracks in Caracas were also members of the conspiracy, but they were prevented from attacking Miraflores because Pérez Jiménez, suspecting an uprising, had taken the precaution of ordering all munitions removed from that garrison.

In the late afternoon, the dictator dispatched four armored columns to suppress the rebellion at Maracay, three of these under the command of Colonel Roberto Casanova, who was loyal to his boss, and a fourth led by Colonel Hugo Trejo, was was secretly sworn to the rebel cause. At about the same time Pedro Estrada, the "Jackal of Güiria", fearful for his life as the most hated man in Venezuela, took refuge with his wife and children in the embassy of Colombia. At 10 p.m. Pérez Jiménez appeared on television to say that the uprising was limited almost entirely to Maracay and that the four armored columns proceeding to that base would crush the rebellion in a few hours.

In this he was correct. Colonel Trejo had led his contingent first to the town of Los Teques, south of Caracas, in the state of Miranda, in order to leave part of his forces to take possession of that center in the name of the rebellion. This manoeuver was not part of the rebel plan, and Trejo was so delayed in arriving at Maracay that eighteen aviators, believing that the revolution had failed, boarded the dictator's private plane and escaped to Barranquilla, Colombia. Colonel Casanova soon arrived at Maracay, took possession of it without firing a shot, and placed Colonel Trejo under arrest.

Only Los Teques remained in the power of the conspirators, and the government announced by radio that the rebels in control there would be bombarded if they did not surrender at once. At six o'clock the following morning Pedro Estrada, apprised of the turn of events, left his embassy refuge, resumed control of SN operations and sent a number of secret agents to Maracay to ferret out all possible information concerning the uprising. Colonel Trejo and all other known conspirators were quickly taken to Caracas and imprisoned.[3]

Although the New Year's Day rebellion in the Armed Forces had failed in its immediate purpose, the situation in Venezuela had not returned to normal, and Pérez Jiménez could not rest easily. The Junta Patriótica flooded the country with leaflets bearing the slogan "Ahora es cuando comienza la lucha" and proposing to set a day for a general strike, including all schools, newspapers, retail businesses, banks, and factories. University and highschool students gathered thousands of signatures on petitions demanding the immediate resignation of the government. Members of long-suppressed labor unions clustered at the gates of factories to discuss the most effective ways of bringing about the fall of the dictatorship.

The 18 aviators who had fled from Maracay to Colombia gave news conferences at which they expressed their detestation of Pérez Jiménez, who had victimized the Armed Forces along with all other sectors of the population. All of the young Air Force rebels had studied in the United States, had great admiration for the democratic freedoms of this country and the American way of life, and expressed consternation at the friendship and support constantly extended to the Venezuelan dictator by President Eisenhower and the State Department.[4]

It was also during the first week of January that Vallenilla Lanz ordered the imprisonment of Father Hernández Chapellín and at least four other priests at the Seguridad Nacional. Archbishop Arias Blanco called on Pérez Jiménez to demand their release, but without success. The dictator announced publicly that the Papal Nuncio Monsignor Formi had no right to receive political refugees like Dr. Caldera. The Vatican sent word that there would be an immediate break in relations between the Holy See and the Caracas regime if the priests were not released.

There is no doubt that during the agitated second week of January there were many complicated plots and counterplots. These were developing in the various branches of the Armed Forces, among the leaders of clandestine political groupings, in labor unions, in the Church hierarchy, and in the new and loosely-knit intellectual group called the Frente Universitario. Certainly the union leaders as well as the political parties represented in the Junta Patriótica wanted to bring about a situation of complete freedom of action for the re-establishment of democratic institutions. But it is clear that not all sectors of the military, financial, and ecclesiastical interests would necessarily favor a return to the hectic days of political campaigns, congressional debates, partisan diatribes in the news media, and perhaps renewed agitation for agrarian reform at the expense of the big landowners and bankers.

Some Venezuelan writers have suggested that Church authorities, while fervently desiring an early end to the Pérez Jiménez regime, did not wish to see a full return to a free democratic system, but hoped that the dictator could be replaced by a more moderate military leader, preferably Chief of Staff General Rómulo Fernández. Such preference on the part of the Church has not been demonstrated, but it is certain that General Fernández, seeing the widespread discontent in all branches of the Armed Forces, began to make demands for drastic changes in the organization of the government.

On January 9 the Venezuelan Navy declared itself in a state of rebellion, and sailed five destroyers out of the Port of La Guaira without the consent of the government. General Fernández, after conferring with the leaders of the naval revolt and with other members of the General Staff, informed Pérez Jiménez that the greatest causes of disaffection were the farcical plebiscite of December 15 and the terroristic methods of the Segurdad Nacional. He demanded the dismissal of the persons responsible.

The dictator, though shaken by the direct challenge to his authority, acceded to the demand in an effort to play for time. He thereupon fired Vallenilla Lanz, planner and organizer of the plebiscite, and Pedro Estrada. Vallenilla, after taking a brief refuge in the Brazilian embassy, boarded a plane for France. Estrada flew at once to the haven of dictator Trujillo in the Dominican Republic, taking with him the archives of the Political Section from the Seguridad Nacional.

Pérez Jiménez, pressured further by the General Staff, then dismissed his entire Cabinet, appointing General Fernández as Minister of Defense, and Rear Admiral Carlos Larrazábal as Minister of the Economy. Most of the other posts, however, were filled with old-guard *perezjimenistas.* The dictator's old friend, Luis Llovera Páez, replaced Vallenilla Lanz in the Ministry of the Interior, and Colonel José Teófilo Velasco, an official in the Military Police, was appointed to succeed Pedro Estrada.

Although Venezuelans rejoiced at the departure of some of their worst enemies, they did not for a moment desist in their efforts to achieve the total overthrow of the regime. On January 10 more than 5,000 citizens gathered in El Silencio in downtown Caracas to demonstrate against the government and to demand its resignation. A pitched battle soon took place with police attempting to disperse the crowd with tear gas and machetes, the civilians responding with sticks, stones, and fists.

As for the changed power alignment resulting from the enforced Cabinet shake-up, there is no indication whatever that the new Minister of Defense shared the objectives of the Junta Patriótica. On the contrary, there is every reason to believe that General Rómulo Fernández was simply another military figure of boundless ambition who hungered for the personal power, wealth, and prestige of the dictator. As such, he was potentially as dangerous to the well-being of the country as Pérez Jiménez himself, but he was soon to reveal that in the game of *coup d'état* he could not match the conspiratorial expertise and tactical manoeuvers of the artillery specialist from Michelena.

For four days following the Cabinet changes, General Fernández remained in the Defense Ministry plotting the way to oust the dictator and to replace him in power. He finally settled on a plan to take his boss into custody at noon on January 14. Pérez Jiménez, informed of this scheme by his own agents, moved quickly to free himself of the threat. On January 13, he called upon some young officers of known loyalty to surround both Miraflores Palace and the Defense Ministry with armored vehicles and machine guns, then immediately summoned General Fernández to his office for a showdown. There, in a situation under his full control, the dictator denounced the plot, fired the general from his ministerial post, and placed him under arrest.

In a swift follow-up, the surprised Fernández was hustled under heavy guard to La Carlota Airport where he was placed aboard a waiting plane and flown to exile in the Dominican Republic. Pérez Jiménez, having emerged the victor in a personal power struggle, once again assumed the post of Minister of Defense and prepared to cope with the rising tide of rebellion of the Venezuelan people.

The third week of January brought a remarkable consolidation of the forces opposed to the dictatorship, a co-ordination owing mainly to the leadership of the Junta Patriótica. At the same time, Pérez Jiménez saw his own support greatly weakened and his position endangered by the events of the preceding days. It was a week of many manifestos signed by hundreds of professional people, businessmen, labor union leaders, professors, and students. Fabricio Ojeda, for the J.P., established firm contact with a new group of civilian and military leaders called the Comité Cívico-Militar to co-ordinate the activities of the two organizations, and the long-planned general strike was set for January 21. Pedro Estrada's successor, Colonel Velasco, in an effort to placate the Church, released the five priests without authorization from the dictator. For this he received a severe reprimand and was ordered to take them into custody again, but the priests could not be located.

Dr. Humberto Fernández-Morán, a scientist of standing in the academic community, was appointed Minister of Education in the hope that he could persuade professors and students to end their disruptive activities. He appeared several times on television, combining his directives with promises of reforms and threats of dire consequences for failure to comply, but teachers and students turned a deaf ear to his entreaties and the riots continued unabated. Priests throughout the country devoted their sermons to denunciation of the tyranny, lent full support to the projected strike, and demanded the resignation of the government.

Pérez Jiménez, perplexed and enraged at the sudden and determined resistance of so many sectors of the population, and feeling the loss of

Vallenilla Lanz and other advisers of long standing, attempted to solve his problem in the only way that he knew: by a combination of deceptive tactics and the application of brute force on the part of the police. To this end, he ordered an indefinite suspension of classes at the Universidad Central, closed the Liceo Andrés Bello and, on January 20, distributed spurious leaflets announcing that the Junta Patriótica had postponed the general strike scheduled for the following day. On the same evening, even as the dictator declared by radio that the strike would be crushed at all costs, his police were battling civilians in all parts of Caracas. An unknown number of citizens were killed by SN agents wielding machetes and firing blindly into crowds, and a great many more were seriously injured and hospitalized.

Since the New Year's Day uprising at Maracay and the ensuing power struggle with General Fernández, Pérez Jiménez no longer had confidence in the loyalty of the Armed Forces, and ordered all soldiers confined to barracks without arms. Hundreds of officers were in jail cells in the underground barracks at Miraflores, the Cárcel Modelo, El Obispo Prison, and Ciudad Bolivar. The dictator was forced to depend entirely on the SN agents trained by Pedro Estrada.

In dramatic intensity and popular violence, the events of January 21 and 22 in Caracas, Venezuela, can find a proper comparison only in such a heroic uprising as that of the Hungarian "Freedom Fighters" of Budapest in 1956 against their Communist overlords. It was a true popular revolution of Venezuelan citizens of all ages and social classes, armed with rocks, clubs, home-made grenades, and "Molotov cocktails", against a ferocious and well-trained police force equipped with armored vehicles, sub-machine guns, rifles, revolvers, machetes, and tear gas. Nevertheless, the general strike set for January 21, despite the government's efforts to prevent it, took place as scheduled.

Precisely at 12 o'clock noon on that day, all editorial offices closed without having printed a single newspaper, church bells rang, factory sirens screamed, thousands of automobiles sounded their horns and, by common consent, shop owners locked their doors and walked into the streets, to be joined by great masses of *caraqueños* who converged toward the center of the city to protest the rule of Pérez Jiménez. Young men representing all of the opposition political parties—*adecos, copeyanos, urredecos,* and Communists—dispatched by the Junta Patriótica, led crowds into all the streets and squares of Caracas to see that businesses were closed in compliance with the strike order. A few stores, mostly owned by Italians and other foreigners, were found open, and these were put to the torch without delay. A number of buses owned by the government and sent to operate as usual promptly suffered the same fate.

Although the greatest crowds and the largest number of police were concentrated in El Silencio on the day of the strike, fighting was general throughout the city. In spite of the 5 o'clock curfew ordained by the regime, the conflict continued until late at night. The SN agents reportedly showed themselves eager to obey the shoot-to-kill orders they had received, slaughtering and injuring rioters on every side, and the people responded with equal ferocity. Students and workers threw Molotov cocktails into police jeeps, incinerating the occupants, while women and children poured boiling water upon the uniformed men from windows and balconies.

Hospitals were unable to care for the great numbers of wounded, and many victims of the fray were tended by their comrades in makeshift centers at the scene of the fighting. Crowds of women of all ages marched in many parts of the city singing the national anthem and chanting *li-ber-tad, li-ber-tad.* Once again Education Minister Fernández-Morán addressed the nation by radio, pleading with students for an end to the riots and promising that if they would cease their activities their comrades would be released from jail. The strife continued.

Tad Sulzc reported to the New York *Times* that guards were removing a great many metal boxes from bank vaults, loading them on trucks, and carting them away. There was no explanation.

On the following morning, January 22, there was a decided lull in the rioting, perhaps from sheer public exhaustion, and the government may have concluded that the crisis was over. A few buses with armed escorts made their rounds. When some downtown shops dared to open for business, groups of workers and students hurled rocks through their windows. Several factories were set ablaze for the same reason. Tension increased steadily throughout the afternoon, with many bloody clashes between police and civilians in various parts of the capital, and the 5 o'clock curfew was again disregarded. At about 6 p.m. a rumor began to circulate that the Armed Forces had risen in rebellion against the dictator, but there was no confirmation.

Inside Miraflores Palace, which was surrounded by a large force of heavily-armed police, Pérez Jiménez relaxed by playing dominoes with Guillermo Pacanins, Governor of the Federal District. The dictator was once again very sure of himself. The public, he said, had spent its fury and must now subside. In a sense, he may have been right: perhaps the unarmed Venezuelan people could never have cast off the tyranny by themselves.

At about 7:30 p.m., however, Pérez Jiménez was appalled to receive word that all branches of the Armed Forces had indeed risen in rebellion against him and were demanding his resignation at once. The senders of the ultimatum were the Chiefs of Staff, meeting as a committee at the Military School, and their spokesman was Rear Admiral Wolfgang Larrazábal. Pérez Jiménez sent a messenger asking the military leaders to come to Miraflores Palace for a conference and promised to do whatever they might ask of him. He added that he would expect them at midnight. He then went home in his armored Cadillac to prepare his family for the expected journey into exile.

During his absence, Colonels Roberto Casanova and Romero Villate, who were present at Miraflores as loyal followers of the dictator, talked by telephone with Larrazábal, and the Rear Admiral invited both of them to join the rebellion. They agreed to do so on condition that they be included in the new governing Junta, and this was accepted. When Pérez Jiménez returned, he was informed that the Chiefs of Staff refused to come to a conference and that the only reply they wanted from him was his immediate departure from the country.

Understanding at last that he had no alternative, the dictator fled in near panic to La Carlota Airport where he boarded the presidential plane "Vaca Sagrada" (Sacred Cow) and flew to the Dominican Republic. With him, besides his wife and children, went several members of his official family: Fortunato Herrera, Soulés Baldó, Pedro Gutiérrez Alfaro, Llovera Páez, and Antonio Pérez Vivas. He was also accompanied by his military aide, Colonel Alberto Paoli Chalbaud, to whom he had entrusted a very heavy suitcase with instructions to make sure that it was placed aboard the plane.

Some time after the flight was under way, Pérez Jiménez discovered that the suitcase was not on board. In the rush to leave before being attacked by angry citizens, Paoli Chalbaud had left it lying on the air field. According to some reports, the ex-dictator flew into a rage and threatened to shoot his aide. Officials who found the suitcase understood why: it contained $1,087,074 in cash besides many bank books and financial records. The only item of clothing was his general's uniform.

Venezuela, for her failure to lend effective and determined support to the democratic and constitutional government of Rómulo Gallegos when it was attacked by a right-wing military clique in 1948, had paid for her apathy and indifference with ten years of totalitarian oppression and corruption. The achivements of the public works program, some of which were useful and worthwhile, would never compensate for the bestiality of Guasina, the torture chambers of Pedro Estrada, the lonely years of poverty suffered by political exiles, the destruction of labor unions, the neglect of education, the abandonment of agrarian reform, and the muzzling of the press. The "transformation of the physical environment", so touted by the dictator, was far from rational, and only a small part of the total price paid by the nation for its lesson in self government was the hundreds of millions of dollars in graft that had gone abroad to support the despoilers in luxury for many years to come.

We must also note that in January, 1958, as in November of 1948, October of 1945, and all previous instances of real and significant governmental change in Venezuelan history, it was the Armed Forces that played the decisive role in determining the political destiny of the country. The participation of the military in the fall of Pérez Jiménez, however, requires some interpretation, for it presents convincing evidence that the Armed Forces, like the Catholic Church, is indeed responsive to public opinion when such sentiment is strong, unequivocal, and united. Military leaders, like bishops and archbishops, are as much citizens of their countries as professors and businessmen, and although their hierarchical organizations have natural right-wing tendencies because of their authoritarian structures, they cannot escape a sense of identification with the general public. If such leaders are, like Archbishop Arias Blanco, sensitive to the mood of the people and to the trend of events, they can, and do, anticipate developments by adopting positions in which they can follow while appearing to lead.

In the case of the united campaign to overthrow the Venezuelan dictatorship, it is clear that although the Church delayed an unconscionably long time in declaring its opposition to the tyranny, it was still far ahead of the military in anticipating the degree to which Venezuelans were nearing the end of their patience. There can be no doubt that by January, 1958, the Chiefs of Staff, as well as officers in all branches of the Armed Forces had for months been reading the leaflets, manifestos, and position papers of the Junta Patriótica, many of which were edited and printed by members of the clergy after the plebiscite of December, 1957. Thus the Church had assumed a position of leadership in the movement at a time when military men were still considering whether or not to follow.

A measure of the responsiveness of the Armed Forces to strong public sentiment is found in the case of Colonels Roberto Casanova and Romero Villate, who had received the assurances of Rear Admiral Larrazábal that they would be included in the new governing Junta. It was well-known, however, that they had both served the dictator in crushing the New Year's Day uprising at Maracay. When their membership in the Junta was announced, public anger and indignation were so pronounced that Larrazábal, as Junta President, was forced to dismiss them from the governing body and send them into exile. They were replaced by two civilians acceptable to the country.

On January 23, after the departure of Pérez Jiménez, the long-suppressed fury of Venezuelans toward the secret police burst forth in a concerted attack on the headquarters of the Seguridad Nacional. Using rocks, gasoline bombs, and some small arms captured in the previous fighting, crowds assaulted the building for hours in the face of savage resistance from the men cornered within who were well armed and knew that they could expect little mercy from the enraged citizenry. When at last the doors gave way and the people rushed into the hated edifice, several agents were dragged into the streets and lynched by the crowd. On the same day, the SN building as well as the homes of Vallenilla Lanz, Fortunato Herrera, Soulés Baldó, and other minions of the dictator were ransacked and looted. Inspector Luis Rafael Castro, Estrada's infamous chief torturer of prisoners, later committed suicide in the Cárcel Modelo rather than face the many charges against him.

Chapter XII

Aftermath and Fallout

Ex-dictator Marcos Pérez Jiménez, who sought refuge on January 23, 1958, with Generalisimo Rafael Leonidas Trujillo Molina, remained under the protection of the "Great Benefactor" less than three weeks. On February 10 he left the Caribbean island to take up residence in Miami, Florida. The legal aspects of his flight from Caracas to Santo Domingo, and from the Dominican Republic to the United States caused much wonderment and comment by journalists at the time, and would later be of importance in the handling of the extradition proceedings brought against him by the Venezuelan government. For reasons never satisfactorily explained, and probably not fully evaluated at the time, the hurriedly-constituted Junta of Admiral Larrázabal issued a diplomatic passport to Pérez Jiménez for his trip into exile on the night of January 22-23.

His decision to leave for Florida so quickly was attributed by some commentators to a supposed falling-out with Trujillo. But this explanation is unconvincing, for it is known that the two leaders subsequently co-operated closely in an effort to overthrow the Betancourt regime in Venezuela. The real reason for his hurry was that the new Junta de Gobierno in Caracas could be expected at any moment to recall Ambassador Luis Chafardet Urgina, a Pérez Jiménez appointee and close friend of the ex-dictator, who was still the accredited representative of Venezuela in Santo Domingo. As it happened, Ambassador Chafardet simply requested the American consul in that city to issue a visitor's permit to a Venezuelan citizen holding a diplomatic passport. Normal procedure required the granting of such a request, and this was done in the case of Pérez Jimenez.

International reaction to the fall of the Venezuelan dictatorship was not lacking. Dr. Jóvito Villalba, the URD leader, who arrived in Caracas from exile on January 26, denounced the United States government for

its support of the Pérez Jiménez regime. Venezuelan students and newsmen demonstrated at the embassies of Franco's Spain, Salazar's Portugal, and Batista's Cuba because the governments of those countries had
publicly congratulated the dictator on the results of the plebiscite of
December 15.[1] Russia's *Pravda,* in a long editorial, hailed the fall of
the Venezuelan tyrant as a blow to United States prestige in Latin
America, and asserted that the Pérez Jiménez economic policy had
made the natural resources of the country a "source of wealth for a
handful of American monopolists".[2]

Representative Charles O. Porter, of Oregon, wrote a letter to President Eisenhower on February 13, suggesting that he congratulate
Venezuela on the overthrow of the Pérez Jiménez regime. The President
did not reply, but Representative Porter received an answer from
Assistant Secretary of State William B. Macomber, Jr., who wrote that
"While we are not in a position to intervene in the internal developments
of the countries of Latin America, we are in a position to feel,—and we do
feel—satisfaction and pleasure when the people of any country deter-
minedly choose the road to democracy and freedom".[3]

As for the alleged policy of non-intervention of the Eisenhower
administration, which did not prevent the President from congratulating
"His Excellency Colonel Marcos Pérez Jiménez" for his "wholesome
policy in economic and financial matters" while conferring upon him
the medal of the Legion of Merit, it is instructive to consider a letter
written by Eisenhower's Ambassador Fletcher Warren to Police Chief
Pedro Estrada after the crushing of the Maracay uprising of January 1,
1958. Mr. Warren, long-time U.S. ambassador in Caracas and close
friend of the Pérez Jiménez clique, had been transferred to Turkey
shortly before the event in question. His letter, dated January 10, 1958,
and sent from the American embassy in Ankara, after expressing
greetings in a friendly and personal way, revealed his point of view
toward the New Year's Day rebellion in the following paragraphs:

> Willa and I were suprised at the attempted coup but note that it
> was put down successfully and quickly. I wish I could come in and
> discuss it with you. According to the Paris papers, you must have
> been very much on the job, as usual.
>
> My cordial and most respectful greetings to your Chief. Willa
> and I send him our best regards for 1958 and trust that it will bring
> him his heart's desire.

Unfortunately Ambassador Warren's letter, which was found in the
files of the Seguridad Nacional after the fall of the dictatorial regime,
came into the hands of the editor of the Communist weekly *Tribuna
Popular,* of Caracas. A photostatic copy of the missive appeared in that
paper on March 15, 1958, showing that it had been typed on the official
stationery of the Foreign Service of the United States of America, with
the State Department seal in the upper left-hand corner, and the signa-

ture of Fletcher Warren in the appropriate place. Its authenticity could not be doubted.[4]

Tribuna Popular, which had resumed publication early in February, 1958, after a year of suspension, had clearly embarked on a campaign to discredit the United States among liberal and democratic governments in Latin America, and in world opinion, by providing evidence of the cordial relations that had existed between members of the Pérez Jiménez regime and U.S. officials. On March 1, the paper devoted an entire page to the montage of photographs, mentioned in a previous chapter of this study, recording the 1954 visit of Pedro Estrada to Washington, D. C.

One week later, the same publication reproduced a letter from Augusto Malavé Villalba, of Acción Democrática, to Under-Secretary of State Rubottom, expressing "surprise and indignation" that the United States had given refuge and protection to Pérez Jiménez and Pedro Estrada. The exiled SN Chief had by then joined the ex-dictator in Miami. On the same page, *Tribuna Popular* published a photo of Ike and the Venezuelan dictator smiling delightedly in each other's company on the occasion of the Conference of American Presidents in Panama in July, 1956.[5]

In retrospect, it was a remarkably unfortunate series of events, some clearly caused by inept diplomacy and defective intelligence in Washington, and others owing to bad luck, that led to the "Nixon incident" in the late spring of 1958. It is generally agreed that despite all that Venezuelans knew about the extreme and continued favoritism shown to their dictator by the American government, there was really very little ill will expressed toward the United States in that country after the tyranny came to an end in late January. A potential source of friction was the imposition at that time of "voluntary" restrictions on the importation of Venezuelan oil because of an oversupply in the United States, a measure often mentioned, but never put into effect, during the Pérez Jiménez period. This particular problem, however, was handled very competently by Washington. A high-level committee was sent to Caracas with facts and figures to explain the necessity of reductions in petroleum imports. The Venezuelan government accepted the restrictions without complaint, and the matter appeared settled. Unfortunately, the favorable impression created by this considerate approach was about to be nullified by a remarkable example of insensitivity in the State Department.

The Larrazábal Junta de Gobierno lodged no protest concerning the letter written by Fletcher Warren to Pedro Estrada, and the Eisenhower administration could easily have found some indirect way to express its regrets for the totalitarian sentiments of its ambassador. Instead, as if to exacerbate the resentments of long-suffering Venezuelans, the State Department chose the week immediately following publication of the Warren letter in *Tribuna Popular* to announce that the United States had granted visas to both Pérez Jiménez and Pedro Estrada. The Communists could not have hoped for a better opportunity to stir up hatred toward the United States. The recently-imposed restrictions on the importation of Venezuelan oil were now examined in a different light. The left-wing weekly suggested that the real purpose of the United States was to weaken the Venezuelan economy, while at the same time harboring Pérez Jiménez and his ex-policeman in Florida, so that the tyrant would be in a position to combine forces with Rafael Trujillo in order to stage a new military *coup* and return to power in Caracas.

If this notion appears absurd and far-fetched to the American reader, we must point out that invasion attempts by exiles were a fairly common occurrence in Venezuela during the long dictatorship of Juan Vicente Gómez, and had been carried out successfully in Cuba and elsewhere in recent times. In any case, the fact that the United States chose to serve as willing host to the exiles could only be regarded as a deliberate affront by the thousands of Venezuelans who had suffered at the hands of the Pérez Jiménez regime.[6]

In early May, 1958, Vice-President Richard Milhous Nixon, accompanied by his wife and staff, began his long-heralded good-will tour through Latin America. Although extolled as an expert in the foreign-relations field, he was reportedly "surprised and mystified" by the hisses and cat-calls with which the crowds greeted him in Buenos Aires and Montevideo. Treated everywhere with cool but correct formality by officials, the Vice-President could evoke little more than hostile stares from masses of ordinary citizens who seemed never to have heard of the slogan "I like Ike". If Mr. Nixon was in any way encouraged by the indifference of Colombians in Bogota, and the apparent apathy or docility of Ecuadorians in Quito, who did not seem quite sure of who he was or why he had come to visit them, he was shocked and appalled at the people of Lima, Peru, who knew very well who he was, remembered the benevolence of the State Department toward their dictator, Manuel Odría, and angrily shook their fists and hurled insults, stones, and over-ripe vegetables at him.

All of this was as nothing, however, compared to the reception accorded the Vice-President in Caracas. In the Venezuelan capital, Junta President Larrazábal, apprised of the extreme hostility demonstrated toward the American official in other parts of Latin America, addressed his countrymen by radio on May 11 to plead for tolerance and civilized conduct. There was complete freedom of speech in Venezuela, he said, but "tomatoes and potatoes do not constitute freedom of speech". If his words had any effect at all, it could only have been to increase the determination of the people to show the North American visitor no mercy.

What Mr. Nixon encountered in Caracas on May 13 was a howling mob of Venezuelans who gave every indication of wishing to tear him to bits, wreaking vengeance on the person of the Vice-President for all of the indignities and deprivations endured in a decade of tyranny. As if still involved in the liberating riots of the previous January, they attacked his car with sticks and stones, smashing all of its windows. When he emerged from the vehicle with his wife, they crowded close to him and spat upon him, screaming over and over the names of Pérez Jiménez and Pedro Estrada, and demanding to know why the United States wished to protect them. The mob continued to spit upon the Vice-President and his wife until both of them were covered with spittle from head to foot.

It is almost certain that if Mr. Nixon had not been constantly protected by Venezuelan soldiers armed with bayonets and tear gas, he would have been seriously injured, and he may well have been lynched. As it was, both he and Mrs. Nixon endured unspeakable indignities from the words and actions of the mob. He was forced to cancel his entire official schedule in the city, for the people would not permit him to "defile" the Panteón Nacional with his presence for the wreath-laying ceremony, nor would they allow him to give any speech.

Somehow the Nixons gained the safety of the American embassy, where the Vice-President stated to newsmen that he realized the vituperations heaped upon him and his wife were not meant for them personally, but expressed the "irritation" of the people because of the sanctuary the U.S. was giving to Pérez and Estrada. He declared that if there were an extradition treaty appropriate to the case between the two countries, he would be glad to turn both men over to the Venezuelan government for trial, and added that he "personally could not think less of either of them".[7]

Obviously it is not possible to condone the vulgar and despicable conduct of the Caracas mob on the occasion of the Nixon visit. The present writer has discussed the matter with many Venezuelan friends, and all of them, without exception, have expressed their disapproval and sense of distress over the incident. It is necessary, however, to place the event in its proper historical perspective. Mr. Nixon was undoubtedly right when he declared to newsmen in Caracas that the attack upon him had been mainly Communist-inspired and directed, "even though not all of the people in the crowd were Communists"; but he was equally correct when he said on a later occasion in Washington that the incident should serve as a lesson to the United States, and that it revealed the need to develop a more enlightened foreign policy toward Latin America. We must, he said, have an attitude of cordiality and support for the democratic governments of the Hemisphere, while remaining cool and aloof from the dictatorships. Obviously the Vice-President was now describing a policy diametrically opposed to the one practiced by John Foster Dulles and the Eisenhower administration, and it remained to be seen whether Mr. Nixon would remember it for the future.

As for the failure of the Larrazábal government to tender a formal apology to the United States for the shameful treatment given to the Vice-President in the Venezuelan capital, we must point out that Washington had never shown the slightest sign of contrition for its consistent support of one of the most brutal and corrupt dictators ever to rule a Latin American nation. It is true that it would have been diplomatically inconvenient, and even unthinkable, for a great power like the United

States to apologize, however indirectly, for the sentiments conveyed in an all-advised letter sent by an American ambassador to a Venezuelan policeman known to his countrymen as the "Jackal of Güiria". In any case, such an expression would have appeared hollow and unconvincing, for it was perfectly clear to the Caracas government that the sympathies manifested in the Fletcher Warren letter were but a faithful reflection of the attitude of the entire Eisenhower administration toward Latin America.

But surely it was unnecessary for Secretary Dulles to choose the week immediately following the publication of that letter, when Venezuelans were still angrily commenting on its implications, to announce the granting of visas to the two most hated members of the overthrown dictatorial regime. Undoubtedly it was that flagrant act, more than anything else, that made it impossible for the Venezuelan government to offer apologies for the "Nixon incident".

There is also the fact that those who attacked him had been brutalized by ten years of police terror, and the Vice-President, despite the expertise attributed to him in the field of foreign relations, clearly did not understand the hostility of Latin Americans during any part of his goodwill tour until he arrived in Caracas. In that city, he undeniably "got the message" that United States relationships with the rest of the Hemisphere left something to be desired. As American blacks have discovered in recent years in the struggle to win recognition of their civil rights, polite representations do not always move powerful government officials to deal fairly with just causes. Sometimes more strenuous measures are necessary.

Pérez Jiménez, meanwhile, had bought a palatial home in Florida. There, well protected by off-duty Miami policemen who were handsomely paid to guard the premises twenty-four hours a day, the ex-dictator lived quietly with his wife and daughters, entertained friends, and exchanged frequent messages with Rafael Trujillo in a vain effort to prepare a return to power in Venezuela. In the wake of the unfortunate Nixon episode, the former ruler also began to confer with representatives of a prestigious New York law firm concerning the possibility of his remaining indefinitely in the United States. Many U.S. newspapers chose the occasion to recall Eisenhower's granting of the Legion of Merit medal to Pérez Jiménez in 1954, although some conservative editors sought to excuse the blunder by saying that it was really John Foster Dulles, rather than the President, who had conferred the distinction upon the dictator. The administration was also under pressure from the Democratic opposition to explain why refuge had been granted to the two Venezuelan exiles in Florida, and on May 21 the Immigration Service announced an investigation into the status of sanctuary of Pérez Jiménez in the United States.[8]

At about the same time, Representative Charles O. Porter, of Oregon, said that he planned to investigate how Pedro Estrada who, unlike the ex-dictator, did *not* have a diplomatic passport, managed to obtain a visitor's visa to the United States while he was in the Dominican Republic. This matter was never clarified, and it is possible that some illegality was involved, as critics of the State Department suggested. In any case, the ex-SN Chief did not wait for his status to be examined. Although his wife had just given birth to a child in a Miami hospital, Estrada promptly boarded a plane for Switzerland. The U.S. Immigration Service stated that it would take steps to prevent his re-entry into the country, and announced at the same time that it had asked the State Department to provide affidavits bearing on the character and background of Pérez Jiménez to determine whether he should be considered an undesirable alien and required to leave American soil.[9] Here the matter rested for many months, and no further action was taken in the case for the remainder of 1958.

On March 26, 1959, Mr. Joseph Savoretti, director of the Immigration Service, told newsmen that he had ordered Pérez Jiménez to leave the United States with his wife and four children by April 15. The State Department, questioned on the point, said that it approved of Mr. Savoretti's order, since the Venezuelan could no longer be considered a "bona fide non-resident visitor".[10]

It is clear that the hard line toward Pérez Jiménez adopted by the American government in the early months of 1959 reflected the new political realities obtaining in Venezuela at that time. Throughout the final months of 1958, a hard-fought campaign characterized by complete freedom of expression and participation by all parties had ended in December with the triumph of Acción Democrática and the election of an older and wiser Rómulo Betancourt to the Presidency of his country. Both before and after the election, the *adeco* leader made no secret of his firm intention to bring legal action in the United States to force the extradition of the exiled tyrant to answer for his crimes in his own land. It was perhaps partly with a view to the avoidance of the long and costly extradition proceedings that the U.S. government ordered Pérez Jiménez to leave the country by April 15. Attorneys promptly appealed this ruling, and the first "temporary" stay of the departure order was granted.

The deportation effort in this case was attended by many difficulties, not the least of which was the absence of provisions concerning political refugees in the extradition treaty between the United States and Venezuela. It was also a precedent-setting undertaking; no exile in the category of chief of state had ever been deported from the United States, and it would clearly be necessary to study all aspects and ramifications of such a case. The ex-dictator was known to possess enormous financial resources for the hiring of whatever legal talent might be necessary, and the famous custom of the American judicial system to permit endless appeals, and to postpone the execution of court orders and injunctions, was certain to work to his advantage.

Nevertheless, the new Betancourt regime made a formal beginning of the case on July 23, 1959, when Venezuelan Attorney General Pablo Ruggeri Parra presented his government's case against Pérez Jiménez before the Federal Court in Caracas. His petition was to authorize the chief executive to send an extradition request to the United States government. Three categories of crimes were alleged against the exiled ruler: 1) Crimes against the Treasury, 2) Crimes against liberty and persons, and 3) Crimes against public faith and national entities.[11]

On August 13, the Venezuelan Federal Court approved the petition and called for the extradition of Pérez Jiménez on civil and criminal charges, including peculation, electoral fraud, and involvement in homicides. Action in the case thereupon moved to the United States where the State Department was still attempting to require the departure of the refugee in compliance with the March 26 order issued by Mr. Savoretti. In an apparent effort to lend more emphasis to its request, the U.S. government charged that Pérez Jiménez had entered the country illegally in the first place. This assertion merely complicated the matter; the Immigration Appeals Board, after sending a special investigator to examine the charge, denied the contention of illegal entry, but nevertheless upheld the deportation order.[12]

Meanwhile, Venezuelan Consul General Aristiguieta in Miami, Florida, filed a complaint in the Federal District Court of Judge Emmet C. Choate, asking the extradition of Pérez Jiménez in the name of his government on charges of murder, attempted murder, and embezzlement. A summons to appear having been issued by the court, and ignored by the ex-dictator, Pérez Jiménez was arrested in his luxurious home on August 26 and held for several hours until he agreed to appear in court as directed. He was released on $25,000 bond, pending a formal hearing of the charges.[13] On the following day, at a press interview held beside the marble swimming pool of his Miami mansion, the exile blamed all of the extradition proceedings on the Reds who, he said, were "out to get him". He also declared that he was in no way worried about his future because he had "faith in the fairness and honesty of American justice".

Attorneys for the two sides were still filing briefs on the case when Pérez Jiménez gave another news conference on September 19. He accused the American press of not reporting the advances made in Venezuela by the Communists since the fall of his regime, and with little regard for the truth, stated that he had always abided by the Constitution of his country during his period of power. He observed that there had always been plenty of "law and order" under his rule, while Acción Democrática allowed Communists to organize and demonstrate freely. In this, at least, he was correct; the Betancourt government permitted much greater freedom for both right- and left-wing political parties than had ever been the case during the decade of dictatorship.

While his extradition case dragged on, Pérez Jiménez was content to remain beside his marble swimming pool and conspire with Trujillo agents in the hope that the Betancourt regime could be overthrown before his deportation to Venezuela. He came very near the realization of this hope on October 6 when President Betancourt sustained near-fatal injuries as an automobile loaded with dynamite was detonated at a short distance from him. According to the Caracas report, the perpetrators of the attempted assassination were Pérez Jiménez agents, and one of them carried a letter outlining the plans for the attack; it was addressed to the Dominican dictator.[14]

There was no further development of importance in the extradition proceedings until December 13, 1959, when Judge William C. Mathes, of the U.S. District Court in Miami, set strict limits on Venezuela's right to inquire into Pérez Jiménez' banking operations in the United States. Only information on transactions that took place on or before December 31, 1958, would be given, and then only on amounts of $1,000 or more deposited or withdrawn. Although this ruling was not pleasing to the Venezuelan government, it was not a serious impediment to investigators concerned with the embezzlement of many millions of dollars, and was probably made as much to protect the privacy of the bank's operations as those of the ex-dictator. With this, Venezuela's legal action against Pérez Jiménez remained almost in a state of suspended animation for nearly a year.

The conspiratorial activities of Trujillo and his Venezuelan colleague, unlike the extradition proceedings, apparently never stopped. Near the end of July, 1960, U.S. officials in Miami confiscated a letter from a Venezuelan courier who proved to be none other than Pérez Jiménez' old friend Luis Chafardet Urgina, former ambassador to the Dominican Republic. The letter, written by Trujillo and addressed to Pérez Jiménez, revealed plans for an attack on Venezuela by Dominican forces in order to restore the former dictator to power. The Betancourt government announced in Caracas that it had evidence that such a plan had been formulated.

On September 7, 1960, the long-delayed extradition hearing was finally held in the Federal District Court at Miami. The plaintiff was again Consul General Manuel Aristiguieta, acting on behalf of the Venezuelan government, and his American attorney was Mr. Howard C. Westwood. Concentrating first on the question of embezzlement, counsel for the plaintiff presented a 75-page memorandum of a general nature prepared the previous April which included a detailed study of Pérez Jiménez' personal known financial condition over a ten-year period. It revealed that in 1949 he had total assets of $33,730, and during his period as President his total salary amounted to $336,810.28. Yet, as already noted, he had attempted to take with him into exile a suitcase containing more than one million dollars; and in that same valise were found bank-deposit slips in his own handwriting that totaled $13,513,576. 39. Although the cash found in the suitcase was recovered by Venezuela, the amount represented by the deposit slips was not. This was presented by the plaintiff as clear proof of embezzlement. For lack of evidence, no mention could be made in court of the vastly greater sums, estimated to be in excess of $200 million, deposited in the dictator's name through the years in secret Swiss bank accounts.

Presented in court on the same occasion by the Venezuelan Consul was a supplementary memorandum, prepared in May, 1960, which focused on a particular instance of graft involving the purchase of tanks in the amount of $6,418,000. The memorandum contained evidence that Pérez, following the custom of such dictators as Batista, Perón, Somoza, and many others, had taken a 10% cut on the deal, a peculation involving more than a half-million dollars in this case.[15]

At the end of the hearing, Mr. David W. Walters, counsel for the defense, asked for dismissal of the charges against the accused on the grounds that the plaintiff had not shown evidence of probable guilt. The motion for dismissal was denied, the case was "taken under advisement" by the court, and another long delay ensued.

On June 16, 1961, in the same Miami court, Judge George W. Whitehurst ruled that Pérez must be extradited to Venezuela on the charge of embezzlement, but threw out the charges of murder and attempted murder. Since the extradition treaty between the United States and Venezuela provides that an accused person can be tried only on the charges under which he is extradited, the ex-dictator appeared to be safe from the consequences of the more serious crimes. Although the Venezuelan government gave assurances that his maximum punishment would not be more than sixteen years in prison, Pérez declared in court that he would be killed at once if he returned home, and his lawyers said that they would fight the ruling and continue appeals "for four or five years, if necessary". The accused was freed on $25,000 bond under a writ of habeas corpus and ordered to remain in Dade County, Florida, to appear at any subsequent hearings.[16] On August 24, on announcement of appeal of the case, his bond was raised to $100,000 at the request of the plaintiff.

More than a year later, on October 1, 1962, the Fifth Circuit Court of Appeals in Jacksonville, Florida, announced that it had taken the Pérez Jiménez appeal under consideration and that a ruling would be made in due time. The grounds of his appeal was that he had been denied due process of law. On December 17, the Appeals Court upheld the extradition ruling of the lower court, the ex-dictator's bond was revoked, and he was confined in the Dade County jail. His attorney immediately announced the filing of an appeal to the U.S. Supreme Court.

In April, 1963, Chief Justice Earl Warren turned down an appeal from Pérez Jiménez to be allowed out of jail on bail, and on May 13 the Supreme Court refused to hear arguments for a review of lower court decisions against him. In his appeal to the Warren Court, filed by attorneys David W. Walters, of Miami, and Eugene Gressman, of Washington, the accused man had two contentions: 1) that federal judges could not act as committing magistrates in extradition proceedings because their findings were subject to review by the Secretary of State, and 2) that financial crimes committed by chiefs of state were political offenses not covered by the United States-Venezuelan extradition treaty. The

Court rejected both of these contentions, turning the entire matter over to the Secretary of State for disposition according to court rulings.

It was clear that Pérez Jiménez, having failed to obtain a favorable decision in his case under the Eisenhower administration, which had always been so kind to him, could have little hope of more generous treatment from President Kennedy, who was known to be an admirer of Rómulo Betancourt and no friend of dictators. For this reason, the exile made a last desperate appeal to the Supreme Court to reconsider its ruling. This, also, was refused, and on June 17, 1963, the case passed into the hands of Secretary of State Dean Rusk.[17]

Secretary Rusk, whose aversion to totalitarian regimes always seemed markedly less pronounced than that of John F. Kennedy, dawdled for weeks over the signing of the extradition order. In July, the ex-dictator's wife, Doña Flor Chalbaud de Pérez Jiménez, bought space in many American newspapers to plead her husband's case, affirming that his return to Caracas would mean his certain death. The terrified exile, remembering Guasina, the torture chambers of the Seguridad Nacional, and his own merciless treatment of such political opponents as Leonardo Ruiz Pineda, Alberto Carnevali, and Valmore Rodríguez, was evidently incapable of believing that a government elected by the people could be more sincere and responsible than his own corrupt regime.

In his hour of need, Pérez Jiménez was not without his champions in the more reactionary sectors of the American political spectrum. Rightwing Representative Henry C. Schadeberg, of Wisconsin, loudly opposed the extradition. The John Birch Society rabidly denounced the U.S. government for its abandonment of this "staunch anti-Communist". And Mr. Robert Morris, former counsel for the Senate Subcommittee on Internal Security, and erstwhile legal adviser to defendant Delfín E. Páez, *perezjimenista* consul in New York, deplored the extradition proceedings as unnecessary and undesirable.[18]

On August 13, the State Department announced that Secretary Rusk, "after exhaustive legal review" by the department's attorneys, had signed the extradition order. Pérez' lawyers thereupon declared that they would make a last-ditch effort to thwart the order by supporting a paternity suit that had been filed against the ex-dictator in a Florida court. A young Spanish American woman named Ilona Marita Lorenz, 26, resident in Miami, had declared that Pérez was the father of her 17-month-old child, and she was suing for support. Obviously, it is impossible to determine, at this point, whether the exile had really fathered a child in Florida, or had merely paid the young woman to begin such a suit in order to frustrate the extradition effort.

Immediately after Rusk's signing of the order, three American lawyers employed in the case by the Venezuelan government left Washington for Miami to press for compliance with the State Department's decision because a Dade County judge, Robert Anderson, had issued an injunction one week previously, forbidding Pérez Jiménez to leave his court's jurisdiction unless he posted a $300,000 bond in the paternity suit. The State Department declared at once that if Judge Anderson did not withdraw his injunction in the face of Rusk's decision, a federal judge would dissolve it.

During the next two-day period, as authorized representatives of the Venezuelan government waited in a nearby hotel to receive custody of their former ruler to transport him to Venezuela, Pérez Jiménez attorneys haggled in court to have the entire case returned to the jurisdiction of the district court on the basis of the paternity suit. They even made a new appeal to the U.S. Supreme Court, asking for a ruling as to whether Pérez was a prisoner of the Federal government or of Dade County, Florida. A plea to Justice Arthur Goldberg for a stay of extradition failed, and the former dictator was turned over to agents of President Betancourt on August 15, 1963, flown at once to Palo Negro Air Field, Venezuela, under heavy guard and transported from there to San Juan de los Morros Penitentiary, in the State of Guárico.

The comfortable private quarters assigned to the fallen dictator, including a sitting room with radio, private bath, and patio, formed a striking contrast to the atrocious conditions endured by his political opponents in that same penal institution during his long period of rule. But his five and one-half years of luxurious living in exile, made possible by his looting of the Venezuelan treasury and the peculiarities of the American judicial system, had come to an end.

Chapter XIII

Conclusion

The present study, as noted in the Introduction, is offered as an interpretive history of Venezuela for the period 1945-1958, with emphasis on the struggle between the emerging liberal-democratic forces and those of the conservative-personalist elements, and the influence of the U.S. State Department in the development of that struggle. In previous chapters of this work, in analyzing the conditions and circumstances involved in the overthrow of the Gallegos regime in 1948, the electoral fraud of November 30, 1952, and the Pérez Jiménez *coup d'état* of that same year, we have found that the policies and practices of the U.S. government, together with the permissive attitudes of the Venezuelan military, the Catholic Church, and the Venezuelan people, were largely responsible for the loss of democratic government in that country, and the ensuing decade of dictatorship. In consideration of this finding, which is made without attributing any proportionate responsibility to each of the other American States, we begin this conclusion by setting forth some important differences in social composition and historical experience between the great English-speaking democracy of North America and the Latin republics to the south.

The United States, self-proclaimed leader of the free world, chief propounder of the Atlantic Charter freedoms, with the highest standard of living ever achieved on this earth, has arrived at its position of unrivalled wealth, power, and prestige through a most felicitous combination of circumstances and events. Blessed by an invigorating climate, virgin lands, and abundant natural resources of every kind, the nation-to-be had as its first settlers men who had come seeking freedom rather than gold. They were not only imbued with the Protestant-Puritan ethic of hard work, self reliance, and the hard virtues of narrow and rigid moral precepts. They were also the inheritors of an Anglo-Saxon tradition of human rights deriving from the Magna Carta which, in the New

World, would develop into concepts of political self-determination giving rise to the Independence movement.

The new nation, though apparently disorganized and chaotic in many ways, possessed the ingredients necessary for political cohesion rather than fragmentation (a predominantly white-Anglo-Saxon-Protestant social composition), even while it expanded from coast to coast through such empire-building notions as Manifest Destiny, and welcomed millions of white European immigrants who would contribute their skills and strengths to the building of an ever-greater and richer nation under one single federal government. Certainly democracy was not born in the United States, but in modified form it found in the free soil of America, in conjunction with free capital and free men, the conditions for vigorous growth as a part of the American way of life.

In contrast, we must note that none of the three ethnic groups that predominated throughout Latin America—Indian, Iberian, and African—had any social tradition of human rights and individual freedom comparable to that which came so easily to North America as a part of its Anglo-Saxon cultural legacy. Of these three groups, the Iberian element, which quickly assumed leadership and domination in language, religion, and social structure, was no less rigidly authoritarian and personalist in tradition than the subjugated American Indians or the imported African slaves. The religion imposed by Spain and Portugal throughout their New World colonies was, of course, Roman Catholicism which, as we have noted, is another thoroughly personalist entity which leaves little or no room for such democratic notions as individual opinion or personal preference, but demands complete and unquestioning obedience to the Church hierarchy and conformity to its doctrines.

During the long colonial period, Church and State were one and the same for all practical purposes. With few exceptions, very little happened, or could have happened, that could pass for a tendency toward responsible self-government. Nor did Independence bring with it any miraculous and sudden infusion of democratic principles and practices. Viceroys and the presidents of *audiencias* were replaced in most cases by war heroes who soon became dictators of one kind or another. Creole clerics took the place of Crown-appointed ecclesiastical authorities. Social stratification continued, and so did the autocratic ways of the new personalist leaders. Democracy could not grow from non-existent roots, and a few great leaders like Sarmiento could only set their countries on the path to self-government, but could not keep them there. With the removal of royal authority the former colonies lost their political unity, and Spanish America tended to revert to the social and political divisions of medieval Spain, with language and religion in common, and various caudillos struggling for power and warring upon one another, thus foreclosing the realization of Bolivar's dream of a Spanish American Federation, or a United States of Spanish America.

It is clear that democracy, so sturdy and well-rooted in the United States that it is taken for granted as a natural part of the American way of life, is a delicate and exotic plant in most of Latin America, always in danger of a sudden uprooting by the more traditional personalist forces represented by the military *coup d'état*. Unfortunately the pressures exerted in Washington by American investors and the U.S. military establishment have rarely tended to make the State Department more zealous in its support of democratic regimes in Latin America.

But why should it matter to the United States whether the nations south of the Rio Grande are ruled by representative governments or by dictatorships of the right or left? The answer is to be found almost exclusively in economic considerations. The record shows that American investors have been able to establish amicable, long-lasting, and mutually profitable relationships with right-wing rulers for the extraction of petroleum, iron, tin, copper, and other natural resources. By contrast, such "popular and revolutionary" regimes as those of Mexico, Bolivia, and Chile have tended to nationalize their mineral wealth, engage in hard bargaining with American extractors, impose increased taxes, and otherwise make investment in their countries less profitable. But the Communist regimes, as exemplified by Cuba, practice outright confiscation of foreign-owned banks, transportation and communication systems, factories, port facilities, etc., eliminating profits and causing total loss of invested capital. For the American businessman who has financial interests in Latin America, even more than for the average U.S. citizen, a Communist take-over of any nation in the Hemisphere is clearly an evil to be dreaded and, if possible, avoided. The question remains as to whether Washington's long-established practice of extending aid and support to right-wing dictatorships is the best means to this end; and even this is only one dimension of the problem.

Certainly it cannot be argued that any American administration has ever sought to export democracy to other nations through force, persuasion, or subversion, as the Soviet Union and the People's Republic of China constantly attempt to establish Communism in all parts of the world. Indeed, democracy, by the nature of the case, has never been, and cannot be, imposed upon any nation: if it is to exist, it must grow, slowly and painfully, from within. It has long been apparent that it is easier, in any given case, for a nation to pass from a fascist regime to a Communist one—*i.e.,* from one totalitarian form to another—than to change from either of these to a free and democratic system. It is in recognition of this fact, and through an interesting inversion of the practice-what-you-preach adage, that the United States, which practices democracy at home, has so often found it expedient to discourage the establishment of representative governments in other parts of the world. Democracy was reputedly born in Greece; but Washington, in the interests of NATO and perhaps with some justification, has so little faith in the capability of the present Greek nation to maintain itself as a viable democracy that the United States continues to support the neo-fascist regime of Colonel Papadopolous, accompanied by routine suggestions that the country should "soon" return to representative government. For similar reasons, but without lip-service to even a pretense of democratic considerations, this country has extended support to Spain's Francisco Franco for the sake of military bases.

It is interesting to note that in all the long years of American involvement in the practice of shoring up fascist-type dictatorships around the world, whether for the sake of maintaining safe conditions for investment or to impede the spread of Communism, neither the morality nor the efficacy of this policy has ever become a major political issue in the United States until very recently. Not until Viet Nam, which has involved neither the protection of democracy nor of American investments, but *has* cost the lives of 50,000 American men and countless billions of dollars of American taxpayers' money, did the United States public become indignant at the immorality and futility of this ill-conceived intervention. As for the supposed efficacy of U.S. protection of right-wing military regimes in Latin America as a policy to prevent Communist takeover, recent developments in Cuba and Chile are instructive as contrasting cases.

Fulgencio Batista, the last right-wing military despot of Cuba prior to the present Communist regime, was as corrupt, brutal, and greedy as Trujillo, Pérez Jiménez, Rojas Pinilla, or any other of the great swarm of dictators who have oppressed and despoiled the nations of Latin America. Batista, like so many of his kind, was wined and dined in his time by the United States government in Washington. His small but efficient military force was trained and equipped by American instructors at the expense of U.S. taxpayers. It is true that his rule was of no benefit to the average Cuban, nor to American taxpayers in general. It was, however, extremely advantageous to a handful of U.S. corporations and individuals who owned and operated Cuban sugar plantations and refineries, banks, transport facilities, night clubs, and gambling casinos. Yet the day arrived when the Cuban masses, led by a political adventurer named Fidel Castro, rose up against their tyrant and forced him to flee into exile with his illicit millions. The long-suffering people of that island, having had no adequate experience in representative government, passed swiftly from a right-wing tyranny to a Communist dictatorship.

It is not that the United States government had no opportunity to land a blow for democracy in the Cuban case, if such had been its intention and desire. In Cuba, more than in any other Latin American republic, Washington had had free rein to do as it would. After the Spanish-American War, as is well known, the island was for years under the direct rule of an American military governor, and until 1935 was subject to the provisions of the Platt Amendment. Yet it was precisely in Cuba, so long subservient to the will of the U.S. State Department, that Communism gained its first successful foot-hold in the Western Hemisphere.

Chile, located far from Washington, at the southern extreme of South America, presents a startlingly different record of political ideology and practice. The Chileans, having won their independence much earlier without the intervention of the United States, soon established an orderly system of self-government that has lasted almost 150 years. Despite her remarkable political stability, Chile had inherited the Iberian patterns of land tenure, social stratification, and other elements that have contributed to the general economic and cultural backwardness of Latin America. In this situation the nation has, in the twentieth century, moved slowly but perceptibly toward meaningful social and economic reforms. electing in 1964 the Christian Democratic Eduardo Frei Montalva, who swore to achieve the desired reforms within the democratic framework. In 1970, dissatisfied with the progress achieved by Frei, despite obstacles deliberately imposed by both right- and left-wing elements, Chileans finally elected the Marxist-Leninist Salvador Allende Gossens, who promised to nationalize the most important sectors of the nation's economy. Although it is still too early to judge either the record of Latin America's first freely-chosen Marxist president, or the fate of that nation's democratic heritage, it is certain that Chile, having established and maintained her political self-determination for a century and a half without the help of the United States, will have a much greater possibility of continuing on the path of freedom if she is unimpeded by the interference of such entities as the CIA and the ITT.

As for Venezuela, the future of representative government in that politically volatile nation cannot be considered assured even if the State Department and U.S. corporations maintain the most favorable and pro-democratic attitude imaginable. Venezuelans, perhaps even more than most Latin Americans, are socially turbulent, chronically dissident, and highly critical of the party in power. Despite the fourteen years of democratically-elected administrations since the fall of the Pérez Jiménez dictatorship—the regimes of AD Presidents Betancourt and Leoni, and the present government of *copeyano* President Rafael Caldera—the historical record is still very lopsided: Venezuelans continue to live, think, and speak much more within the tradition of personalist one-man rule than within the democratic norms of constant debate of issues and the presentation of conflicting points of view.

The people of Venezuela, like those of other nations, also tend to remember the virtues of past administrations, but perceive only the defects of present ones. During the decade of military rule, 1948-58, citizens yearned for the democratic freedoms that were so sadly lacking; but in the 1960s they rarely recalled Guasina, the SN raids on private homes, the torture chambers of Pedro Estrada, the electoral frauds, or the great peculation practiced by the dictatorship. Constitutional government and democratic freedoms, when present, are held in small esteem, and citizens are wont to assert that under Pérez Jiménez there was more employment; public disorder was not permitted; the bolívar held strong at 3.35 to the dollar under military rule, but suffered devaluation by the subsequent democratic regime.

Some students of Venezuelan affairs, including several investigators whose works are listed in the Bibliography of this book, have taken a favorable view of the record left by the military rulers of the period

1948-58. They allege, for example, that in 1968 Pérez Jiménez, living in exile in Spain after his release from prison by the Leoni regime the previous year, proved that he enjoyed popular support in Venezuela by being overwhelmingly elected to the Senate by the State of Táchira; that Rómulo Betancourt was, and is, a rabble-rousing demagogue motivated throughout his lifetime only by a desire for political power; that the post-Pérez Jiménez administrations, however democratically elected, have engaged in peculation and that they have a mediocre record of achievement in carrying out all of the reform programs that they propagandized so thoroughly during the electoral campaigns; and that Vallenilla Lanz was correct in declaring that Venezuela is a backward country of lazy and shiftless *criollos* for whom democratic practices are entirely unsuitable.

Some, but not all, of the above assertions are undoubtedly true. The 1968 election of the exiled Pérez Jiménez to the Senate from his native State of Táchira, a region with a longtime clerico-military tradition, is in no way surprising. It is also no more indicative of national standing than the election of Sam Yorty as Mayor of Los Angeles or that of James O. Eastland as Senator from Mississippi. As revealed by the documented facts presented in this study, Pérez Jiménez was never able to win a single national election except through the use of fraud and the application of police-state methods of intimidation.

As for Rómulo Betancourt, there is no doubt that he inspired violent hatred as well as great admiration among Venezuelans. He is likely to be a subject of controversy for some time to come, and it is probably too soon to attempt a definitive historical judgment of his accomplishments and career. It is true that a great many Venezuelans, especially non-*adecos* of almost any political coloration, have few kind words for him. Industrialists, land barons, and clerics remember his persistent efforts in behalf of organized labor, agrarian reform, and legislation unfavorable to parochial interests, and they denounce him accordingly. Political opponents, perhaps recalling that Betancourt often bested them, both before and after the decade of military dictatorship, in campaign oratory, parliamentary manoeuver, and organizational ability, condemn him as an astute and unscrupulous operator interested only in attaining his own objectives, without regard for the divisions and bitterness that he left in his wake. In short, it is not surprising that Betancourt, a conscious imitator of many of the methods and techniques of FDR, succeeded in alienating the corresponding sectors of Venezuelan society. Competent studies by U.S. scholars, treating the Betancourt administration of 1959-64, have already appeared. In another decade or two, when partisan passions have cooled and personal resentments have abated, Venezuelan investigators themselves may produce balanced and reasonable reports on the *adeco* leader.

The records of the AD and Copei regimes since the fall of the Pérez Jiménez dictatorship in 1958 do not fall within the scope of this study, but the allegations of shortcomings of those administrations as a rationale in favor of military rule rather than representative government merit some comment. Even if these democratically-elected governments, once in power, committed all the blunders, peculations, and criminal acts of which the military regimes were guilty—*a most unlikely possibility*—, there is still a vast and important difference in the context of governmental behavior and public reaction.

Since January, 1958, Venezuela has enjoyed freedom of the press, freedom of assembly, and freedom to petition for redress of grievances— in short, all of the basic freedoms that are the only guarantee of governmental responsibility in the United States. Certainly it is not the mere existence of a *constitution* that impels officials to restrain their cupidity or aggressive impulses; even the most repressive dictatorships are well supplied with these fine documents. It is, rather, the knowledge that their behavior is ever subject to the scrutiny of political opponents, that their failures and misdeeds will be fully reported by the news media, and that they may have to answer for them in court, or be voted out of office at the next election. Political processes in the United States are by no means free of scandals associated with campaign contributions, conflicts of interest, secret deals with big business or labor unions, padded payrolls, kickbacks, and even underworld connections. Yet few Americans will suggest that this country would be better off under a military dictatorship.

The notion that Latin Americans in general, and Venezuelans in particular, are somehow necessarily incapable of representative government must be rejected as unfair, overly pessimistic, and incompatible with the historical record. It is not that the Latin nations of this Hemisphere, in order to be acceptably democratic, must imitate the United states in their governmental structures and political practices. The histories of such nations as Mexico, Costa Rica, Chile, and Uruguay are convincing evidence that much variety is possible under the common principle of representative government based on certain indispensable rights and freedoms.

The central fact concerning recent and current developments in Venezuela is not, as some writers have asserted, the "oil revolution" alone. Of clearly greater importance is the way in which this natural resource is managed, or mismanaged, by the government of that country. The slogan *Sembrar el petróleo* can be a meaningful symbol of intelligent utilization, or a mere catchphrase for illicit personal enrichment and self-aggrandizement. Venezuela has had experience in both types of utilization and, as noted throughout the chapters of this study, the results cannot be expressed in terms of black and white. Even the most corrupt and tyrannical of regimes, not excluding even those of Juan Vicente Gómez and Marcos Pérez Jiménez, have carried out programs of lasting benefit to the nation. And even the most admirable of popularly-elected administrations have been guilty of waste, ill-conceived programs, and the subordination of the national welfare to political expediency.

But it is the finding of this study that Venezuela, like other Latin American nations, has realized, and can continue to realize, greater progress within the general framework of representative government than under any kind of totalitarian regime. Undoubtedly such self-determination would also redound to the long-term advantage of U.S. taxpayers and the American citizenry in general,—although not necessarily to the immediate benefit of those business interests engaged in the extraction of Latin America's mineral wealth. Will Washington hearken sufficiently to these realities, in resistance to the lobbying and blandishments of giant U.S.-based conglomerates with billions of dollars invested in those countries, the pressures of the Pentagon and of politicians and journalists imbued with anti-Communist hysteria?

The outlook is not reassuring. Despite the deplorable "Nixon incident" of May, 1958, in Caracas, and the Vice-President's subsequent statements in favor of a more pro-democratic U.S. policy toward Latin America, the actions and programs of both the Johnson and Nixon administrations are convincing evidence that the interests of the American "military-industrial complex", as perceived even by President Eisenhower, are still paramount in the determination of U.S. conduct toward the rest of the world.

But the Venezuelan people demonstrated clearly in January, 1958, that they were able to seize control of their own political destiny, force an end to an intolerable tyranny, and embark once more upon the path of self-determination. The Eisenhower-Nixon-Dulles policies had been a strong influence, along with Venezuela's own inexperience and divided interests, in prolonging a military dictatorship, but the will of the people themselves proved decisive. Venezuela is now in her fifteenth consecutive year of representative government, the longest such period in her history. With each day that passes, the possibility of a democratic tradition grows stronger.

Notes

Notes to the Introduction

1. Rómulo Betancourt, *Venezuela: Política y Petróleo*, Fondo de Cultura Económica, Mexico, D.F., 1956, p. 99.
2. Austin F. Macdonald, *Latin American Politics and Government*, Thomas Y. Crowell Company, New York, 1949, pp. 417-418.
3. Betancourt, p. 95.
4. Isaías Medina Angarita, *Cuatro años de democracia*, Pensamiento Vivo, C.A., Caracas, 1963, p. 22.
5. Betancourt, p. 134.
6. Edwin Lieuwin, *Venezuela*, Oxford University Press, New York, 1965, p. 58.
7. Edwin Lieuwen, *Petroleum in Venezuela. A History*, University of California Press, Berkeley, 1954, pp. 90-97.
8. Betancourt, pp. 152-163.
9. Medina Angarita, pp. 91-121.
10. Macdonald, p. 422.

Notes to Chapter I

1. Ramón David León, *Hombres y sucesos de Venezuela*, Tipografía Americana, Caracas, 1952, pp. 71-75.
2. *Ibid.*, pp. 76-80.
3. Ladislao Tarnói, *El nuevo ideal nacional de Venezuela. Vida y obras de Marcos Pérez Jiménez,* Ediciones Verdad, Madrid, 1954, p. 39.
4. Román Delgado Chalbaud began his military career in the service of Dictator Cipriano Castro shortly after the turn of the century. When Juan Vicente Gómez seized power in 1908, Delgado found himself supporting that tyrant. Although accustomed from birth to the personalist tradition and possessed by an unquenchable desire to rule his country, Delgado appears to have been convinced that he could also give Venezuela a more enlighten-

ed form of government. After World War I, seeing that Gómez had the support of the powerful U.S. petroleum interests, he decided to overthrow the dictator by means of a trick rather than an armed uprising.

In 1919, as Chief of the Armada, Delgado was stationed at Ocumare de la Costa in command of the Venezuelan "fleet", a tiny collection of cruisers, sloops, and other small craft used to patrol the coast. The flagship, a little vessel of Spanish make originally named the "Isla de Cuba" had been sunk off Santiago de Cuba during the Spanish American War. Refloated and repaired, it was purchased by Venezuela and renamed the "Mariscal Sucre". It was Delgado's plan to invite Gómez, on the occasion of the latter's birthday, to come aboard for a celebration, then seize him and overthrow the dictatorship. The old tyrant did not fall into the trap. Like Stalin, Porfirio Díaz, and other despots, he had an uncanny ability to detect seditious intentions. In this case his agents, sent to arrest Delgado on suspicion of treason, found a set of manacles, leg irons and chains engraved with the tyrant's name. The 90-pound shackles not only revealed Delgado's intentions, but provided Gómez with the means of ironic revenge. The naval commander soon found himself in a dungeon of the infamous La Rotunda Prison in Caracas, laden with the shackles he had intended for the dictator. For further details on this event, see Normand H. Dupray, *Aves de rapiña sobre Venezuela*, 2nd ed., Editorial Siembra, Buenos Aires, 1958, pp. 51-56.

In 1926, after seven years in the Caracas dungeon, Román Delgado was released. He lost no time in joining his wife and son in France and organizing a new plan to overthrow the Gómez regime. In 1929 he set forth in a ship named the "Falke" with the financial support of a millionaire Venezuelan expatriate, Antonio Aranguren, who lived in London and reportedly represented the British petroleum interests of Royal Dutch-Shell, the latter having been consistently rebuffed by Gómez in favor of American oil magnates. The plan was to sail secretly into the Caribbean, launch a surprise attack on the port city of Cumaná, capital of Sucre State, this action being co-ordinated with a simultaneous assault within the city by Delgado's agents who were to capture Governor Emilio Fernández.

The "Falke" set forth from Hamburg, Germany, heavily loaded with armaments purchased in that country, then picked up 125 Venezuelan revolutionaries off the coast of Poland. From there the voyage to the Venezuelan coast was completed without mishap. This adventure, like all previous conspiracies against Gómez, was doomed to failure. On Sunday morning, Aug. 11, 1929, Gov. Fernández led his troops in a furious resistance to the rebel landing which was thoroughly repulsed, though both he and Román Delgado Chalbaud lost their lives in the encounter. Financier Aranguren and Delgado's son, Carlos, both aboard the "Falke", then sailed back to Europe. The New York *Times,* Aug. 11, 1929, and for several days following, gives lengthy accounts of this adventure.

5. Ana Mercedes Pérez, *La verdad inédita*, Editorial Colombo, Buenos Aires, 1953, pp. 19-89, reports details of this meeting in the form of interviews with the military participants. See also Rómulo Betancourt, *op. cit.,* pp. 188-192.

6. Pérez, *op. cit.,* pp. 37-38.

7. *Ibid.,* p. 88.

8. *Ibid.,* p. 77.

9. Betancourt, *op. cit.,* p. 189.

10. Julio Diez, *Historia y política,* Pensamiento Vivo, C.A., Caracas, 1963, pp. 6-17, gives a full account of the Escalante candidacy, the Medina-López feud, and related matters. See also Laureano Vallenilla Lanz, *Escrito de memoria,* Versailles, 1961, pp. 215-221; and Betancourt, *op. cit.,* pp. 192-195. The government's point of view is set forth in Isaías Medina Angarita, *Cuatro años de democracia,* Pensamiento Vivo, C.A., Caracas, 1963, pp. 43-49.

11. Medina, *op. cit.,* pp. 45-46, indignantly denies that he had ever wished to establish Biaggini as a puppet President, insisting that it was his greatest desire to bring about constitutional reform that would result in direct election of the President by the people. Unfortunately, Medina destroys his own credibility in this instance by failing to mention the visit of Gallegos, or the AD proposal, acceptance of which could well have prevented the *coup* of October, 1945.

12. Medina, *op. cit.,* pp. 48-49, asks accusingly: "Why did Acción Democrática, which calls itself a democratic party, abandon the civic struggle for the barracks revolt? Why did Acción Democrática, which one year earlier, attacked in a public document the *coup* of

some sargents, support and stimulate that of some officers?" Dupray, *op. cit.,* p. 91, referring to the indignation of President Gallegos when, in 1948, a group of officers attempted
to interfere in his conduct of government says: "Gallegos forgot how, in October, 1945, his
party incited the military to revolt and to interfere in political matters." On the other hand,
Vallenilla Lanz, *op. cit.,* p. 233, makes an accusation in the opposite direction, asserting
that "Acción Democrática took no part whatever in the events of October 18. It was a
matter of military men."

13. *El Nacional,* Caracas, Oct. 10 to Oct. 17, 1945, gives full coverage to these events.

14. Medina, *op. cit.,* p. 175. Vallenilla Lanz, *op. cit.,* p. 223, lends credibility to this
assertion of Medina by recalling that on the morning of Oct. 19, 1945, he had urged the
President to send loyal forces against the insurgents barricaded within Miraflores Palace,
with the suggestion that "those people won't withstand a good charge." He quotes Medina
as replying, "Perhaps, but that would spread chaos and create for Venezuela a worse situation than we have already."

Notes to Chapter   II

1. Rómulo Betancourt, *Venezuela: Política y Petróleo,* Fondo de Cultura Económica,
Mexico, D.F., 1945, p. 199.

2. Rodolfo Luzardo, *Notas Histórico-económicas, 1928-1963,* Editorial Sucre, Caracas,
1963, pp. 136-138, reproduces the full text of the Communiqué. Luzardo calls attention
to the inclusion of the Soviet Union among the "democratic nations" mentioned by the Junta. It is, indeed, probable that the principal drafter of the Communiqué to the Nation was
Betancourt himself, and his youthful enthusiasm for Marxism comes readily to mind; but
it is necessary to orient the foreign-policy statement within the time and circumstances of
its inception. It is clear that the Communiqué was not intended for domestic consumption
alone, but sought to clarify the position of the Provisional government in international
relations. The term "democratic", then, may be considered diplomatic usage. The first
Russian ambassador to the AD Junta was Foma Andreevich Trebin, who arrived in Caracas on Feb. 12, 1946. See *El Nacional,* Caracas, Feb. 13, 1946, for an account of this
event. Betancourt's later writings make clear that he knew the difference between the representative democracies of North America or Western Europe and the "people's democracies" of Eastern Europe.

3. For details of these court proceeding, see *El Nacional,* Caracas, for Feb. 8, Mar. 3,
Mar. 16, Mar. 19, June 25, and July 15, 1946.

4. Laureano Vallenilla Lanz, in his previously-cited *Escrito de memoria,* p. 231, declares flatly that the entire anti-graft trial was based on the desire for revenge and political
advantage on the part of Betancourt and other AD leaders. He bitterly resented the inclusion in the crime list of his father-in-law, Dr. Adolfo Bueno, whose only crime, he said,
was having cured Dictator Gómez of a urinary infection for which he was rewarded with
a gift of land in Zulia State which later proved to be rich in oil. Vallenilla also accuses Junta
members of shielding their own relatives from the same investigation. Former President
López Contreras, *El triunfo de la verdad,* Mexico, D.F., 1949, offers a defense of his administration against the accusations of *peculado* and makes anti-*adeco* claims similar to
those of Vallenilla. Rodolfo Luzardo, *op. cit.,* p. 139, asserts that "It was indeed time to
turn back upon the old crimes, and to take account of the previous abuses of power. But
the way in which the measure was carried out proved to be impolitic because of the
magnitude of the lists and the errors in them. The result of haste necessitated by the very
circumstances of the moment." In the same work, p. 158, Luzardo says that the two ex-
Presidents, at least, should have been excluded from the defamatory lists out of respect for
the high office they had held. He states further that the ignominy inflicted upon the former
Presidents elicited public symaphty for them and contributed to the eventual downfall of
the AD government.

5. *El Nacional,* Aug. 31, 1948, contains an account of the devolution of property to 23 such exonerated persons. However, as pointed out by Luzardo, *op. cit.,* p. 158, this eventual absolution "would never be sufficient to repair the humiliation wrongfully inflicted."

6. On Oct. 18, 1948, shortly before its overthrow by the *cuartelazo,* Pres. Gallegos signed the Law of Illicit Enrichment, sponsored by his party, which contained these same requirements and provided severe penalties for financial betrayal of public trust. See Betancourt, pp. 228-229; also *El País,* Caracas, Oct. 19, 1948. This anti-graft legislation, fixing norms and prescribing limits for the financial behavior of both elected and appointed officials, placed Venezuela somewhat ahead of the United States in this respect. Few, if any, American administrations of either party have been free of the taint of financial scandal involving conflict of interest, lobbying, influence peddling, expensive gifts, or the diversion of campaign funds to private use. As of this writing, Congress has passed no effective legislation to control this problem.

7. For a severe and frankly partisan denunciation of the extreme negativism of Copei during the campaigns of 1946 and 1947, see Valmore Rodríguez, *Bayonetas sobre Venezuela,* Editores e Impresores Beatriz de Silva, Mexico, D.F., 1950, pp. 157-163. Valmore Rodríguez, longtime AD leader, was Interior Minister under the Betancourt administration of 1945-46 and President of the Senate in the Gallegos government of 1948. See also Betancourt, pp. 211-212. It is good to note, however, that the Copei underwent a meaningful change of political philosophy during the Pérez Jiménez tyranny of the 1950s. For an account of this evolution and the collaboration of Copei with the government after the fall of the dictatorship in 1958, see Robert J. Alexander, *The Venezuelan Democratic Revolution,* Rutgers University Press, New Brunswick, 1964, pp. 84-88.

8. *El Nacional,* Mar. 26, 1946, contains some typical URD speeches. Criticism and evaluation of this party are found in Alexander, pp. 97-104; Valmore Rodríguez, pp. 163-172; and Betancourt, p. 212.

9. On the shifting alliance, strategic manoeuvers, and in-fighting of the Venezuelan Communists between the October Revolution and the national elections of Oct. 27, 1946, see *El Nacional,* Oct. 22, 1945, Oct. 27, 1945, Nov. 30, 1945, Jan. 16, 1946, and June 17, 1946. See also Robert J. Alexander, *The Venezuelan Communist Party,* Hoover Institution, Stanford, 1969, pp. 9-16.

10. This method of balloting, and the colors assigned to each party, were determined by the Supreme Electoral Tribunal and published in the Venezuelan press. See *El Nacional,* Oct. 10, 1946.

11. Luzardo, p. 142.

12. Much of the trouble between *copeyanos* and other parties, including AD, stemmed from provisions embodied in the Junta's "Decree 321", on education, explained near the end of Chap. III. See also, Chap. III, Note 32.

13. *El Nacional,* July 20, 1946.

14. Betancourt, pp. 213-214; and the New York *Times,* Oct. 30, 1946.

15. Luzardo, p. 144; and *El Nacional,* May 9, 1947.

16. The Junta's view of Article 77 is found in Betancourt, pp. 216-217. For contrary opinion, see Luzardo, pp. 164-165.

17. Betancourt, p. 214.

18. *Ibid.,* pp. 220-222.

19. For election results by states, see *El Nacional,* Jan. 6, 1948.

20. *El Nacional,* Feb. 25, and Mar. 19, 1948.

Notes to Chapter III

1. Rómulo Betancourt, *Venezuela: Política y Petróleo,* Fondo de Cultura Económica, Mexico, D.F., 1956, pp. 243-245.

2. *Ibid.,* p. 252.

3. *Ibid.,* pp. 262-263.
4. *Ibid.,* p. 274. Despite the efforts of the AD government to establish such pilot-plants in 1948, and further efforts in the same direction after the restoration of democratic government in 1959, the present writer must report that he found, during the summer and autumn of 1965, that natural gas was still being burned off rather than saved in many of the Venezuelan oil fields. At night, from the highway that passes through the extensive oil fields of El Tigre, in Anzoátegui State, great natural gas flares could be seen for miles in all directions.
5. Betancourt, pp. 275-277, and *El Nacional,* June 22, 1947.
6. Betancourt, p. 300; and Alexander, p. 32.
7. Betancourt, pp. 277-285.
8. *Ibid.,* p. 313.
9. *Ibid.,* p. 317.
10. *Ibid.,* p. 322.
11. *Ibid.,* pp. 322-323.
12. *Ibid.,* pp. 334-335, and p. 821, Notes 5 and 6.
13. *Ibid.,* p. 339.
14. *Ibid.,* pp. 339-340.
15. *Ibid.,* pp. 344-349.
16. *Ibid.,* p. 352.
17. *Ibid.,* p. 357.
18. *Ibid.,* pp. 359-360.
19. *Ibid.,* pp. 330-331.
20. *U.S. Army Area Handbook for Venezuela,* prepared by Special Operations Research Office at American University. U.S. Government Printing Office, Washington, D.C., 1964, pp. 97-101.
21. Alexander, pp. 159-193.
22. Betancourt, pp. 366-368.
23. Luzardo, p. 157. Vallenilla Lanz, p. 273, ridiculing the AD government's pride in its irrigation efforts in the interior, asserts that in the Caracus suburb of San Agustín there was a pot-hole so enormous that the street was impassable and the people, using it as a garbage dump, nicknamed it "The 18th of October".
24. Betancourt, p. 375.
25. *Ibid.,* pp. 377-381.
26. *Ibid.,* pp. 385-387.
27. *Ibid.,* pp. 388-389. Note: the present author found in 1965 that, despite some years of AD control of industry, Venezuelan leather products were still fairly crude. Fine-quality purses, brief cases, belts, shoes, and similar accessories were still being imported from elsewhere in Latin America, particularly from Mexico.
28. *Ibid.,* p. 388.
29. *Ibid.,* pp. 390-397.
30. *Ibid.,* pp. 397-405.
31. Luis B. Prieto, *De una educación de castas a una educación de masas,* Editorial Lex, Havana, 1951, p. 115.
32. *El Nacional,* June 2, 1946; Luzardo, p. 145; and Betancourt, pp. 411 and 832, Note 3.
33. Betancourt, pp. 413-423.
34. *Ibid.,* pp. 422-423.
35. *Ibid.,* p. 439.
36. *Ibid.,* pp. 440-444.
37. Rómulo Betancourt, *Trayectoria democrática de una revolución,* Imprenta Nacional, Caracas, 1948, pp. 29-86.
38. Luzardo, pp. 141-142.
39. *Ibid.,* p. 158.

Notes to Chapter IV

1. Rómulo Betancourt, *Venezuela: Política y Petróleo,* Fondo de Cultura Económica, Mexico, D.F., 1956, pp. 468-469.

2. Normand H. Dupray, *Aves de rapiña sobre Venezuela,* 2nd ed., Editorial Siembra, Buenos Aires, 1958, pp. 87-88. Laureano Vallenilla Lanz, *Escrito de memoria,* Versailles, 1961, p. 274.

3. Rodolfo Luzardo, *Notas histórico-económicas, 1928-1963,* Caracas, 1963, pp. 149-150.

4. Betancourt, pp. 468-469.

5. *El Nacional,* Caracas, June 26, 1948.

6. *Ibid.,* July 5 and 10, 1948.

7. Betancourt, p. 467.

8. *El País,* Caracas, Oct. 19, 1948.

9. Vallenilla Lanz, p. 275.

10. *Ibid.,* p. 278.

11. Luzardo, pp. 154-156. As previously noted, Dr. Luzardo was acquainted with all, or nearly all, of the persons involved in this matter. He knew many people in the Armed Forces as well as in the government, thus had access to reliable sources of information.

12. All Caracas papers carried the text of this Decree on Nov. 21, 1948.

13. The best single source of information on these events is Luzardo, pp. 154-156. Others are: Vallenilla Lanz, *op. cit.,* pp. 280-290; and Dupray, *op. cit.,* pp. 88-92. Vallenilla and Dupray, although fairly accurate in factual matters of persons, times, and places, show little historical objectivity. Vallenilla's extreme right-wing tendencies, like the Marxist predilections of Dupray, have resulted in equally grotesque distortions in the interpretation of events. Anyone who still imagines that Delgado Chalbaud was loyal to the constitutional government of Pres. Gallegos and free of conspiratorial intentions should read the brochure of Rodolfo Luzardo, *Alfredo,* Tipografía Chacao, Caracas, 1961, p. 8.

14. Betancourt, of course, was not present at this meeting, but reports, *op. cit.,* p. 471, the verbatim dialogue of Delgado and Pérez Jiménez as recounted later by Mario Vargas. According to the Vargas account, Delgado thrust himself into the Presidency ahead of Pérez more or less by the force of his personality. According to Vallenilla, *op. cit.,* p. 291, who was also present, there was no disagreement whatever about the leadership of the Junta.

15. Betancourt, *op. cit.,* p. 476, asserts that "both fractions" of the Communist Party (*i.e.,* the Reds and the Blacks) also rushed to congratulate the Junta. Dupray, *op. cit.,* p. 93, declares that his Party did not approach the Junta, for it "did not wish to see itself accused of being a usurper, reactionary or fascist", and that it was only Caldera and Villalba who "dared to defy the wrath of Betancourt, and offered their collaboration to the new government". Vallenilla Lanz, *op. cit.,* p. 291, mentions the "almost euphoric Caldera and Villalba" at the time of their visit to the Junta, but says nothing of the Communist leaders.

16. Betancourt, p. 477. Valmore Rodríguez was eventually released by the Junta when it appeared certain that he had no hope of survival. Taken by ship to the United States, he made a surprising recovery, living for six years in exile and working to restore constitutional government in Venezuela.

17. Luis Colmenares Díaz, *La espada y el incensario, la Iglesia bajo Pérez Jiménez,* Caracas, 1961, p. 5, begins his book with the statement: "On November 24, 1948, Col. Sam (*sic*) Adams, military attache of the United States Embassy in Caracas, arrived at the Ministry of Defense; he was going to direct the overthrow of the government of Rómulo Gallegos, elected eight months earlier by popular vote." This version of the event, without basis in fact, persists in Venezuela to the present day.

18. The New York *Times,* Dec. 7, 1948.

19. Jose Rodríguez, *¿Quién derrocó a Gallegos?,* Tipografía Garrido, Caracas, 1961, p. 7.

20. Ramón David León, *Hombres y sucesos de Venezuela,* Tipografía Americana, Caracas, 1952, pp. 57-68. See also Vallenilla Lanz, *op. cit.,* pp. 289-290; and Dupray, *op. cit.,* p. 91.

21. León, pp. 58-59.

22. Vallenilla Lanz, p. 307. This charge against Betancourt appears to have been made first by Federico Landaeta, *Cuando reinaron las sombras,* Madrid, 1955, p. 45. Landaeta, an apologist for the most reactionary and brutal of Venezuela's military regimes, including that of Juan Vicente Gómez, speaks of "eighty-seven million dollars that Betancourt sent to Canada for his expenses." Neither Landaeta nor Vallenilla offers any proof for these damaging assertions.

23. Luzardo, pp. 159-162.

24. *Documentos oficiales relativos al movimiento militar del 24 de noviembre de 1948,* Oficina Nacional de Información y Publicaciones, Caracas, 1949. This work contains various statements, proclamations, and decrees issued by the Junta of Delgado Chalbaud during its first year in power. Also included are reprints of several press conferences in which Delgado, Pérez Jiménez, and Llovera Páez attempt to explain and justify the *coup* of Nov. 24, 1948.

25. Betancourt, pp. 231-287.

26. Betancourt, p. 469. The question of recognition as an instrument of U.S. foreign policy is a much-debated matter. For more on the subject of recognition of dictatorial regimes, see J. Lloyd Mecham, *A Survey of United States-Latin American Relations,* Houghton Mifflin Company, New York, 1965, pp. 175 and *ff.* Prof. Mecham, who sees little wrong and much to praise in U.S. policy in Latin America, avoids mention of the State Department's recognition of the Odría regime. He finds that Latin America itself is largely, if not wholly, to blame for the failure to "use non-recognition as an instrument in defense of democratic practices and principles." A more forthright and perceptive evaluation of the matter is found in Jerome Slater, *The OAS and United States Foreign Policy,* Ohio University Press, Athens, 1967, p. 243 and p. 261, Note 10. Slater points out that the phrasing of Resolution 35 of the Final Act of the Bogotá Charter "could be, and in fact was, later used to legitimize United States diplomatic recognition of Latin American dictatorships coming to power in *coups* against democratic governments."

27. Luzardo, p. 152.

28. Colmenares Díaz, *op. cit.,* devotes his entire book to a denunciation of the alleged "fascist sympathies and anti-democratic doctrines" of the Catholic Church in Venezuela.

Notes to Chapter V

1. The New York *Times,* Dec. 7, 1948.

2. *El Heraldo,* Caracas, Nov. 25, 1948.

3. Rómulo Betancourt, *Venezuela: Política y Petróleo,* Fondo de Cultura Económica, Mexico, D.F., 1956, p. 478.

4. Laureano Vallenilla Lanz, *Escrito de memoria,* Versailles, 1961, p. 295.

5. *Ibid.,* p. 299. See also Rodolfo Luzardo, *Alfredo,* Tipografía Chacao, Caracas, 1961, p. 9, on a plot to kidnap Betancourt on the plane which was to take him from Maiquetía to Curaçao.

6. J. Lloyd Mecham, *A Survey of United States-Latin American Relations,* Houghton Mifflin Company, New York, 1965, pp. 175-176.

7. *El Universal,* Caracas, Jan. 22, 1949.

8. *El libro negro de la dictadura. Venezuela bajo el signo del terror, 1948-1952.* Written and published by the Comité Ejecutivo del Partido Acción Democrática, Editorial Centauro, Mexico, D.F., 1952, p. 273.

9. Betancourt, pp. 523-524.

10. Robert J. Alexander, *The Venezuelan Democratic Revolution,* New Brunswick, Rutgers University Press, 1964, p. 38.

11. Betancourt, pp. 524-529.

12. *Libro negro de la dictadura,* pp. 268-276.

13. *El Universal,* Jan. 13, 1949; and the New York *Times,* Jan. 13, 1949.
14. Betancourt, pp. 539-542.
15. The New York *Times,* Mar. 29, 1949, and Mar. 31, 1949.
16. *El Nacional,* Apr. 20, 1949; and the New York *Times,* Apr. 20, 1949.
17. *El Universal,* Jan. 28, 1949.
18. The New York *Times,* Jan. 24, 1949.
19. *El libro negro de la dictadura,* pp. 153-197.
20. Betancourt, pp. 479-482.
21. *Libro negro de la dictadura,* pp. 119-122, and 153-154.
22. *El Nacional,* June 29, 1949.
23. Betancourt, pp. 647-650.
24. The New York *Times,* Sept. 28, 1949.
25. *Ibid.,* Feb. 16, 1950.
26. *Ibid.,* Mar. 10, 1950.
27. Vallenilla Lanz, pp. 315-316.
28. *El Nacional,* Mar. 24, 1950.
29. *Ibid.,* Mar. 31, 1950.
30. *Ibid.,* Apr. 14, 1950.
31. *El Universal,* Apr. 22, 1950; and New York *Times,* Apr. 26, 1950.
32. *Ibid.,* May 4, 1950.
33. *El Nacional,* May 7, 1950.
34. *Ibid.,* May 14, 1950.
35. Betancourt, pp. 483-484.
36. *Ibid.,* p. 483.
37. Vallenilla Lanz, p. 318.

Notes to Chapter VI

1. *Sumario del juicio seguido a las personas indiciadas de haber cometido el asesinato del Coronel Carlos Delgado Chalbaud, Presidente de la Junta Militar de Gobierno.* Oficina Nacional de Información y Publicaciones, Caracas, 1951.

2. Another figure, not heretofore mentioned, formed a clear link between Pérez Jiménez and Rafael Simón Urbina. Víctor José Cedillo, personal secretary to the Defense Minister, had also served Urbina in the same capacity several years previously. An implacable enemy of democratic institutions, and an unconditional admirer of police-state methods and military strongmen, Cedillo was later to be decorated by Spanish Dictator Francisco Franco for services rendered to the fascist cause. As former secretary and hanger-on of Delgado's assassin, the Defense Minister's secretary must have known very well the kind of persuasions by which the flamboyant Urbina could be made the principal actor in the plot against the President. Author of a collection of mediocre verse entitled *El cofre de la Cenicienta,* Cedillo was best known for the great quantity of political satire and personal invective that he published in the Caracas press against opponents of the military regime. In March, 1954, nearly four years after the death of her husband, Sra. de Delgado Chalbaud wrote from London an open letter to Pérez Jiménez accusing him of planning the crime and pointing out the obvious function of liaison performed by Víctor José Cedillo in that plot. This letter, although not published by any Venezuelan paper, was widely reproduced elsewhere in Latin America, and elicited from Cedillo a virulent denunciation of Delgado's widow which the Caracas press was required to print. See Rómulo Betancourt, *Venezuela: Política y Petróleo,* Fondo de Cultura Economica, Mexico, D.F., 1956, pp. 844-847.

3. *El Universal,* Caracas, Dec. 4, 1951. The principal sources for study of the Delgado assassination, in addition to the above-listed *Sumario,* are: Betancourt, pp. 482-485 and 844-847; Dupray, the entire book; Rodolfo Luzardo, *Notas histórico-económicas, 1928-*

1963, Editorial Sucre, Caracas, 1963, pp. 168-169; and Laureano Vallenilla Lanz, *Escrito de memoria*, Versailles, 1961, pp. 318-327.

4. Vallenilla Lanz, pp. 323-325, naturally reports this matter in a somewhat different light. According to him, Dr. Gabaldón, from Trujillo State, was about to fill all of the government posts with *trujillanos*, whether competent or not. To belittle the Gabaldón candidacy, Vallenilla also informs us that Pérez Jiménez had already offered it, as one might offer a theater ticket, first to Foreign Minister Luis Emilio Gómez Ruiz, and then to Minister of Public Works Gerardo Sansón; both allegedly turned it down.

5. *El Nacional*, Caracas, Nov. 28, 1950.

Notes to Chapter VII

1. *El Nacional*, Caracas, Nov., 28, 1950.
2. Only slightly less unfortunate were the other appointments: Pedro Emilio Herrera as Minister of Development, Carlos Tinoco Rodil as Minister of Labor, Pedro José Lara Peña to the Ministry of Agriculture, and Simón Becerra in the Education Ministry.
3. *El Nacional*, Feb. 2, 1951.
4. *Ibid.*, Apr. 19, 1951.
5. *Ibid.*, May 19, 1951.
6. *Ibid.*, May 20, 1951.
7. *Ibid.*, May 10, 1051.
8. The New York *Times*, July 28, 1951.
9. *Ibid.*, Apr. 21, 1951; and Betancourt, *Venezuela: Política y Petróleo*, Fondo de Cultura Económica, Mexico, D.F., 1956, pp. 486 and 847-849.
10. *Libro negro de la dictadura*, p. 91. According to this source, Adolfo Salvi was Governor of Cojedes State for only a few months, but during that time was able to accumulate more than one million bolivars through a partnership in a construction business to which he granted contracts for the erection of public buildings in the city.
11. Edwin Lieuwen, *Venezuela*, Oxford University Press, New York, 1965, p. 142.
12. Laureano Vallenilla Lanz, *Escrito de memoria*, Versailles, 1961, pp. 331-332.
13. *El Nacional*, Sept. 1, 1951.
14. *Ibid.*, Oct. 7, 1951.
15. The New York *Times*, Oct. 13 and Oct. 14, 1951.
16. Valmore Rodríguez, former Senate President exiled in New York, wrote a letter to the New York *Times*, Oct. 21, 1951, in which he denied that Acción Democrática used or approved of terroristic methods of any kind. He denounced the Junta's reports of the riots as an attempt to justify a personal dictatorship by Pérez Jiménez. Betancourt, *op. cit.*, pp. 487-488, offers a similar interpretation. On the other hand, Vallenilla Lanz, *op. cit.*, p. 332, represents the Columbus Day incident as an authentic attempt on the lives of his Junta friends.
17. *El Nacional*, Oct. 14, 1951. See also Betancourt, *op. cit.*, p. 488.
18. *El Nacional*, Oct. 22, 1951; and Betancourt, *op. cit.*, p. 489.
19. *El Nacional*, Oct. 31, 1951. Both letters were published verbatim.
20. *Ibid.*, Jan. 31 and Feb. 23, 1952.
21. Vallenilla Lanz, pp. 332-333, mentions a "heated debate" in the Council of Ministers as to whether students should be sent to Guasina. According to him, Foreign Relations Minister Gómez Ruiz registered such strong objection that students were excepted from this extreme punishment. However, José Vicente Abreu, *Se llamaba SN*, Editorial Arte, Caracas, 1964, *2nd ed.*, pp. 231-254, lists many students in the first shipment, as well as in subsequent ones. See also *Libro negro de la dictadura*, pp. 194-197; and Betancourt, *op. cit.*, pp. 490-500. It is from these three books that most of our information on Guasina is derived.
22. *Libro negro de la dictadura*, p. 181.

23. Abreu, pp. 158-159.

24. *El Nacional,* Feb. 28, 1952.

25. *Ibid.,* Mar. 27, 1952.

26. Betancourt, p. 632.

27. The New York *Times,* Apr. 16, 1952, carries the report of the alleged plot. The same paper, May 17, 1952, prints a letter from Prof. Robert J. Alexander on the same subject; and on June 30, a letter from Valmore Rodríguez on this and related matters.

28. *Ibid.,* Nov. 23, 1952.

29. *Ibid.,* Apr. 7, 1952.

30. See, for example, Alfred P. Jankus and Neil M. Malloy, *Venezuela, Land of Opportunity,* Pageant Press, Inc., New York, 1956; also specifically for 1952, the New York *Times,* Jan. 4, 1952.

31. Betancourt, pp. 590-592.

32. *El Nacional,* Aug. 30, 1952.

33. Betancourt, p. 552.

34. *Ibid.,* p. 552; and *El Universal,* Caracas, Sept. 30, 1952.

35. *El Universal,* Oct. 2, 1952; and Betancourt, p. 552.

36. The main sources of information on the life and death of Ruiz Pineda are: Rodolfo Luzardo, *Alfredo,* previously cited; Betancourt, *op. cit.,* pp. 553-554 and 854-856. Falsified reports appear in *El Universal,* Oct. 22, 1952, and in Vallenilla Lanz, *op. cit.,* p. 336. The collected writings of Pineda have been edited by Ramón J. Velásquez, editor of *El Nacional,* and published in book form: Leonardo Ruiz Pineda, *Ventanas al Mundo,* Editorial Arte, Caracas, 1961.

Notes to Chapter VIII

1. Mario Briceño Iragorri, *Sentido y vigencia del 30 de noviembre,* Editorial Doctrina, Caracas, 1961, p. 42. In a manifesto dated Sept. 13, 1952, Rómulo Betancourt set forth the official position of Acción Democrática with respect to the Nov. 30 election. In that document AD published some 100 telegrams that had been sent to various officials from Interior Minister Llovera Páez which indicated that a massive electoral fraud on the part of the government could be anticipated. It was for this reason that AD recommended a boycott of the election. The manifesto made clear that *adecos* within Venezuela were free to vote for other candidates, such as those of URD or Copei, if it appeared that such action might "contribute to the recuperation of national sovereignty." See Betancourt, *Venezuela: Política y Petróleo,* Fondo de Cultura Económica, Mexico, D.F., 1956, p. 550.

2. Briceño Iragorri, p. 44.

3. *Ibid.,* p. 46.

4. Laureano Vallenilla Lanz, *Escrito de memoria,* Versailles, 1961, p. 343.

5. Betancourt, pp. 554 and 856.

6. Cited in Betancourt, p. 551.

7. Cited in Betancourt, p. 551.

8. *El Universal,* Caracas, Nov. 21, 1952.

9. *Ibid.,* Nov. 27, 1952.

10. Vallenilla Lanz, p. 344 and *ff.*

11. *Ibid.,* p. 345.

12. *El Universal,* Dec. 1, 1952.

13. The New York *Times,* Dec. 2, 1952.

14. Vallenilla Lanz, pp. 347 and 350.

15. Reproduced in Mario Briceño Iragorri, pp. 58-59; also in Betancourt, pp. 558-559.

16. Rodolfo Luzardo, *Notas histórico-económicas, 1928-1963,* Editorial Sucre, Caracas, 1963, pp. 170-171.

17. Betancourt, p. 560; and Vallenilla Lanz, p. 355.

18. The New York *Times*, Dec. 3, 1952.
19. Mariano Arcaya, *Ante una infamia*, Caracas, 1963, p. 5; also Vallenilla Lanz, p. 363.
20. Luzardo, p. 171; and Vallenilla Lanz, pp. 356-357.
21. Betancourt, p. 558; and Vallenilla Lanz, pp. 356-357.
22. Quoted in Betancourt, p. 559.
23. The New York *Times*, Dec. 5, 1952.
24. *El Universal*, Dec. 6, 1952. On impounding of the ballot boxes, see Briceño Iragorri, *op. cit.*, pp. 63 and 79. It is significant that Vallenilla Lanz does not mention his confiscation of the electoral evidence. He does assert, *op. cit.*, p. 357, that "friends of the regime have gone to various places in the interior with the object of supervising the count. There have been frauds in favor of the opposition candidates whose victory all over the country is not as overwhelming as they have claimed."
25. Vallenilla Lanz, pp. 365-366. Dr. Caldera, President of Venezuela at this writing, has left no known record of the alleged interview with Vallenilla.
26. *Ibid.*, pp. 366-367; also Briceño Iragorri, p. 64.
27. *El Universal* and *El Nacional*, Dec. 17, 1952.
28. Betancourt, pp. 560-561; also Briceño Iragorri, p. 64.
29. Vallenilla Lanz, p. 371, makes much of the fact that, as Interior Minister, he adhered strictly to the letter of the Electoral Law in opening the Constituent Assembly on Jan. 9, since the text had stated that it should take place "40 days after the election". The political opposition, he said, had forgotten that December has 31 days, and had therefore supposed that the Assembly would convene on January 10.
30. Vallenilla Lanz, who privately admitted "without regrets" his masterminding of the electoral fraud, nevertheless attempts, without notable success, p. 371, to attribute to the activities of the Assembly some semblance of dignity, if not of legitimacy, by asserting that "everything took place with the greatest normality."
31. Vallenilla Lanz, p. 371; also *El Universal*, Jan. 10, 1953.
32. Published in *El Nacional*, Apr. 10, 1953, under the heading of "Disposiciones Transitorias".
33. *Time Magazine*, Apr. 8, 1953.
34. *El Nacional, El Universal,* and *La Religión*, Apr. 20, 24, and 25, 1953.
35. Betancourt, p. 858, Note 10.
36. *Ibid.*, p. 561.
37. J. Lloyd Mecham, in his interesting and well written book *Church and State in Latin America*, University of North Carolina Press, Chapel Hill, 1966, p. 110, leaps nimbly from an event of 1946 to the year 1957 with these two sentences: "The image of the Church was improved by its stand against the dictatorship of Marcos Pérez Jiménez. In a pastoral letter of May 1, 1957, Archbishop Rafael Arias of Caracas subscribed to labor's right to freely organize and share in the country's riches." It is obvious that the suppression of an entire decade of the Church record on social justice in this crucial period of Venezuelan history creates an impression that is, indeed, very misleading. Archbishop Arias wrote his pastoral letter several years *after* Pérez Jiménez came to power. We shall examine it in a later chapter.
38. Mecham, p. 248.
39. *Ibid.*, pp. 249-251.
40. See Jerome Slater, *The OAS and United States Foreign Policy*, Ohio State University Press, Athens, 1967, pp. 239-245.
41. Slater, pp. 121-129.
42. Vallenilla Lanz, p. 358.
43. *El Universal*, Apr. 25, 1953.
44. The New York *Times*, Jan. 30, 1953. An article by Sam Brewer attributes the "whispering campaign" to left-wing elements who wished to discredit the State Department. Briceño Iragorri, pp. 59 and 203-204, attributes the story to Pérez Jiménez himself for the reasons already suggested.
45. The New York *Times*, Oct. 12, 1955.
46. Betancourt, p. 557 and pp. 856-857, Note 7.

Notes to Chapter IX

1. *Memoria del Banco Central de Venezuela,* Caracas, 1955, p. 15.
2. The New York *Times,* Jan. 7, 1953.
3. Edwin Lieuwen, *Venezuela,* Oxford University Press, London, 1965, p. 142.
4. The New York *Times,* Aug. 30, 1953.
5. *Ibid.,* Sept. 13, 1953.
6. *La Esfera,* Caracas, May 22, 1953. Also the New York *Times,* May 24, 1953, and May 29, 1953; also Vallenilla Lanz, *Escrito de memoria,* Versailles, 1961, pp. 380-384 and 394.
7. *El Universal,* Caracas, Feb. 25, 1953.
8. Romulo Betancourt, *Venezuela: Política y Petróleo,* Fondo de Cultura Económica, Mexico, D.F., 1956, pp. 562-563.
9. *Ibid.,* pp. 563-564; and *El Nacional* and *El Universal,* June 12, 1953.
10. The New York *Times,* Jan. 26, 1953.
11. Vallenilla Lanz, p. 361, explains that Pérez Jiménez reminded him on assuming office that the old dictator Juan Vicente Gómez had always given orders directly to his police chief, and that he wished to continue the same practice. According to Vallenilla, his boss told him that he was "not built for giving out certain kinds of repressive orders." Vallenilla gladly accepted this arrangement.
12. Betancourt, pp. 571-572.
13. *El Nacional,* June 21, 1953.
14. Betancourt, p. 715. See also Robert J. Alexander, *The Venezuelan Democratic Revolution,* Rutgers University Press, New Brunswick, 1964, p. 46.
15. The New York *Times,* Sept. 4, 1953.
16. *Time Magazine,* Sept. 21, 1953.
17. Betancourt, pp. 579-581.
18. The New York *Times,* Dec. 14, 1953.
19. Betancourt, p. 579.
20. *Ibid.,* p. 580.
21. *Ibid.,* p. 577.
22. *Ibid.,* p. 582.
23. *El Nacional,* July 25, 1953.
24. Betancourt, pp. 635-636 and 868.
25. Vallenilla Lanz, p. 368.
26. *El Nacional,* Oct. 1, 1953.
27. *El Universal,* Oct. 21, 1953.
28. *Time Magazine,* Feb. 28, 1955.
29. *El Universal,* Jan. 2, 1954.
30. Rómulo Betancourt, "La Opinión Continental frente a la X Conferencia Interamericana", *Cuadernos Americanos,* No. 5, Septbre-Octbre, 1953, Vol. LXX, pp. 7-37.
31. Quoted in the original Spanish in Betancourt, *Venezuela: Política y Petróleo,* Fondo de Cultura Economica, Mexico, D.F., 1956, p. 568. See also The New York *Times,* Feb. 26, 1954.
32. The New York *Times,* June 23, 1954; and Betancourt, p. 568.
33. *Venezuela bajo el Nuevo Ideal Nacional,* Imprenta Nacional, Caracas, 1956, pp. 109-234.
34. Betancourt, p. 627. In the period 1950-1961 the Federal District received a total of 291,518 migrants from other points, including 126,745 foreign immigrants. See Chi-Yi Chen, *Movimientos migratorios en Venezuela,* Instituto de Investigaciones Económicas de la Universidad Católica Andrés Bello, Caracas, 1968, p. 188.
35. *El Nacional,* June 17, 1954.
36. *El Universal,* July 18, 1954.
37. *Ibid.,* Oct. 22, 1954. The text of the Eisenhower citation given in this work is translated from the Spanish version published in the Caracas press.
38. The New York *Times,* Nov. 8, 1954.

39. *Ibid.*, Nov. 12, 1954.
40. *Ibid.*, Sept. 15, 1955.
41. *Ibid.*, Oct. 28, 1955.
42. Rodolfo Luzardo, *Notas histórico-económicas, 1928-1963,* Editorial Sucre, Caracas, 1963, p. 172.
43. *La Religión,* Caracas, Nov. 13, 1954.
44. *Tribuna Popular,* Caracas, Mar. 1, 1958.
45. Vallenilla Lanz, pp. 403-404.

Notes to Chapter X

1. Rómulo Betancourt, *Venezuela: Política y Petróleo,* Fondo de Cultura Económica, Mexico, D.F., 1956, p. 534.
2. *Ibid.,* p. 535.
3. *Ibid.,* p. 536.
4. *El Universal* and other Caracas papers were given copies of this telegram by Vallenilla Lanz; they published it verbatim on Apr. 29, 1955, together with the reply from Pérez Jiménez.
5. *El Universal,* Apr. 29, 1955.
6. Betancourt, p. 852, Note 4.
7. *El Universal,* May 3, 1955. The regime's rationalizations of its conduct in the matter are found in *Venezuela bajo el Nuevo Ideal Nacional,* pp. 68-69.
8. *Venezuela bajo el Nuevo Ideal Nacional,* p. 27.
9. Luis Cova García, *Fundamento jurídico del Nuevo Ideal Nacional,* Caracas, 1955, p. 27.
10. The New York *Times,* Mar. 15, 1955.
11. *El Universal,* May 4, 1955.
12. *Memoria del Banco Central de Venezuela,* Caracas, 1958, p. 81.
13. *Ibid.,* p. 193.
14. *Idem.*
15. *El Nacional* and *El Universal,* Feb. 24, 1956; also Robert J. Alexander, *The Venezuelan Democratic Revolution,* Rutgers University Press, New Brunswick, 1964, p. 45.
16. Betancourt, pp. 657-658, bases his argument on an unedited monograph by J. P. Pérez Alfonso, *Nuevas concesiones de petróleo.*
17. *Memoria del Banco Central,* 1956, p. 24.
18. *Ibid.,* p. 25.
19. *Ibid.,* pp. 238-239.
20. *Memoria del Banco Central,* 1957, p. 261.
21. *Venezuela bajo el Nuevo Ideal Nacional,* Sec. IV, no pagination.
22. *Ibid.,* Sec. IV.
23. *La visita al Perú del Presidente de Venezuela,* Ministerio de Relaciones Exteriores, Caracas, 1955, p. 139.
24. *El Universal,* Aug. 7, 1955.
25. *El Nacional,* July 22, 1956; also *Tribuna Popular,* Caracas, Mar. 8, 1958.
26. *El Nacional,* Sept. 22, 1957.
27. *Ibid.,* Feb. 28, 1957.
28. *El Nacional,* July 7, 1957; also the New York *Times,* July 7, 1957. An additional satisfaction for Pérez Jiménez at the time of his quarrel with the Argentinians was the greeting received from Pres. Eisenhower, who cabled "felicitations and hearty good wishes to Your Excellency and to the people of Venezuela from the people of the United States."
29. According to Norman Dupray, *Huyen las aves de rapiña,* pp. 133-137, Herrera was one of the closest confidants of Pérez Jiménez, accompanied him on his state visit to Lima, and was exceedingly wealthy, having for years the monopoly of the Federal District lottery,

and a very large share of the race track profits in the capital. He reportedly owned several large buildings in downtown Caracas and had deposited many millions of dollars in foreign banks. It is a fact that he accompanied the dictator and his family on their private plane when they fled into exile on Jan. 23, 1958.

30. Mariano Arcaya, *Ante una infamia*, Caracas, 1963, pp. 11-13.

31. The New York *Times*, Feb. 4, 1956, and Feb. 5, 1956.

32. *Ibid.*, Feb. 22, 1956.

33. *Ibid.*, Mar. 1, 1956. In this case the *Times* erred in indicating Mariano Arcaya as its source of information. It was his cousin Ignacio Luis Arcaya, also living in New York, who provided the details on the student riots. See Mariano Arcaya, *op. cit.*, p. 19.

34. Arcaya, *op. cit.*, p. 32.

35. Various aspects of the Arcaya case are extensively treated in articles by Milton Bracker in the New York *Times*, June 5, 1956, and June 24, 1956. The most complete treatment of the matter is found in Arcaya, *op. cit.*, which is devoted entirely to it.

36. The New York *Times*, Oct. 28 and Nov. 1, 1956.

37. *Ibid.*, May 31, 1957.

38. *Ibid.*, Aug. 28, 1957. Tad Szulc, in a *Times* article of Nov. 12, 1957, reported that Pérez Jiménez spokesmen explained that Caldera had been arrested because it was feared that his influence with the Church hierarchy would result in increased clerical opposition to the dictatorship. Other sources indicated that the arrest had taken place because Caldera had refused to pledge that he would not run as a coalition candidate against Pérez Jiménez in the election.

39. *El Nacional*, Nov. 5, 1957.

40. The New York *Times*, Nov. 8, 1957.

41. *El Nacional*, Nov. 28, 1957.

42. The New York *Times*, Nov. 29, 1957.

43. Paul Hefferman, in a financial report to the New York *Times*, Feb. 13, 1955, wrote that the Pérez Jiménez regime was "entangled in financial practices that smack of the Dark Ages", and that "her fiscal slip is beginning to show". He explained that even at that time, there was no "visible control" of the government's unfunded debt and that no one knew how much it was.

44. Laureano Vallenilla Lanz, *Escrito de memoria*, Versailles, 1961, p. 453.

45. *Ibid.*, p. 451; also Normán Dupray, p. 23.

46. Alexander, p. 60.

47. Vallenilla Lanz was so proud of his editorials in *El Heraldo* that he selected a large number of them for publication in two volumes. See Bibliography.

48. José Umaña Bernal, *Testimonio de la revolución en Venezuela*, Caracas, 1958, pp. 92-94.

49. *Ibid.*, pp. 73-77, gives details on the founding, organization, and activities of the Junta Patriótica.

50. Vallenilla Lanz, pp. 453-454.

Notes to Chapter XI

1. The New York *Times*, Dec. 10, 1957.

2. *El Nacional*, Caracas, Dec. 16, 1957; also Normán Dupray, *Huyen las aves de repiña*, Técnica Impulsora, Buenos Aires, 1959, pp. 28-29.

3. The best source of information on details of the Venezuelan events of January, 1958, is José Umaña Bernal, *Testimonio de la revolución en Venezuela*, Caracas, 1958. Secondary sources: the dispatches of Tad Sulzc to the New York *Times*, and Vallenilla Lanz, *Escrito de memoria*, Versailles, 1961.

4. The New York *Times*, Jan. 7, 1958.

Notes to Chapter XII

1. The New York *Times,* Feb. 5, 1958.
2. *Ibid.,* Feb. 13, 1958.
3. *Ibid.,* Feb. 26, 1958.
4. *Tribuna Popular,* Caracas, Mar. 15, 1958.
5. *Ibid.,* Mar. 8, 1958.
6. Article by Tad Szulc in the New York *Times,* May 18, 1958.
7. *Ibid.,* May 12, 14, and 18, 1958. Richard M. Nixon, *Six Crises,* Doubleday and Company, Inc., Garden City, N.Y., 1962, pp. 183-234, presents the Vice President's own account and interpretation of his encounter with the mob in Caracas.
8. The New York *Times,* May 22, 1958.
9. *Ibid.,* May 24, 1958.
10. *Ibid.,* Mar. 27 and 28, 1959.
11. Dario Parra, *Venezuela: "Democracia" vs. "Dictadura",* Madrid, 1961, pp. 1-5.
12. The New York *Times,* Aug. 22, 1959.
13. *Ibid.,* Aug. 27, 1959.
14. *Ibid.,* Oct. 17, 1959.
15. *Ibid.,* Sept. 6, 1960.
16. *Ibid.,* June 17, 1961.
17. *Ibid.,* May 14 and June 18, 1963.
18. *Ibid.,* July 16, 1963.

Bibliography

Abreu, José Vicente, *Se llamaba SN,* 2nd ed., Editorial Arte, Caracas, 1964.

Acción Democrática, Comité Ejecutivo, *El libro negro de la dictadura. Venezuela bajo el signo del terror, 1948-1952,* Editorial Centauro, Mexico, 1952.

————(Seccional Zulia), *Un reto a la dictadura,* 2nd ed., Editorial Cordillera, Caracas, 1959.

Allen, Henry J., *Venezuela, a History,* Doubleday, Doran and Company, Inc., New York, 1940.

Alexander, Robert J., *Prophets of the Revolution,* The Macmillan Company, New York, 1962.

———— , *The Venezuelan Democratic Revolution,* Rutgers University Press, New Brunswick, 1964.

———— , *The Venezuelan Communist Party,* Hoover Institution, Stanford, 1969.

———— and Porter, Charles O., *The Struggle for Democracy in Latin America,* The Macmillan Company, New York, 1961.

Arcaya, Mariano, *Ante una infamia,* Caracas, 1963.

Arcila Farías, Eduardo, *Econômia colonial de Venezuela,* Fondo de Cultura Económica, Mexico, D.F., 1946.

Así progresa un pueblo (Anonymous), Talleres Gráficos Ilustraciones, S.A., Caracas, 1956.

Banco Central de Venezuela, *Memoria,* Tipografía Londres, Caracas, 1955.

————, *Memoria,* Artegráfica, C.A., Caracas, 1956.

————, *Memoria,* Artegráfica, C.A., Caracas, 1957.

————, *Memoria,* Artegráfica, C.A., Caracas, 1958.

Bergamín, Rafael, *20 años en Caracas, 1938-1958,* Gráficas Reunidas, S.A., Madrid, 1959.

Bermúdez, Roldan, *Aquella farsa,* Caracas, 1949.

Betancourt, Rómulo, "La Opinión Continental frente a la X Conferencia Interamericana", *Cuadernos Americanos,* No. 5, Sept.-Oct., 1953, Vol. LXXI. pp. 7-37.

————, *Trayectoria democrática de una revolución,* Tomos I y II, Imprenta Nacional, Caracas, 1948.

————, *Venezuela: Política y Petróleo,* Fondo de Cultura Económica, Mexico, D.F., 1956.

Briceño Iragorri, Mario, *Cartera del Proscrito,* Editorial Las Novedades, Caracas, 1958.

————, *Sentido y vigencia del 30 de noviembre,* Editorial Doctrina, Caracas, 1961.

Cárdenas, Rodolfo José, *El combate político,* Editorial Arte, Caracas, 1965.

Chen, Chi-Yi, *Movimientos migratorios en Venezuela,* Instituto de Investigaciones Económicas de la Universidad Católica Andrés Bello, Caracas, 1962.

Colmenares Díaz, Luis, *La espada y el incensario,* Caracas, 1961.

Cova García, Luis, *Fundamento jurídico del Nuevo Ideal Nacional,* Caracas, 1955.

Diez, Julio, *Historia y política,* 2nd ed., Pensamiento Vivo, C.A., Caracas, 1963.

Discursos y documentos oficiales con motivo del fallecimiento del Coronel Carlos Delgado Chalbaud, Oficina Nacional de Información y Publicaciones, Caracas, 1950.

Documentos oficiales relativos al movimiento militar del 24 de noviembre de 1948, Oficina Nacional de Información y Publicaciones, Caracas, 1949.

Dupray, Normand H. (pseudonym of Juan Bautista Fuenmayor). *Aves de rapiña sobre Venezuela,* 2nd ed., Editorial Siembra, Buenos Aires, 1958.

Dupray, Normán (pseudonym of two anonymous authors), *Huyen las aves de rapiña,* Técnica Impulsora, Buenos Aires, 1959.

Estados Unidos de Venezuela, *Sumario del juicio seguido a las personas indiciadas de haber cometido el asesinato del Coronel Carlos Delgado Chalbaud, Presidente de la Junta de Gobierno,* Oficina Nacional de Información y Publicaciones, Caracas, 1951.

Febres Cordero, Julio, "Génesis, infancia y madurez del periodismo en Venezuela", in *Universalia,* Vol. I, No. 2, Sept.-Oct., 1964.

Feo Calcaño, Guillermo, *Democracia vs. Dictadura,* Caracas, 1963.

Fergusson, Erna, *Venezuela,* Alfred A. Knopf, New York, 1939.

Foreign Areas Studies Division, *U.S. Army Area Handbook for Venezuela,* Special Operations Research Office, American University, Washington, D.C., 1964.

Furtado, Celso, *Obstacles to Development in Latin America,* Doubleday and Company, Inc., Garden City, N.Y., 1970.

Gabaldón Márquez, Joaquín, *Archivos de una inquietud venezolana,* Caracas, 1955.

———, *Gacetillas de Dios, de los hombres y de los animales,* Caracas, 1957.

———, *Páginas de evasión y devaneo (1948-1958),* Caracas, 1959.

Gallegos Ortiz, Rafael, *La historia política de Venezuela,* Tomo I, Imprenta Universitaria, Caracas, 1960.

García Ponce, Servando, *Apuntes sobre la libertad de prensa en Venezuela,* Cuaderno 15, Escuela de Periodismo, Universidad Central de Venezuela, Caracas, 1961.

Gil, Federico G., *Latin American-United States Relations,* Harcourt Brace Jovanovich, Inc., New York, 1971.

Hamill, Hugh M., Jr. (ed.), *Dictatorship in Spanish America,* Alfred A. Knopf, New York, 1965.

Instituto Venezolano de Investigaciones de la Prensa, *¿Qué publicó la prensa venezolana durante la dictadura?* Escuela de Periodismo de la Universidad Central, Imprenta Universitaria, Caracas, 1959.

International Bank for Reconstruction and Development, *The Economic Development of Venezuela,* The Johns Hopkins Press, Baltimore, 1961.

Jankus, Alfred P. and Malloy, Neil M., *Venezuela, Land of Opportunity,* Pageant Press, New York, 1965.

Landaeta, Federico, *Cuando reinaron las sombras,* Gráfica Clemares, Madrid, 1955.

León, Ramón David, *Hombres y sucesos de Venezuela,* Tipografía Americana, Caracas, 1952.

Lieuwen, Edwin, *Petroleum in Venezuela. A History,* University of California Press, Berkeley, 1954.

————, *Venezuela,* 2nd ed., Oxford University Press, New York, 1965.

López Contreras, Eleazar, *El triunfo de la verdad,* Edición Genio Latino, Mexico, D.F., 1949.

Luzardo, Rodolfo, *Andanzas de América,* Editorial Sucre, Caracas, 1962.

————, *Alfredo,* Tipografía Chacao, Caracas, 1961.

————, *Venezuela: Business and Finances,* Prentice-Hall, Inc., Englewood Cliffs, N.J., 1957.

————, *El Petróleo,* Lit. y Tip. del Comercio, Caracas, 1940.

————, *Notas histórico-económicas, 1928-1963,* Editorial Sucre, Caracas,

————, *Rio Grande,* Editorial Sucre, Caracas, 1965.

Macdonald, Austin F., *Latin American Politics and Government,* Thomas Y. Crowell Company, New York, 1949.

Mancera Galletti, Angel, *Civilismo y militarismo,* Caracas, 1960.

Mecham, J. Lloyd, *A Survey of United States-Latin American Relations,* Houghton Mifflin Company, New York, 1965.

————, *Church and State in Latin America,* Rev. ed., University of North Carolina Press, Chapel Hill, 1966.

Marsland, William D. and Amy L., *Venezuela through its History,* Thomas Y. Crowell Company, New York, 1954.

Medina Angarita, Isaías, *Cuatro años de democracia,* Pensamiento Vivo, C.A., Caracas, 1963.

Ministerio de Relaciones Exteriores de Venezuela, *La visita al Perú del Presidente de Venezuela,* Dirección de Información Exterior, Caracas, 1955.

————, *Venezuela, 1955,* Tipografía La Nación, Caracas, 1955.

Nixon, Richard M., *Six Crises,* Doubleday and Company, Inc., Garden City, N.Y., 1962.

Obras dadas al servicio durante el Primer Año de Gobierno del Coronel Marcos Pérez Jiménez, Imprenta Nacional, Caracas, 1953.

Pacanins, Guillermo, *Siete años en la gobernación del Distrito Federal,* Tipografía Vargas, S.A., Caracas, 1965.

Palabras del Dr. Germán Suárez Flamerich, Presidente de la Junta de Gobierno de los Estados Unidos de Venezuela, el 24 de noviembre de 1951. Oficina Nacional de Información y Publicaciones, Caracas, 1951.

Parra, Darío, *Venezuela: "Democracia" vs. "Dictadura"*, Taller Gráfico Cies, Madrid, 1961.

Paz Galarraga, Jesús A., *Violencia y suspensión de garantías*, Caracas, 1963.

Pérez, Ana Mercedes, *La verdad inédita. Historia de la Revolución de Octubre, 1945*, 2nd ed., Editorial Colombo, Buenos Aires, 1953.

Pérez Jiménez, Marcos, *Pensamiento político del Presidente de Venezuela*, Imprenta Nacional, Caracas, 1954.

————, *Alocución dirigida a los venezolanos*, Imprenta Nacional, Caracas, 1955.

Porter, Charles O. and Alexander, Robert J., *The Struggle for Democracy in Latin America*, The Macmillan Company, New York, 1961.

Proyecto de Ley de Presupuesto General de Ingresos y Gastos Públicos para el Año Fiscal 1956-1957, Imprenta Nacional, Caracas, 1956.

Rangel, Domingo Alberto, *Los andinos en el poder*, Caracas, 1964.

Ray, Talton F., *The Politics of the Barrios of Venezuela*, University of California Press, Berkeley and Los Angeles, 1969.

Rivas Rivas, José, *Historia gráfica de Venezuela*, Tomo I, Primera Parte, Pensamiento Vivo, C.A., Caracas, 1963.

————, *Historia gráfica de Venezuela*, Tomo II, Pensamiento Vivo, C.A., Caracas, 1962.

————, *Historia grafica de Venezuela*, Tomo III, Pensamiento Vivo, C.A., Caracas, 1962.

Rodríguez, José, *¿Quién derrocó a Gallegos?*, 2nd ed., Tipografía Garrido, Caracas, 1961.

Rodríguez, Valmore, *Bayonetas sobre Venezuela*, Mexico, 1950.

Ronning, C. Neale (ed.), *Intervention in Latin America*, Alfred A. Knopf, New York, 1970.

Serxner, Stanley J., *Acción Democrática of Venezuela*, University of Florida Press, Gainesville, 1959.

Sigmund, Paul E. (ed.), *Models of Political Change in Latin America*, Praeger Publishers, New York, 1970.

Slater, Jerome, *The OAS and United States Foreign Policy*, Ohio State University Press, Columbus, 1967.

Szulc, Tad, *The Winds of Revolution*, Frederick A. Praeger, New York, 1963.

————, *Twilight of the Tyrants*, Henry Holt, New York, 1959.

Tarnói, Ladislao, *El nuevo ideal nacional de Venezuela; vida y obra de Marcos Pérez Jiménez,* Ediciones Verdad, Madrid, 1954.

Ugarte Pelayo, Alirio, *32 meses de gobierno en el Estado Monagas,* Imprenta Nacional, Caracas, 1952.

Umaña Bernal, José, *Testimonio de la revolución en Venezuela,* Tipografía Vargas, S.A., Caracas, 1958.

Vallenilla Lanz, Laureano (the elder), *Cesarismo Democrático,* 4th ed., Tipografía Garrido, Caracas, 1961.

Vallenilla Lanz, Laureano (the younger), *Editoriales de "El Heraldo" por R. H.,* Vols. I and II. No date or place of publication.

————, *Escrito de memoria,* Versailles, 1961.

Venezuela bajo el Nuevo Ideal Nacional, Imprenta Nacional, Caracas, 1956.

Vizcarrondo Rojas, Germán, *Cuando los bandoleros se imponen,* Tipografía Garrido, Caracas, 1947.

Note on Periodical Sources

In preparing the present study, tne author consulted, over a period of several months, a variety of Venezuelan periodicals at the National Library in Caracas. These included: *Ahora, El Gráfico, El Heraldo, Elite, El Nacional, El País, El Popular, El Universal, Fantoches, La Prensa, La Religión, ORVE, Tribuna Popular,* and *Ultimas Noticias.* Also used extensively were such U.S. periodicals as the New York *Times,* the Christian Science *Monitor, Time Magazine, Newsweek, Coronet,* the *Wall Street Journql,* and *U.S. News and World Report.*

Index

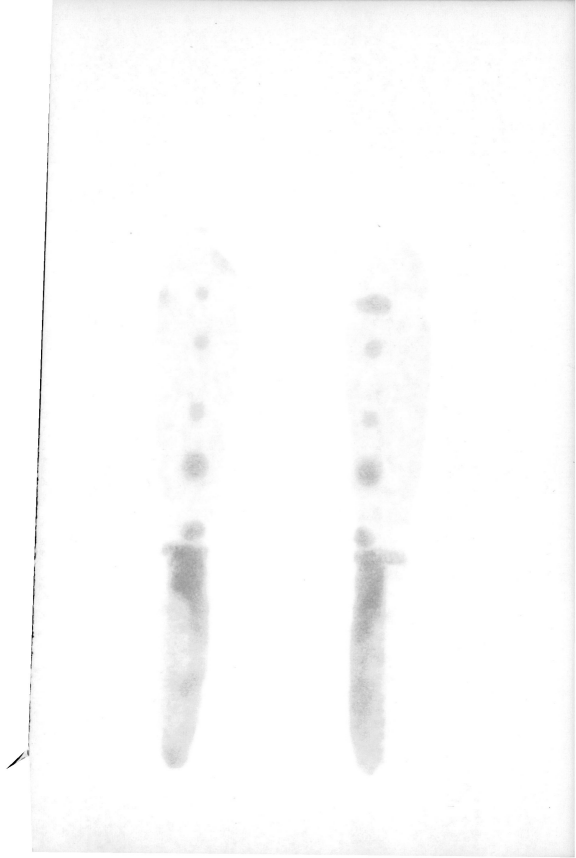

DATE DUE

DEC 12 2003	
APR 25 2013	

GAYLORD   PRINTED IN U.S.A.